Modern Networking

Fundamental Concepts

Declan Moran

Table of Contents

Colophon **1**

Preface **3**

Who this book is for 3

The Chicken and the Egg 3

Why networking is difficult, and why its not. 4

Fundamental Concepts (Volume 1) 4

Acknowledgments 5

Conventions used in this book 6

Metaphor as a tool 7

Book Website 7

Aetheria 8

1. Foundations—understanding and describing networks **11**

What is a Network? 11

Nodes and Ports 11

Infrastructure 13

Communication Technology 14

Network Interface Cards 15

Abstraction and Standardization 17

Layers of Abstraction 17

Models — network layers 18

Layer-Specific Devices 18

Summary 20

Conclusion 21

2. Lower Layers—physical networks and LANs **25**

Layer 1 25

Media 25

Electromagnetic Waves and the Role of Media 27

Nodes—analog-digital converters 28

Networks (Bitstreams) 28

Layer 2 28

Interfaces 29

Packets (Frames) 29

Nodes — addressed packet processors 32

Switches ... 32
Networks (LANs) ... 35
Lower Layer Landscape ... 37
Limitations ... 40
Summary ... 43
Conclusion ... 44
3. Middle Layers — encapsulation, logical addressing, routing and conversations ... 49
Metropolea ... 50
Layer 3 ... 52
Logical Addressing ... 52
Packet Encapsulation ... 55
Protocols ... 55
IP ... 58
IP Addresses ... 60
Subnets ... 61
Routers ... 67
The Internet (Simplified) ... 73
The Internet (Realistic) ... 76
Packet Fragmentation ... 80
ICMP (Diagnostics) ... 81
Layer 4 ... 83
Port Numbers — interface sharing and network endpoints ... 83
Packet Encapsulation ... 84
Packet Delivery — order and reliability ... 84
UDP - the minimalist approach ... 85
TCP — the reliable conversation manager ... 85
Choosing between TCP and UDP ... 86
Summary ... 87
Conclusion ... 89
4. Upper Layers and Applications ... 95
Layer 5+ ... 95
DNS - FQDNs (dotted strings) for IP addresses ... 95
Host Configuration ... 102
URLs ... 104
HTTP ... 108
Client-Server and *Peer-to-Peer* models ... 117
The Web ... 120
Other Protocols ... 122
Overlay, Virtual, and Software-Defined Networks ... 123
Layer Sets ... 123

Virtual Devices and Interfaces ... 123
Virtual (Software) Networks ... 124
Overlay Networks ... 124
Software-Defined Networks ... 126
Combinations ... 127
Summary ... 128
Conclusion ... 129
5. Security ... **137**
Access Control ... 138
Identity ... 140
Credentials ... 142
Cryptography ... 146
Applications of Cryptography ... 147
Cryptographic Keys ... 149
Authenticating Cryptographic Keys ... 152
Cryptographic (Algorithm) Schemes ... 155
Security in Practice ... 156
Group and individual Trust ... 156
Layer 2 ... 157
Layer 3 ... 158
Layer 4 ... 158
Layer 5+ ... 161
Cascading Encryption Layers (Keys) ... 165
VPNs ... 166
Firewalls ... 167
Identity Management ... 170
Service Provider Federation and Single Sign-On (SSO) ... 171
Protocols and Flows ... 172
Role-Based Access Control (RBAC) ... 173
JSON Web Tokens (JWTs) ... 174
Social Login ... 175
Delegated Authorization ... 176
Anonymous Networks — Dark Web ... 179
Tor ... 180
Summary ... 182
Conclusion ... 184
Afterword ... **191**
Index ... **193**

Modern Networking — Fundamental Concepts

Revision: 1.0.53
modern-networking.com

Preface

When I was starting out in software, one of my senior colleagues sent me a network related snippet he suggested I integrate into my code base. I was having some difficulty understanding it, and asked if he could explain it to me. He said (a little impatiently), that it was part of *the basics* all software developers must know. A little taken aback, I replied that if he would be so kind as to recommend me a book where these basics are explained, I would be happy to read it. Initially, he didn't reply. But the next day he approached me and said he had been thinking — that there indeed wasn't any such good book he could recommend. It's now over 20 years later, and the networking landscape isn't any simpler. This book is my attempt to help you understand the basics of networking so you don't have to figure it out alone like I did.

Who this book is for

This book should provide a good starting point for any technically savvy reader who wishes to acquire a solid grounding in the fundamentals of networking. Those who have previous exposure but feel some of the dots don't yet connect (e.g., software developers, system administrators, and computer science students) should feel particularly at home. Experienced cloud engineers or network specialists will not likely find much new here, but those wishing to become such specialists may well find this book a very good first step in the right direction.

Whatever the background of the reader, I hope they will discover, that once they master the fundamental concepts, that a shroud of mystery lifts from networking, and what's left presents a very logical and satisfying mosaic. In a world where technologies come and go at a rapid pace, networking is an area with a bright future, where, with a solid grasp of the *fundamental concepts*, the limits are defined largely by one's creativity.

The Chicken and the Egg

It can sometimes be difficult to explain a concept clearly and succinctly without, in the process, at least mentioning a related concept that hasn't been explained (independently) yet, and vice versa. For example, a good explanation of what a chicken is, may require mentioning that they lay eggs. And a good explanation of an egg might require mentioning that they are often laid by chickens. But which to explain first—the chicken or the egg? No matter what the choice, the result is less than ideal. But this seems to be an unavoidable consequence, and one may need to read a little further before the current concept becomes fully clear. Rest assured, however, that this book shall strive not to hide any eggs, but to place them as close and clearly as possible to their respective chickens.

Why networking is difficult, and why its not.

> *"When I use a word, it means just what I choose it to mean—neither more nor less."*
>
> — Humpty Dumpty in Lewis Carroll's, Through the Looking-Glass

Unfortunately, Humpty seems to have no small following in networking circles. A single term is often used in different contexts to mean different things, or different terms in separate places for a single concept. Often sources use terms inconsistently or don't clearly define what they mean by them, forcing you to consult other sources, which in turn use the term you're trying to clarify in yet a different way.

Another challenge is the sheer size of the subject. There is a lot of ground to cover in networking—hardware, software, layers, security, cloud—the list goes on, and it's not getting any shorter. It's very easy to get lost *down a rabbit hole* of details at various points, and lose sight of (and possibly motivation to grasp) the bigger picture.

In this book, I strive to use terms consistently, and pursue as best as possible (chicken-egg paradox notwithstanding), a top-down approach. Throughout the text, you'll find sections designated as tips or cautions—these provide additional insights but can be safely skipped on your first pass without hindering your understanding of subsequent material. I also make ample use of footnotes to isolate edge cases, elaborations or precision not crucial for a basic understanding, and to better highlight the central concepts.

The book focuses on *modern* networking, and as such omits discussion of unusual configuration or legacy hardware. The hope is that once the reader grasps the core concepts, in a big picture setting, using the terms presented, it will put them in a much better position to navigate other sources or further pursue any more specialized directions.

Fundamental Concepts (Volume 1)

This book lays the essential groundwork for understanding modern computer networks. Whether you're a technical professional or someone who simply wants to demystify networks, it will give you a clear and accessible introduction to the fundamental concepts. The fundamental concepts one must understand in order to understand the topic as a whole. And it strives to present them as *simply as possible — but no simpler.*

You'll explore everything from network basics to more advanced ideas like security, protocols, URLs, and the layered structure of networks. Key principles such as nodes, ports, abstraction, standardization, and network domains are covered, along with concepts spanning all network layers — from physical connections to higher-level services. It deliberately keeps code and configuration listings to a minimum, preferring instead more intuitive, easily understandable explanations, without sacrificing clarity in the process.

If you're planning on diving into the planned follow-up volume *(Modern Networking - Software and Techniques)* which focuses on more advanced, hands-on techniques, code samples, and troubleshooting recipes, this first volume will provide the conceptual background you need to confidently apply those practical skills, and what is (or must be) happening behind the scenes rather than just following instructions blindly. Even if you're not interested in writing code or configuring networks, this book will still give you valuable insights into the networks that underpin our digital world. By the end, you'll have a solid understanding of how networks function, empowering you to make sense of the technology around you.

Acknowledgments

This book is the fruit of the combined efforts of many people, without whom it would not exist in its present form. I would like to sincerely thank everyone involved, particularly the following:

Oliver Moran, whose eagle eye, deep technical competence and remarkable capacity to think from first principles shaped this work profoundly. His tireless attention to detail, cognitive flow and consistency, along with our many fruitful discussions, elevated the quality of this book in countless ways.

Kevin Sandermann and *Marcus Mechmann*, who devoted considerable time and effort to sharing their vast knowledge, despite the demands of leading teams of 100+ cloud and DevOps experts and architecting Azure and AWS infrastructure for world-renowned organizations. I had the great fortune of receiving their guidance, always delivered with patience and grace, and the book benefited enormously from their contributions.

Gerry Siegemund, for his unwavering support, congenial spirit and professional encouragement.

Florian Moran, whose impressive ability to think outside the box, ask deeply insightful questions, and recognize patterns others miss, brought fresh perspectives to every chapter.

John Devins, former senior editor at O'Reilly, who convinced me to begin writing this book. I'm deeply grateful for his support, encouragement, patience and gracious nature. Without him, this book would likely never have existed.

Oliver Feeley an inspirational English teacher, who motivated, enriched and could make even the mundane seem somehow captivating.

Scott Meyers who brought technical writing to a new level with clarity and elegance, writing with the simplicity that comes from true understanding.

Jonathan Griffiths, whose pertinent and insightful feedback greatly improved the content and clarity, and whose meticulous eye caught numerous typographical mistakes.

For substantial feedback, valuable insights and thorough error checking: *Raymond Goggins, Sergey Antonyukov, Aoibhe Fleming, Tino Kreutzberger, Max Darscht, Markus Ewers, Lennart Graewe, Karsten Ludwig Hauser, Björn Wellegehausen, Thomas Moran, Tim Tenhagen-Krabbe, Christoph Schlosser, Irina Bartmann, Evelyn Moran, Andreas Belke, Pierre Totzki, Niklas Mevenkamp, Stephan Linz, Maeve Moran, Kaltrina Nuredini, Sean Fleming, Jonathan Johnson.*

For various helpful comments and constructive contributions: *Irene Grusla, Carlos Eduardo Niño, Kaveh Faghihi, David Petroff, Reinhard Meinel, Craig Scott, Matthew Filipovich, Florens Dietz, Sara Hunter, Melissa Potter.*

If I have forgotten anyone, please let me know.

Conventions used in this book

The following typographical conventions are used in this book:

> **Sidebar Title**
>
> Here's a sidebar. Sidebars are great for setting aside a section of text that is related to the surrounding content but that doesn't necessarily fit into the main flow.

This is a tip or suggestion.

This is a caution or warning

Cross-References and Index Entries

Cross-references are highlighted like hyperlinks on the page. If you have an electronic version of this book, you can click on the highlighted text to jump to the *target* location. For example, clicking on electromagnetic wave will jump you to the section *Electromagnetic Waves and the Role of Media*. This helps mitigate the *chicken-and-egg* problem.

If you're reading a printed version, you can still follow these cross-references by looking up the highlighted term in the index. The index contains two types of entries: cross-reference terms (like *electromagnetic wave*) that point to their target sections, and traditional index entries (like section titles and key concepts). For example, both *electromagnetic wave* and *Electromagnetic Waves and the Role of Media* may appear in the index pointing to the same page number, allowing you to navigate by either the link text you encountered or by the section title itself.

Metaphor as a tool

Metaphor and analogy can be helpful tools for understanding new concepts. I felt this might be particularly so in the case of networking. Even the best tend to have limits where they break down, and are no longer valid or even counterproductive. Though I came up with some metaphors and analogies that help clarify isolated concepts in networking, try as I might, I couldn't manage to find existing ones that would serve the big picture understanding, without breaking down somewhere important. So I decided to create some new ones — short science fiction stories, Aetheria, and a sequel called Metropolea in chapter 3, which, I hope, might be easily relatable for the target audience. I hope the reader will indulge this unusual interlude in an otherwise factual book. My hope is that, at various places in the rest of the book, the reader may be able to draw parallels with concepts (or people) from the narrative, that help them see where the individual pieces fit into a bigger picture. Those who would prefer to skip it can, however, feel free to do so.

Book Website

The companion website for the book is *modern-networking.com*. Please keep an eye on it for new editions, bonus content and extra information, such as *Frequently Asked Questions*—and answers.

Aetheria

In a kubit of Lumia, the home planet of the Aetherians, Dalvin lay on what we would have called a bed (if there had been a bed). The Zertax crystal his uncle had sent him glowed subtly. It was one of the few material objects in his kubit, the majority of which was a motor sensory simulation created by the kubit's electromagnetic field — what we might have called a wireless virtual reality (if it had been virtual). It vibrated imperceptibly at frequencies that resonated with Dalvin's theta waves, helping him to relax and stimulating his creativity.

That the Aetherians had become a dominant civilization in that sector of the Andromeda galaxy was due, in no small part, to the invention of the Flux Transporter. Dalvin's great-great-grandmother, Radia, had designed the first functioning prototype—a device capable of creating a precise subatomic blueprint of an object. This blueprint could then be transmitted through a tachyon stream faster than the speed of light through the subspace medium to a remote receiver, where advanced nanotechnologies could assemble an object that was an exact replica of the original.

Dalvin gazed at the crystal and thought of his great-great-grandmother, caught up in the controversy surrounding the proposed use of the technology to transport blueprints of sentient beings, with optional (and costly) enhancements. Though she herself received little credit in her lifetime, she had shaped the lives of so many. His uncle, on one of his many voyages, had found the crystal on a moon of Targon and sent it by Flux to Dalvin.

Once her prototype of the Flux Transporter was made production-ready, the prime planets and major moons all hurried to erect high-performance flux interfaces, each of which broadcast its subatomic signals into the medium and received those broadcast by the others. However, as more and more interfaces were created, interference between the individual signals competing for space in the medium caused more and more transports to fail.

That's when the Stellar Switch was created—a magnificent feat of engineering even for the Aetherians. It was the size of a small protoplanet, with 100 times more portals than the number of inhabited worlds in all the Aetherian star systems (at the time). Each interface on a planet or moon was assigned its own dedicated portal on the switch, to which it sent its subatomic signal in a focused beam directly, instead of polluting the medium. And from which it directly received signals from others, the switch forwarding the signals reliably and instantaneously. In fact, it worked so well it was easy to forget it was there at all.

That was a century ago—an aeon at the current rate of Aetherian technological advancement, during which the Aetherians had created their first Dyson Sphere in less time than it took Khufu to build the Great Pyramid. Most of the sphere was flux transported on-site using a winding fleet of interface (WiFi) satellites that orbited the home star.

Neighbouring stellar systems (some of which possessed rare crystals) that were colonized (or assimilated) by the Aetherians had their own Flux networks, centered on their own stellar switches. But not even the Aetherians were able to build a switch big and powerful enough to span multiple star systems. The individual stellar networks, each with their own switches, were never designed to facilitate the sending of an object managed by one switch to a destination interface in a distant part of the galaxy—possibly separated by a convoluted web of thousands or more switched networks, constantly changing and updating with the individual stellar systems themselves.

Dalvin shifted his focus to the holographic display, his retina dancing commands to his personal Comanche 64 quantum computer, interacting with it almost telepathically as the crystal continued to vibrate. Sometimes he wasn't sure where his thoughts ended and those of the computer began. Were the holograms generated by the computer reacting to him, or the other way around? Did his thought cause information to flow in his brain, or did the flow cause the thoughts? Are we more than our thoughts? Do we perceive reality, or does it create a perception of us? Action and reaction dancing in a quantum blur as the crystal hummed in harmony. Oscillations in the invisible spectrum, simple photons carried like foam on the tide of an expanding and contracting universe, bits of existence, emergent sentience, collective reality.

Dalvin didn't know it yet, but 11 versions of himself would one day experience the Aetherian advance to a Type 3 civilization, to which one of them would make a decisive contribution. And upon their Flux Transportation would be engineered the galaxy-spanning Interstellar Protocol (IP).

For my mother who taught me to read and write, and my father who taught me to learn — I owe you both so much. For my children Merlin, Jolinus, Rosalin, Oliver, and Florian who fill me with pride and joy. For Irina, who brings love into the world.

1. Foundations – understanding and describing networks

This chapter provides the essential foundation for understanding what a computer network is, and what it is not. We'll begin by defining the basic building blocks of modern networks and explore the core concepts needed to navigate more complex network structures.

You'll learn about nodes (the devices that make up the network), ports (the entry and exit points for information), and the media through which data flows between them. From there, we will introduce fundamental ideas like layers of abstraction and standardization, which help to simplify and organize the complexities of networks.

The chapter will also dive into important concepts such as broadcast domains, collision domains, and network interface cards (NICs), and how networking differs from other kinds of communication technology. These ideas set the stage for understanding the interactions and relationships between devices on a network, helping you see how and why networks are structured the way they are.

By the end of this chapter, you'll have a solid grasp of the basic principles that form the backbone of all networks, giving you the conceptual framework to explore more advanced topics, and specific types of networks, in the chapters to come.

What is a Network?

In the most general sense, a network is two or more separate entities somehow connected, together with any infrastructure required to connect them. In the context of this book, I will be discussing *modern computer networks*—the entities are computerized and the connections between them are for communication.

Nodes and Ports

A network device is a (computerized) device equipped with the hardware and software it needs to take part in network communications. A computer network is composed of one or more (network) *devices* called (network) *nodes* connected by *media*, as illustrated in Figure 1.

Each of the devices can be almost anything (as long as they have the appropriate software and hardware): a high-end server, a desktop pc, a smartphone, a Raspberry Pi, or a tiny sensor measuring temperature. They are all *computerized devices* and, being integrated into a network through which they can communicate with one another, makes them nodes of that network. All network nodes are devices, but not all devices are network nodes. Just like all footballers are people, but not all people are footballers. Being capable of and motivated to play football, makes certain people footballers, and being integrated into a team makes those footballers players of that team.

Media are discussed more in the next chapter (remember the *chicken and the egg*?). For now, you can just consider them to be cables (joining the nodes). Each node has one or more *ports*, each of which acts like a *door* between the device and the rest of the network. A network node needs at least one port, since without one there is no way in or out and thus no possibility to *attach* to the network. Any port can be the *door* to at most one node, but a node may contain multiple ports. The rest of the network only *sees* (or cares about) the ports. It's a bit like a courier delivering a package who may not see if multiple doors on a large building are multiple entrances/exits to a single business office or each a separate entrance to a separate (independent) business office. They just care about the single door they need to use to deliver the package, and if they can identify (e.g., from a number written on the door) that it's the correct *address*. What is otherwise happening in the building or whether other doors also lead in or out of the same building, and if so what's behind them, need not concern the courier.

There are two basic types of network nodes: those that make use of (the services of) the network, and those that help provide (services to) the network. Consider again the analogy with a package delivery system, in the context of which one can distinguish two different types of buildings: those of the users of the system who are the original source and final (intended) destination of packages, and those of the logistics company who may need extra buildings to temporarily store and process packages while in transit. The users never address a package to one of the storage facilities of the logistics company, and aren't generally aware of or interested in which, if any, logistics company building a package enters or leaves on its journey to its final destination. The details may vary over time (if, for example, the logistics company needs to add or remove buildings as part of an expansion or temporarily to avoid roads under maintenance or make better use of new improved ones) or from one package to another (packages sent further may need to be stored or processed more times), of which the users of the system may remain blissfully unaware. The primary concern of the users is that their packages get delivered reliably and speedily.

There are no accepted standard terms to distinguish nodes that are users of the network from nodes that service the network. This is unfortunate, as having names for important concepts one regularly talks about is very useful (as even Humpty Dumpty would surely agree). So in this book, I will use the terms network *user nodes* and *service nodes* respectively. Similarly, there is no standard term for ports on service nodes to distinguish them from those (called *interfaces*) on user nodes, so I will refer to the former in this book as *service ports*.

One can distinguish two fundamental types of nodes on a network: *user nodes* — which use the services of the network, and *service nodes* — which help provide it.[1] Note that, as devices, there is no fundamental difference between user nodes and service nodes apart from their roles in the network. Consider people in a restaurant, where the staff represent service nodes, and the customers represent user nodes. Fundamentally, there is no inherent difference between them (each is, in principle, capable of either working or dining in a restaurant). However, in any particular restaurant, each person can only play one of these mutually exclusive roles.

Infrastructure

The network service nodes, together with any media (e.g. cables) that connect nodes, make up what is called the *infrastructure* of the network, as illustrated in Figure 2. You can think of it as the logistics company, together with any pathways, roads, and buildings they use before initial pickup and after final delivery.

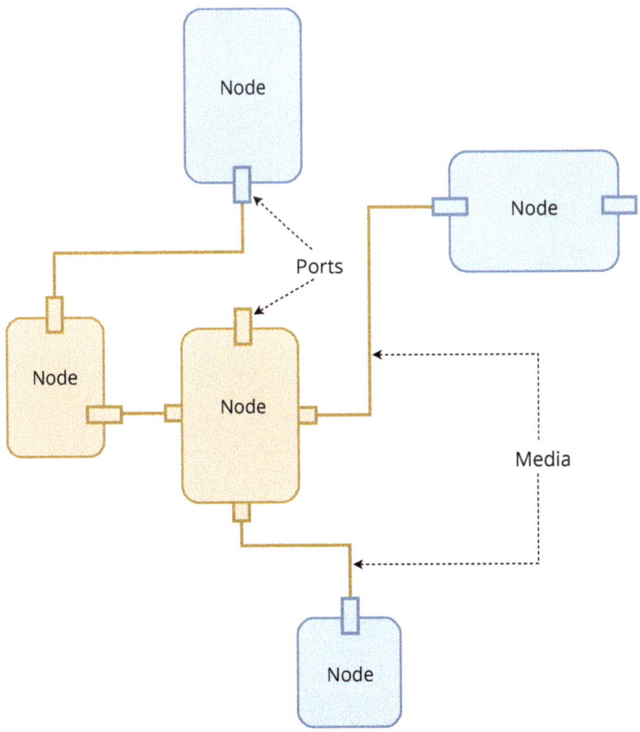

Figure 1. **Structural View**—*the components of the network. A network is composed of nodes and media (such as cables), which connect the nodes at their ports. There are two types of nodes—user nodes (shown in blue) which make use of (the services of) the network, and service nodes (shown in brown). Together, the service nodes and media form what's called the infrastructure of the network—see Figure 2.*

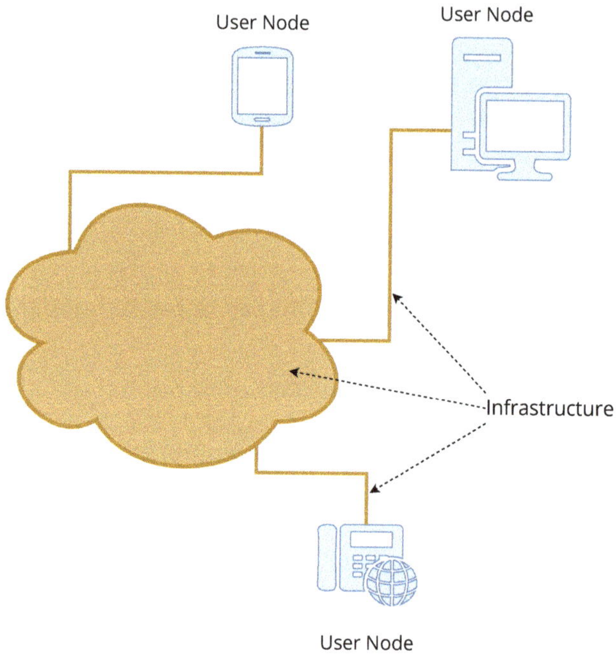

Figure 2. **Functional View** *of a network—The infrastructure (shown in brown) provides a service for user nodes (shown in blue), which enables the user nodes to exchange information with one another. The details of the infrastructure itself, and how it is (internally) composed, is neither readily apparent nor of interest to the users of the network. The user nodes only care if they can exchange information reliably with one another. Compare Figure 1*

Network

A computer network can be defined as one or more *ports* located on *(user)* nodes[2] that are connected by *infrastructure*, through which they communicate by exchanging information with each other. The ports act like doors, on their respective nodes. Each node requires at least one port to access the network, which are the original sources and final destinations of all packets of network information sent by one to another. The infrastructure is composed of *(service)* nodes and media such as cables. See also *Figure 2*.

Communication Technology

Networking (technology) can be seen as a subset of *communication* (technology) where the emphasis is on enabling effective communication between *many interfaces*, more *widely distributed*, in more *complicated topologies*. Other communication technologies, such as USB, FireWire, RS-232 (Serial), Bluetooth etc, are neither designed with these use cases in mind nor suitable for such communication, and as such will not be the subject of this book[3].

Network Interface Cards

Devices like PCs often have their ports located on a *Network Interface Card (NIC)*. In addition to the ports themselves, as can be seen in Figure 3, such cards also contain specialized hardware (chips) that are typical of (shared) resources used to pre-process information before sending, and post-process information after it arrives at the ports.

Figure 3. A **Network Interface Card (NIC)** *with two Ethernet ports (the slots) and one Wi-Fi port (the antenna). Also shown is an Ethernet cable that can be inserted into one of the Ethernet ports. On the end of the cable, you can see a semi-transparent connector, that helps it fit into the slot. Though important, for example, for technicians installing network equipment, as far as this book is concerned, you can consider such connectors to be part of the medium, as they play no significant role in the networking concepts discussed here.*

Though a single node can contain multiple ports, all of them need not necessarily all be on a single network. Some may be on one network, some on another (separate/independent) network, and some on no network at all.

Broadcast and Collision Domains

The **Broadcast Domain** is the set of (other) interfaces on the network an interface can successfully send information to. Ideally, this will be all (other) interfaces on the network.[4]

The **Collision Domain** is the set of (other) interfaces information reaches (as an unintended side effect) when an interface (intentionally) sends information to specific interfaces. The smaller the collision domain, the better.

Imagine a large room full of people. When a person wants as many people as possible to hear what they are saying, they speak loudly. The (maximum) number of people who actually hear what they are saying is the speaker's *broadcast domain*. Ideally, this would be everyone in the room. When a speaker wants just the person standing closest to them to hear, they speak quietly and directly to their partner. Those other than this partner who still hear (and who as a result may feel like their own private/direct conversations are being disturbed) are like the speaker's *collision domain*. The direct/private conversations of these people interfere (unintentionally) with each other. Ideally, this would be nobody.

Domains as discussed here may seem a little contrived or academic at first, but they play an important role which will become clearer in later chapters, so it's well worth taking note of them now.

In many sources, the terms *Node* and *Host* are often confusingly used when a *port*[5] is actually meant.

Don't confuse *port* as defined here with *port number*—often confusingly abbreviated to just *port*, which has a different (software related) meaning.

The term *domain* is unfortunately used in different contexts to mean different things. Don't confuse the concepts of *broadcast* and *collision domain* as described here with others such *administrative domain*, *routing domain* and *DNS domain*—see *Domains*.

Abstraction and Standardization

Layers of Abstraction

Conceptually, one can divide a complicated topic into different *layers of abstraction*. Where answering questions or solving problems in higher layers, relies on the existence of answers to questions or solutions to problems in lower layers. The trick is defining layers with boundaries between them that are as clean as possible, so that a person thinking at one level of abstraction is seldom forced to digress to a different level of abstraction to complete their thoughts or solve their problems. Instead, they can focus on just knowing *what* solutions and answers *other layers provide* without having to get caught up in the details.

Just as a biologist may know that life on earth would hardly be possible without Carbon, by virtue of its being able to form so many different kinds of complex molecular bonds with so many different kinds of atoms. But what exactly a molecular bond is and why life couldn't have just as easily formed based on silicon instead, they can feel free to leave to chemists or molecular biologists who prefer spending their time and mental energy at that level of abstraction. In turn, they may profit from the results and answers of quantum physicists who focus on an even lower layer of abstraction, who themselves are not overly concerned about how all their results will be used by those at higher levels.

And if at some future stage a particle physicist were to discover a new elementary particle, or some new properties of an existing one, though it may radically affect their research and view of reality, it may have little or no (disruptive) effect on that of the researcher who has spent the last 3 years observing primates in the Ngogo jungle.

Such a layered approach also proves very helpful when trying to understand or implement computer networks. The lower layers are the most fundamental, each higher layer making use of the solutions to problems and questions answered in the layer below, in such a way that there is as little as possible *spill over* from any layer into the layer above. Boundaries are chosen that cleanly (as possible) separate the concerns of adjacent layers. Each lower layer provides to the layer above it, clear succinct answers, and easy to use solutions, which hide the complexity and detailed nature of the processes involved in finding these answers or solutions.[6]

In order to function correctly, every layer depends on the functionality of all layers *below* it. But higher layers tend to offer a broader range of functionalities to a wider audience. In this sense, for example layer 1 can be considered the most *fundamental* layer of all, since without it, no network communication at all is possible. (*Think*: operating system (lower layer) and the apps (higher layer) you as a smartphone user actually use. Or a small handful of elementary particle types giving rise to possibly infinite variety of sentient species).

Models — network layers

Deciding on a *model* for such a layered abstraction is tantamount to choosing what layers to use and what to call them. In computer networking, there are two common models: The *OSI Model* (which is the older of the two and divides the subject matter into 7 layers) and the *TCP/IP Model* (which divides the *same* subject matter into 4 layers).[7]

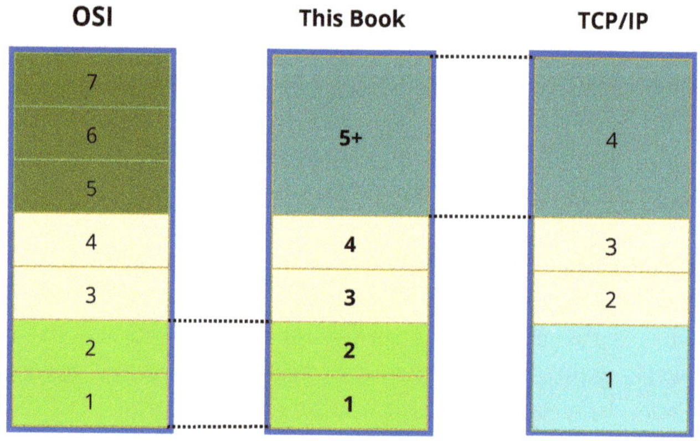

Figure 4. **Layer Models.** *The layers used in this book correspond to the lower two of the OSI model, and the top layer of the TCP/IP model (but referring to it as layer "5+" as a reminder that it corresponds to all of the OSI layers 5 and above) together with intermediate layers 2 and 3 that both the other models have in common.*

Layer-Specific Devices

It's not uncommon to see a node being referred to as a being an *layer n device*, or that it *operates at layer n*, or is *layer n enabled* (where *n* is any layer number in the *model* being used).

Switches and *Routers* will be introduced and explained later in this book. For now, however, note that you may often read that a *switch is a layer 2 device*, whereas a *router is a layer 3 device*. This means that a router has characteristics of, or exhibits behaviour that are the subject matter of, layer 3. Similarly, for a switch and layer 2. What's maybe not so obvious, but important to note, is that this (by definition of our layers of abstraction) means that a router is also both a layer 2 device and a layer 1 device. Similarly, a switch being a layer 2 device also makes it (by definition) a layer 1 device.

When we say a device *operates at* a specific layer, we generally mean this is the *highest* layer it can be considered operating at. Implied is however, that it also operates at all layers below this too.[8] So in general, if a node *is a layer n device* this means this is the *highest* layer it can be considered being in, or operating at, but by induction, that it is also a layer *n-1 device*, a layer *n-2 device*, ... and a *layer 1 device*, for every layer number n in our model.[9]

Official Standards

Standards are formally established guidelines and specifications that ensure consistency, quality, and interoperability across different products and technologies. They provide a common framework that manufacturers and developers follow to create compatible and reliable solutions.

Consider a possible *standard* for Lego. Though maybe not so formally documented or complicated as that for networking technology, its purpose and value would be analogous. The standard might specify requirements for the studs (the raised circular *bumps* on the top of Lego pieces) and tubes (the hollow circular *holes* on the underside of Lego pieces that fit over the studs). It may mandate their size, positioning, and distribution. A product team designing a new Lego set must adhere to these specifications to ensure compatibility with existing sets.

Adhering to the specifications of the Lego standard involves extra effort and *compliance* on the part of the product team, but both users and manufacturers benefit. Users can freely combine pieces from different sets to create designs beyond what any single team envisioned. This compatibility makes Lego more appealing, leading to increased sales. Manufacturers benefit not only from more customers, but also from the ability to reuse specialized pieces created by other teams, reducing development costs and time to market. This creates a "win-win-win" cycle of value for users, manufacturers, and the ecosystem as a whole.

Standards in networking serve a similar purpose, but in a far more complex field. The layered approach to networking makes it possible to create specific standards for the part of the technology covered by specific layers (which by design are separated by clear borders). For instance, Ethernet and Wi-Fi are collections of standards covering Layer 1 and Layer 2. Any manufacturer wishing to sell standards-compliant equipment must meet the specifications, such as ensuring proper cable shielding, defined in these standards. This ensures quality, interoperability, and user trust. It's also common to hear terms like Ethernet or Wi-Fi used to refer both to the technologies themselves and to the standards governing them.

Saying a node *operates at a given layer*, implicitly implies it operates at all lower layers also.

Don't confuse the *TCP/IP model* discussed here with the so-called *TCP/IP protocols* used within the intermediate layers of *all models* discussed here.

Summary

- A computer network is composed of devices called *nodes* connected by *media*, through which they can pass information to one another
- The nodes are connected to the media, and thus the rest of the network, through their *ports* which act like doors through which the information passes in and out.
- Each node needs at least one port to join a network.
- A node may have multiple ports, in which case each port may be used to join a different network. Thus, a single node may simultaneously be part of multiple networks.
- On devices like a PC, ports are often recognizable as the antennas used for Wi-Fi, or the slots into which an Ethernet cable is inserted.
- The ports (along with any other possibly shared, hardware resources needed for pre- or post-processing the network information) are often located on a so-called Network Interface Card (NIC).
- The *infrastructure* of the network is composed of the media and devices whose role it is to make the network *function*. The network will not function (as well) without them. These devices are referred to as *service nodes* in this book.
- Devices like your smartphone, or pc which can optionally join an existing network, and whose role it is to use the network and benefit from its functionality, are called *user nodes* in this book.
- A port on a user node is also called an *interface*.
- The set of other interfaces an interface can intentionally send information to is called the *broadcast domain*.
- The set of other interfaces that information (unintentionally) reaches when an interface (intentionally) sends information to specific interfaces is called the *collision domain*.
- Ideally, the broadcast domain would be all (other) interfaces on the network, and the collision domain would be empty.

- Dividing larger complex subject matter into separate layers of abstraction facilitates understanding, and focusing attention (more) independently on one such part at a time.
- The lower layers typically encompass more fundamental considerations of the subject matter.
- Higher layers typically encompass more big-picture considerations.
- Higher layers benefit from clear answers and simpler solutions to complex questions, the details of which are *hidden* inside lower layers.
- The more independent the layers are, and the more clearly defined their boundaries, the better.
- A *model* for such layered abstractions is a choice of layers and a means of referring to them.
- The OSI and TCP/IP models are two common models for networks, and this book uses a

combination of both.

- Saying that a device is in or operates at a certain layer, generally means this is the *highest* layer it can be considered being a part of, or operating in. Such a device implicitly operates at all lower layers too.
- Official standards are formal guidelines and specifications that benefit all involved.
- Ethernet and Wi-Fi are two such standards.

Conclusion

In this chapter, you've established a solid foundation for understanding modern computer networks. We explored key concepts such as nodes, ports, and network infrastructure, clarifying how devices connect and communicate. You learned to distinguish between user nodes and service nodes, and gained insight into essential ideas like broadcast domains and collision domains, and standardization.

We also discussed how layers of abstraction can help manage network complexity by isolating different aspects of functionality, making networks easier to understand and troubleshoot. This book uses a custom model that blends elements of the OSI and TCP/IP models for a practical, comprehensive approach. As we explore each layer in the chapters that follow, you'll see how they work together to create functioning networks. Finally, we touched on the importance of official standards like Ethernet and Wi-Fi, which ensure compatibility and efficiency in real-world networks.

With these key principles in mind, you're ready to explore how data physically moves through networks — starting with the cables, signals, and local connections that form Layer 1 and Layer 2 in the next chapter. These are significant first steps toward one of the main goals of this book—building up an understanding of how the internet works—a network so large and complex it connects billions of devices worldwide.

[1] more precisely, one could see this division as being at the level of ports rather than at that of a node as a whole. However, it's very rare for a single device to be *both* a user *and* provider of a single network, so classification at the node level is acceptable in this context. Furthermore, as we shall later, the role a node plays in a network, depends on what layer we are talking about. *Routers* for example, are service nodes at layer 3, but user nodes at layer 2. Layers will be discussed more in *Layers of Abstraction* and layer 2 and 3 in detail in *Layer 2* and *Layer 3*

[2] we will see in the next chapter that such ports are called *Interfaces*

[3] Several of these other communications technologies are however very similar to Ethernet/Wi-Fi in their design

[4] Large broadcast domains increase vulnerability to Layer 2 attacks that can cause *DoS (Denial of Service)* - making resources unavailable to legitimate users). In *ARP spoofing*, fake address announcements reach all devices at once. *MAC flooding* forces switches to broadcast all traffic when their address tables overflow. In networks with multiple interconnected switches, *STP (Spanning Tree Protocol)* prevents loops. *STP manipulation* involves sending false messages to become the *root bridge* (the central switch others calculate paths through to prevent loops), potentially redirecting traffic or causing instability. These attacks exploit the shared nature of broadcast domains —one attacker can impact all connected devices, which is why modern networks favor smaller, segmented broadcast domains through *VLANs*.

[5] or an *interface*

[6] Imagine studying a complicated topic like the social dynamics in one of the most advanced species on our planet like primates, dolphins or elephants. One could think for example, about how the interactions in a group are motivated by the need to secure food and under what conditions a focus on individual success actually benefits each member in the long term more than a collective, cooperative approach (*think*: the first farmers in human history, who provided enough food for cities to eventually emerge, filled by many individuals freed from the need to directly forage or hunt for food. Instead, they are able to specialise in other ways to contribute to and shape their societies). This may in turn beg the question of what exactly is food. Or how and why certain kinds of food are more available in certain regions, or how it contributes to size difference or longevity of individuals, in turn playing a role in the social hierarchy of the respective groups. Regions with more food may lead to the prospering of larger groups with more complicated hierarchies, or individuals playing more significant roles for longer due to increased longevity. This in turn may lead one to think about ecology, biology, and even the biochemistry involved in favouring the growth of certain kinds of plants or digesting different kinds of food. This is a lot of ground to cover and not everyone studying social dynamics will be equally interested in all of these aspects, and all the associated scientific disciplines mentioned, at least in the same detail. But nonetheless, to be able to satisfactorily answer *any* question on the topic in detail requires a familiarity with a *diverse range* of complicated topics. Going from the bottom up instead, a physicist may argue that a full understanding of anything that exists (including food, primates and social structures) isn't possible without also understanding elementary particles. After all, elementary particles make up atoms, which make up molecules, which make up simple organisms, and food, which give rise to more complicated species and social dynamics. If elementary particles behaved fundamentally differently, this would give rise to different chemistry and different versions of what we call life. Most likely it would in fact lead to the existence of no life at all, since even tiny changes in the fundamental constants of nature would cause huge changes in the universe and make life as we know it unthinkable. However, if every social scientist first had to learn all about quantum physics before even being able to consider why chimpanzees tend to live in groups of less than 100, there would probably be very slow progress in answering such questions.

[7] The TCP model combines layers 1 and 2, and layers 5, 6 and 7 respectively of the OSI model into two single layers. The TCP model is generally regarded as the more practical of the two. It covers the same subject matter as the layers 5, 6 and 7 of the OSI model in its single layer 4. This is because it became apparent that the upper divisions originally chosen by the OSI model were not always as practical as intuitive as they might in modelling real world networking. Its merging of the two lower layers is mainly attributed to the boundary between them often being less than clear in practice. Each of the two models refers to the layers not only by number (as shown in *Figure 4*) but also by name. Unfortunately their naming differs significantly, and can sometimes seem less than fitting, which is why I shall in this book refer to them solely by number. In this book I shall effectively use the OSI model but condense the subject matter of layers 5-7 into a single layer as the TCP/IP model does - at the level of

detail in which this books treats layers 1 and 2, if feel distinguishing them adds clarity

[8] An ethologist may say that elephants they are studying are highly emotional and intelligent sentient beings that exhibit advanced social dynamic behaviour, whereas a rock in the desert does not. The elephants fall clearly into the layer of abstraction the zoologist is interested in, but the rock does not. A quantum physicist, on the other hand, may not differentiate between the two at all. Both elephants and rocks are made up of the same (type of) elementary particles, that obey the same fundamental laws of physics that the physicist is interested in, at this lower layer of abstraction. An elephant being a magnificent, socially advanced being does not mean it's not also composed of elementary particles that at a fundamental level behave the same as those in rock, and thus for the physicist both, as are many other objects, are collections of elementary particles. But the elephant is a collection of elementary particles that is also much more - a sentient social being. In an abstract layer model, we might say the elephant *operates in a higher layer* - that of sentient beings. It also operates, like the rock, in the lower layer of *collection of elementary particles*

[9] Technically, its individual ports of a device which operate at given layer, but since It's very uncommon (though not impossible) for the individual interfaces not to all operate at the same layer(s), one often speaks of the *layer of operation of the node* as a whole

2. Lower Layers – physical networks and LANs

In this chapter, we'll dive into the two most fundamental layers of networks: layer 1 and layer 2. You will learn that layer 1 is the only layer that *exists* between separate physical devices – all other layers operate within the devices themselves. When data needs to move from one device to another, layer 1 provides the actual physical path through electromagnetic signals in cables or air. Everything else – the processing, packaging, routing decisions – happens inside the devices at their respective layers. Layer 1 is the bridge between them.[1] You'll gain a clear understanding of the media that carry these signals between the nodes.

Layer 2 serves as the crucial interface that connects devices to the layer 1 bridge. With incoming signals, it receives bit streams from layer 1 and reconstructs the data into manageable *packets* (also known as *frames*). For outgoing signals, it decomposes the packets into bit streams for layer 1 to send them. Layer 2 also manages *addressing* – assigning unique identifiers to each device's network ports so that data can be directed to specific destinations and devices know which signals are meant for them.

We'll also look at the limitations of these lower layers and the LANs (Local Area Networks) they form, which will help you appreciate their crucial yet somewhat constrained role in larger networks like the internet.

Layer 1

All network communication involves the transmission of *electromagnetic waves* through a medium, as described in more detail in *Electromagnetic Waves and the Role of Media*. Layer 1 is concerned with the details of this transmission, as well as the conversion of the waves to and from a *stream of bits* at each end of the medium, as illustrated in *Figure 5*.

Media

The media used in modern networks are almost exclusively one of *Copper Cables*, *Fibre Optic cables* or *Air*[2]. See also *Lower Layer Landscape*. A medium *unconditionally* connects all ports attached to it, so that every packet sent by any port arrives at ever other port attached to said medium. The more ports attached, the more potential (collision) problems can occur, since it becomes more likely two different ports may try to send packets simultaneously, which then *collide*, resulting in communication difficulties. Such connections (of three or more ports) over a single medium can be at best *half-duplex*, i.e. the nodes involved try to observe a policy of *"transmit if quiet—back off on collision"*, thus endeavouring to recover from any collision problems. Examples are *Ethernet Bus* and *Wi-Fi*. The use of an Ethernet Bus (a medium) to connect more than 2 ports has been largely superseded by the use of a switch (an *intelligent* node that operates at layer 2 which will be discussed more in the next chapter) in modern networks.

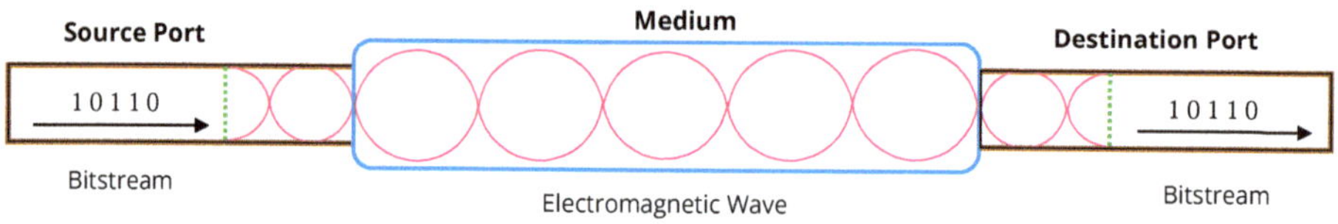

*Figure 5. A **Bitstream** coming out of a source port is encoded into (the modulation of) an **electromagnetic wave** which is transmitted to the other end of the medium, where the output bitstream is reconstructed (in the same order) as input to the destination port. The digital information the bits represent are encoded into analogue waves and vice versa*[3]*. Though not explicitly shown, the source and destination ports are each located on a node (as ports always are).*

Bits and Bitstreams

A *bit* is the smallest unit of information—with two possible values, which we often represent as 1 and 0 (*think*: light switch, which can be either *on* or *off*). Computers *naturally* use binary (two values) because their processing is built on transistors—tiny electronic switches that *either* are conducting electricity *or* not. Modern computer chips contain billions of these microscopic switches. All data that computers process and transmit—text, images, videos—is ultimately represented as long sequences of bits. See also *Decimal, Binary, and Hexadecimal*. By *stream* of bits is meant that the bits *pass* a certain point in a specific order and can only be processed one at a time in this order. *Think*: drops of water falling out of a tap. You can't *get* any drop until after those before it have fallen first. You can collect a cup full of water, but only after you have patiently waited for each drop to fall into the cup in the particular order in which they fell.

When using cables is feasible, an even better solution is to ensure that each cable connects exactly 2 ports. This creates a so-called *point-to-point* connection. Modern cables are generally *full-duplex* which means that 2 packets can travel in opposite directions simultaneously (like a road where cars going in each direction have their own separate *side* of the road), thus completely avoiding the collision problem, for the 2 ports connected. *Think*: you have a road with no intersections, with two sides (one for each direction of travel) and cars all travel at the same speed.[4]

Electromagnetic Waves and the Role of Media

Even though one often talks about seemingly different physical phenomena, such as *radio* waves, *infrared* radiation, *optical* signals in fibre cables, *voltages* in copper wires etc. being used to implement network communications, these can all be viewed as different aspects of a single fundamental physical process — the propagation of electromagnetic waves.

Visible light, radio waves and infra-red radiation are all forms of electromagnetic waves—they just have different frequencies, and our eyes happen to be able to *see* one but not the others. Voltages are just a consequence of the forces electric charges exert when they repel or attract each other, and the charged particles in a copper wire don't really move (far). They just oscillate back and forth, constraining the electromagnetic waves, which is what actually propagates down the wire. (This is equally true of electric power supply cables—the power company doesn't actually deliver any *new electrons* to your home along the electricity cables, but rather electromagnetic waves, which *contain* the energy).

The role of any media, is not so much to enable the waves to propagate (electromagnetic waves can, in fact, propagate most easily and rapidly through vacuum), but for the body of the medium to *not hinder* the propagation, and for the boundary (if any) of the medium to *keep the waves inside*. The cladding on an optic fibre keeps light (waves) inside through (total internal) reflection. And the free electrons oscillating back and forth on the surface of a copper cable play a similar role for the radio waves propagating along it.

A medium like a cable (e.g. used for Ethernet) can be likened to a water pipe. The interior of the pipe (which is ideally empty except maybe for some air) doesn't hinder the water from flowing though it, and the boundary (shell) of the pipe keeps the water inside. So, as much as possible of the water flowing into one end later flows out of the other end. When you turn on a tap connected to a garden hose, all the water that flows into the hose at the tap (assuming no leaks or defects) will reach the plant at the other end of the hose. Electrons bunch and spread in a wave-like pattern, akin to a compression wave in a spring where segments push and pull, creating a push-pull effect where the energy falls off with the square of distance between charges. This wavelike electromagnetic field, relies on the free electrons in the conductor to propagate it.

In the case of Wi-Fi, the medium (such as air) doesn't generally have a physical boundary to contain the waves, so they aren't confined. The waves emanate from their source and spread in all directions. This is more like using a sprinkler, which sprays water broadly across the garden. This approach is convenient because it waters multiple plants without needing to connect each one individually with a hose. However, it also means that only a fraction of the water reaches the plants you intend to water. A significant portion is wasted when it lands on rocks, paths, or even outside the garden, and sometimes on things like your shoes where it's unwanted. Wi-Fi offers the convenience of not requiring direct connections with cables, but it also has the disadvantage of wasting energy to generate waves that never reach useful destinations. This is what people typically call electromagnetic waves or radiation, moving freely without a physical guide.[5]

Nodes — analog-digital converters

Most layer 1 nodes transform incoming waves to bit streams, and vice versa, as illustrated in *Figure 5*. It's not always essential for their operation, however, that they do, i.e. they may operate in a purely analogue fashion working just with waves directly without any conversion to/from *bits*. What's important to note, however, is when a layer 1 service node does convert to/from bits as shown, that they do *not change the values of the bits* or in any way *make logical decisions* based on these values. The primary purpose of the transformation (if any) is to prevent signal degradation and enhance noise reduction, ensuring the integrity and reliability of the transmitted data. And this is often also the main purpose of the layer 1 service nodes.

Networks (Bitstreams)

A layer 1 network is composed of one or more user nodes, and zero or more service nodes, all joined by media. The service nodes and media together form the infrastructure of the layer 1 network. Such a layer 1 network is sometimes called a *physical network*, but, as with many terms in networking, it's unfortunately not used consistently. For this reason, I shall refer to it simply as a *layer 1 network* in this book. It forms a *single collision domain*, which is identical to its *single broadcast domain*.[6] This single collision domain, however, makes it unsuitable for the inclusion of more than a few nodes, since as previously mentioned, the more nodes in a single collision domain, the more likely collisions will occur. And more collisions means a less responsive and less reliable network. Furthermore, the fact that it only handles streams of bits rather than whole *packets* of data makes it somewhat cumbersome to use. After all, it's entire packets, and not just individual bits, that we actually want to send and receive. Which leads us to the topic of the next chapter, and up to a higher layer of abstraction.

Segment is sometimes used to describe one or more layer 1 nodes connected only by a single type of medium (but it's not uncommon, however, to observe its use in other contexts to mean something different — often some less clearly defined section of a network in the context of a higher layer).

Link is sometimes used to describe a segment where the medium is a single *cable* (*point-to-point*) and, more confusingly, in the context of layer 3, sometimes also as a synonym for a whole *Subnet*.

Layer 2

Layer 2 is concerned with *packets* (which, in the context of layer 2, are often also referred to as *frames*),[7] as well as their conversion to and from a *stream of bits*.

Interfaces

Ports on nodes which are not layer 2 infrastructure nodes are also called *interfaces*.[8] Only interfaces can serve as original sources or final destinations of layer 2 packages.

Hash and Checksum

A *hash* (or *checksum*) is a relatively small, effectively unique value that can be calculated for any particular body of data (including text). It's a bit like a *fingerprint* of the data in question. For each (finger of each) person, there is an (effectively) unique corresponding fingerprint. Similarly, for each body of data there is an (effectively) unique hash which can be derived from it, and can be used to *identify* the data. Changing any part of the data, no matter how small, will (almost always) result in a different hash value.[9]

Hashes are used in *Cryptography* to detect even deliberate tampering whereas more simple checksums (like *FCS* in the trailer of layer 2 packets) are designed to detect accidental corruption during transmission. Hashes are preferred when certainty of uniqueness is more important than speed and simplicity of calculation.

Packets (Frames)

A packet is the smallest independent *chunk* data gets handled as, before it's disassembled into a sequence of bits for layer 1 to transmit, or after it's assembled from a sequence of bits layer 1 has transmitted.

Assembly and Disassembly

Packet *assembly* is the construction of a packet from a sequence of bits (at a destination port) after transmission by layer 1. Packet *disassembly* is the deconstruction of a packet into a sequence of bits (at a source port) so layer 1 can transmit them. Here, the details (in what they refer to as the *MAC sublayer*) of the Wi-Fi and Ethernet standards differ significantly.

The process of assembly and disassembly may seem trivial, but consider an air traffic controller at a busy airport. Their (very non-trivial) job is to ensure that as many aeroplanes as possible can take off and land safely in limited airspace (and land), which means minimizing the separation between planes, but without them ever getting dangerously close. But aeroplanes (like weather and passengers) don't always behave as expected. A build up on the runway may require planes waiting to land to circle the airport temporarily, and of those waiting to depart to join a waiting queue somewhere. Similarly, network nodes work hard to ensure bits can *take off* and *land* as efficiently as possible, applying various techniques to adapt when network conditions aren't ideal, in order to keep performance high, while minimizing any danger of *bit collisions* and data loss. Additionally, every node has to agree on the exact location of the bits in a packet. Do they get filled with incoming bits from the top up, bottom down, left to right etc? Even if all the pixels of an image you send arrive at your friend's phone, you might not be very happy if every pixel doesn't end up there in the same place as it was on your phone.

Structure

A packet consists of a *payload* (sometimes also called *body*), together with a *header* and a *trailer*, as illustrated in *Figure 6*. The payload is the actual data the sender wants to send (*think*: *contents of a letter*). The sole purposes of the header and trailer are to store extra information used to help deliver the payload reliably (*think*: *address* and *stamp* on the *envelope*). The details of packet structure (in what is referred to as the *LLC sublayer*) are largely similar in both the Ethernet and Wi-Fi standards.

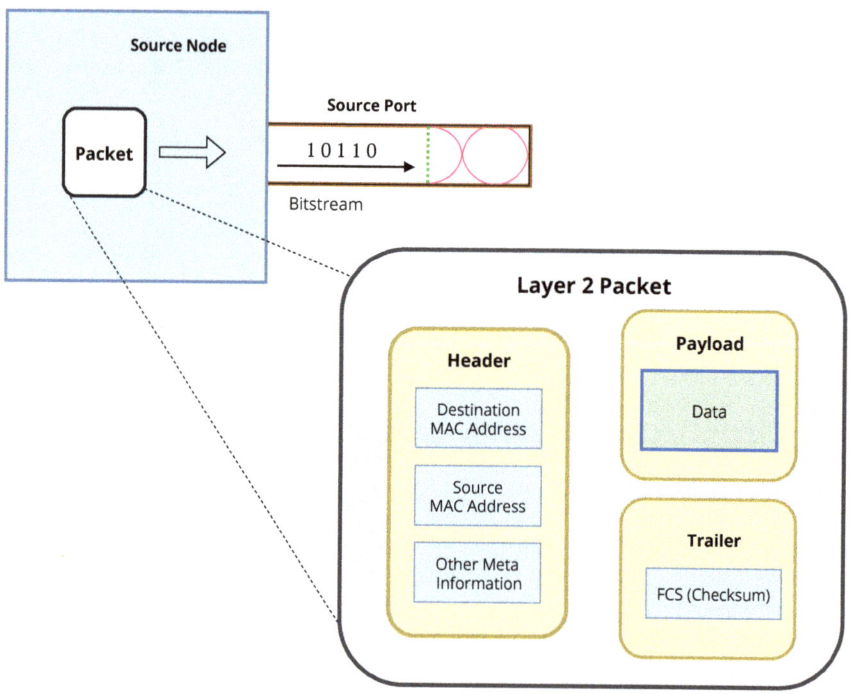

Figure 6. **Packet (Layer 2)** *and its structure showing the main fields*[10] *such as Destination Address, Source Address, and Data, in their respective groups (Header and Payload). Note that, though the image illustrates a package being disassembled at a source port, the assembly at a destination port is completely symmetrical.*

Header

- **Destination** Address. This identifies[11] the intended recipient interface(s).
- **Source** Address. This identifies uniquely the sending interface.
- **Other** Meta Information, used to facilitate reliable and efficient transmission[12].

Payload

This contains the actual information (content) the sender wishes to transmit. The payload is sometimes also referred to as the *body* of the packet[13]

Trailer

Contains the **Frame Check Sequence (FCS)**, a *checksum* which can be used by the receiver to check if the packet arrived correctly.[14]

MAC Address

The address used for an interface in layer 2 is known as a *MAC* (or *hardware*) *address*.[15] They are *burned* into the hardware (e.g. on the *NIC*) by the manufacturer and cannot subsequently be changed.[16]

The addresses in a layer 2 packet are always those of the interfaces originally sending and intended to ultimately receive the packet, respectively, and never those of ports on any service nodes the packet may pass through on the way. (Even though the manufacturer also burns such an address into the ports of all nodes, not knowing how they will later be used—i.e. as user or service nodes). Just like the addresses on a packet a courier is delivering is never that of any building they use to temporarily store or process the package on its journey, but those of its final destination and original sender.

Nodes — addressed packet processors

As mentioned in *Layer-Specific Devices*, layer 2 nodes (can) do everything layer 1 nodes (can) do. In particular, transforming bit streams into waves and vice versa at their ports, as illustrated in *Figure 5*. Unlike layer 1 nodes, however, they can (and often do) also actively *interpret* the incoming *bit patterns*, and make *logical decisions based on these values_about how to behave. A layer 1 service node will, for example, always resend the same bit pattern on its output port, that it has received on its input port. A layer 2 service node, however, may (depending on how it's configured) make a logical decision not to _forward* certain incoming bit patterns through its output port. It may just *drop* them instead.[17]

Only being able to access the bits of data one at a time in whatever order they happen to be arriving does not lend itself ideally to further processing. Imagine someone tells you over the phone, one point at a time, what the colour is of every pixel in an image you wish to analyse. You probably wouldn't find it conducive to do this analysis while they're still speaking. First you might construct the complete image, so you could *see* all pixels at once, or be able to shift your focus at will to various parts of the image in any order you wish in order to analyse it. Similarly, layer 2 nodes don't try to make any of their logical decisions based on the values of the bits in the stream while they are still incoming. Instead, they first construct whole packets from them, which they can subsequently analyse and further process much more effectively.

Switches

The most important type of layer 2 service node is a switch. Its main function is to perform the logical processing described above based on the address fields of the incoming packets. Each interface that should be added to a given layer 2 network is typically attached directly to a single port on the switch that acts like a *central switchboard* for that network. See *Figure 7*. Every time a packet arrives (by which I mean an em wave arrives, which gets transformed into a bitstream which gets assembled into a layer 2 packet), the switch analyses the destination address of the packet. It then forwards the package on its other port(s) (by which I mean it disassembles the layer 2 packet into a bitstream which gets output as an em wave) to which it *knows* the destination interface(s) is attached. This way, no other attached interfaces except the intended destinations get packets not intended for them.

This effectively maximizes the broadcast domain (any interface can send a packet to any other interface), while reducing the size of the collision domain (no node will receive any packets not intended for it, but it may still receive too many simultaneously, which collide with one another).

How does the switch *know* which interface is attached at which of its ports? Nodes can effectively join and leave a layer 2 network without *warning*, and with them any interfaces they attach to the switch. The answer is that the switch *learns* which interfaces are attached by *observing* not only the destination addresses of packets it receives, but also the *source address*. Every time a packet arrives at a given switch port, it updates its internal *list* of which interface is attached to which port. This internal list is called the switch's CAM Table. See *CAM Tables* for further details.

Sophisticated switches often use (intelligent) *buffering* to avoid multiple (simultaneous) packets arriving at a single destination interface, which might lead to congestion/collisions. The switch is careful not to forward any more than one packet at a time to a single interface (*think*: giving one car a head start on a road before letting another set off in the same direction from the same starting point). This, combined with modern full-duplex cables (see *Media*) for the connections between the interfaces and the switch, can completely eliminate the collision domain. No interface will receive any more than one packet at a time, and every such packet will have been intended for this interface. The full-duplex cables ensure that every interface can also send and receive simultaneously.

Of course, when exiting interfaces are removed or new ones added, or a switch is replaced, the performance of the network is less than optimal, as the switch gradually learns what interfaces are attached where. However, even in the (temporary) worst-case scenario where the CAM table is still completely empty, the network performance is still significantly better than it would be without the switch, thanks to features like buffering.

Imagine, by way of analogy, a switch to be like an efficient *airport shuttle bus system*. It gets passengers from their respective gates to the parked aircraft waiting outside. The passengers don't have to concern themselves about where their aeroplane is parked or how to get there. Without it, the passengers would have to walk out the gate and *somehow* find their way to their respective aircraft, possibly wandering around, getting lost and colliding with one another or ground crew vehicles in the process. And the bigger the airport (more gates, more waiting aircraft, more collisions, and longer distances to walk), the more necessary the shuttle bus system becomes.

A network *switch* is more like a regular *switchboard* than a (single) *regular* switch (like a light switch), since it internally contains multiple regular switches, each of which can be individually turned on or off, depending on what should be connected or disconnected.

In the older days, a telephone switchboard was managed by an *operator*. When a call came in, a light would blink next to the caller's line. The operator would then ask, "Number, please?" (analogous to the switch learning the source MAC address from the incoming frame and associating it with the port it arrived on). Once the caller provided the number of the person they wanted to reach (the destination MAC address), the operator would manually plug a cable from the caller's line into the recipient's line, establishing a direct, dedicated connection between those two specific parties.

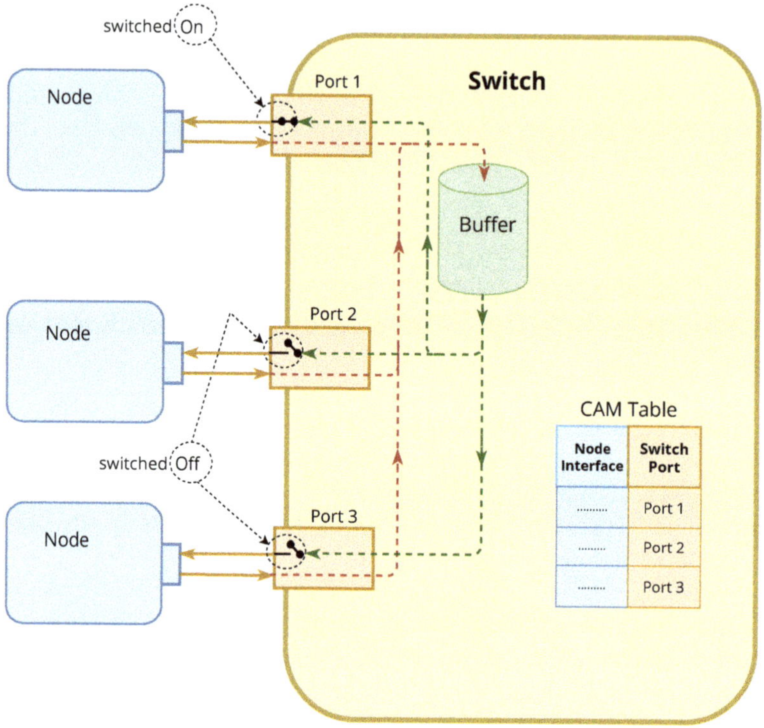

Figure 7. **A Switch** *(which contains multiple traditional "on-off switches") is a critical layer 2 service node which forms the core of most modern layer 2 networks (LANs). It can efficiently connect a large number of interfaces (for simplicity, just 3 are shown here). If multiple nodes try to send simultaneously, it queues the packets in a buffer, and forwards them sequentially. It also ensures that only intended recipients receive any packet by switching the respective outputs on/off depending on the destination address in the packet.*

Network Topology

Many networking introductions start with "*network topologies*" such as *ring*, *star*, and *mesh* as foundational concepts. Emphasizing these terms made more sense when network ports could be both *addressable* (i.e. interfaces) themselves and could serve as *pass-through* points for other ports. They are less relevant in modern networks where there is a clear separation between infrastructure and user nodes, as illustrated in *Figure 2*. Topology is still relevant for *infrastructure design*—how the infrastructure nodes are connected strongly influences network properties (e.g. performance and reliability), but this is specifically the topology of the infrastructure of the network—not that of the network as a whole. The simple ring/star/mesh labels are not very helpful for big-picture understanding of modern networks, where pure-infrastructure devices like *switches* connect interfaces that are purely users of the network.

CAM Tables

As mentioned above, a switch *remembers* which interface (of a user node) is attached at which of the switch's ports, by *noting* the information in its so-called *CAM (Content Addressable Memory)* table. The CAM table of a switch maps the address of each (connected) interface (address) to a port on the switch. When an incoming packet arrives at a port of the switch, the switch looks up the destination address of the packet in its CAM table. This tells it where the destination interface(s) of is connected to the switch. It then forwards the packet out on the corresponding port. (Switches may also use additional columns in their CAM table to note other information such as which VLAN, if any, the interface belongs to, and when the entry was last updated). The CAM table of a switch is typically empty to begin with (when the network is first set up), and it builds up the CAM table incrementally over time.

Every time an incoming packet arrives, the switch uses the **source** address of the packet to **update** its CAM table. If it already has an entry mapping the source interface (address) to the port it received the packet on, it updates the entry if necessary (which may happen if interfaces get reconnected to different ports). If not, it adds a corresponding entry to the CAM table.

When a switch receives a packet for whose **destination** interface (address) it does not have an entry in its (CAM) table for, it floods the packet - i.e. resend the packet on every port to which an interface is connected (within the respective broadcast domain) except the one on which the packet arrived.

So in summary, for each packet arriving at a particular switch port, the switch makes a *note* (in its CAM table) in order to *remember* that the interface with this *source address* is attached to this port. And to figure out which of the switch's ports it should forward the packet in question out of, so that it reaches the (user node interface corresponding to the) *destination address* in the same packet, it looks for a *note* it previously made (when said port received an earlier packet from the interface that is now the destination of the current packet).

Networks (LANs)

The infrastructure of two or more layer 1 networks can be joined by layer 2 service nodes to form the infrastructure of a combined layer 2 network, also known as a *LAN (Local Area Network)*. As mentioned in Switches, an optimal (and typical) configuration is when all the layer 1 infrastructures are single full-duplex point-to-point connections between the interfaces and ports on a switch. A single switch per LAN is the most common and simple to maintain configuration, but it's not impossible to have multiple switches, with one being the primary switch *in charge* of the others, to which it delegates some of the work.

To say that a switch is an important type of layer 2 service node is a bit of an understatement.

They are more like the *rock stars* of layer 2, and sophisticated (and correspondingly expensive) switches can connect thousands of interfaces in a highly optimized fashion, with advanced features like the buffering mentioned above. Many organizations who value performance and security invest significant amounts of money in correspondingly sophisticated switches.

A LAN, like a layer 1 network, forms a *single broadcast domain*, but, unlike a layer 2 network, it forms multiple small collision domains, or more often than not, *no collision domains* at all. This makes it able to accommodate many more interfaces much more reliably than a layer 1 network, and the switch with its conditional forwarding plays a key role here.

A LAN is often *defined* as a set of nodes managed by a single organization and/or restricted to a limited geographical area. While these are typical characteristics (as the name suggests) of existing LANs, they are not defining characteristics. Any more than say, *likes to swim* and *lives in the sea* are defining characteristics of a fish. It's very possible, for example, to create a LAN that is neither local nor managed by a single organization.[18] A defining characteristic of a LAN is the (exclusive) use of MAC addresses — every source interface must know the (permanent) *MAC address* of the intended destination address, before it can send that interface a packet. We will see in later chapters how this distinguishes a LAN from networks of *Layer 3* and above. The application of *conditional logic based on these MAC addresses* (leading to a reduction or elimination of collision domains, by layer service 2 nodes like a switch), distinguishes a LAN from layer 1 networks.

LAN

A layer 2 network. It connects ports on nodes which can communicate at layer 2, by exchanging packets of data using layer 2 (*MAC*) addresses. Most LANs are either:

- *Point-to-Point* : Two nodes connected directly by a medium (such as an Ethernet cable). See also *Link*.
- *Switch based*: multiple ports connected (by media) through a switch.

Despite LAN being an abbreviation for *Local Area Network* (and some definitions to the contrary), a LAN need not be restricted to a local area.

Destination Address Types

A destination address is always one of three types:

Unicast

The address is that of a specific existing interface[19]. When an interface receives a packet with its address in the destination of the header, it knows that the packet is meant specifically for it (alone). When a switch receives such a packet on one of its ports, it will forward it on the port connected to the recipient interface.

Multicast

The address is within a reserved range, representing a group of interfaces configured to know they belong to that group. When an interface receives a packet with a value in the destination of the header, that corresponds to a group the receiving interface belongs to, it knows that the packet is meant for it (as well as all other interfaces in the group). When a switch[20] receives such a packet on one of its ports, it will forward it out of each of its ports where an interface in said group is connected (excluding the one it received it on).

Broadcast

An address representing all connected interfaces (usually all **1s**). When an interface receives a packet with this value in the destination of the header, it knows that the packet is meant for it and all other interfaces in the network. When a switch receives such a packet on one of its ports, it will forward it out of each of its ports where an interface is connected (excluding the one it received it on).

Lower Layer Landscape

Three technologies dominate the landscape at layer 2: *Ethernet*, *Wi-Fi* & *Cellular*. Whereas at layer 1 *Fibre Optics*, *Wi-Fi* & *Cellular* are becoming increasingly popular. See *Figure 8*. Note that Ethernet, Wi-Fi, and Cellular [21] are *Official Standards* covering all aspects of *both* layer 1 *and* 2.

Some of these technologies lend themselves to pick-and-mix from different layers, e.g. layer 2 Ethernet (*think*: packets) can be used on top of layer 1 Ethernet or layer 1 fibre optics (*think*: type of cables). Whereas some (e.g. layer 2 Wi-Fi and cellular) can be combined only with their dedicated layer 1.[22]

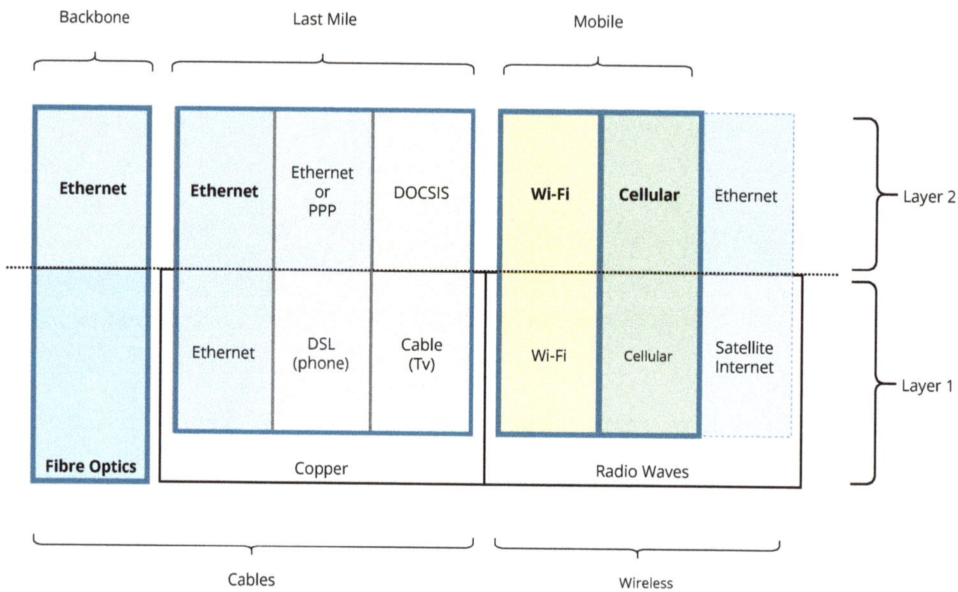

Figure 8. Layer 1 signals travel either through cables or wirelessly. The internet backbone (much of which is under the ocean) uses fibre optics, while the "last mile" to homes and businesses still commonly uses copper cables (though fibre is increasingly replacing them), and to mobile devices usually wireless.

The history of networking reveals an interesting reversal. Early internet access *hijacked* existing infrastructure never designed for data. Dial-up modems (1990s) repurposed telephone lines — unshielded copper wires designed for 4 kHz voice — using mostly analogue circuitry internally to convert bits into audio tones that could travel over these voice lines at 56 kbps. *ISDN (Integrated Services Digital Network)* improved on this with digital signal processors and dedicated channels for voice and data, eliminating the *can't use phone and internet simultaneously* problem. *DSL (Digital Subscriber Line)* pushed further by using digital processing to split the telephone line into multiple frequency channels — voice on low frequencies, multiple data channels on high frequencies — reaching up to 1 Gbps+ over the same thin, unshielded copper originally installed for analogue phones.[23] Similarly, cable internet using *DOCSIS (Data Over Cable Service Interface Specification)* hijacked unused frequency bands in TV coaxial cables, carving out channels for bidirectional data alongside television broadcasts.

However, purpose-built networking technologies (e.g. Ethernet, Wi-Fi, Fibre Optics) evolved so rapidly that the trend completely reversed. Instead of forcing data through infrastructure built for voice and television, we now eliminate that legacy infrastructure entirely and run everything — including phone calls and TV — as IP packets over data networks. Modern *phone service* is just *VoIP (Voice over IP)*, and television is streaming video over the same fibre that carries email and web traffic. The global telephone system, once entirely separate with circuit-switched connections,[24] has been absorbed into the packet-switched internet. This reversal is driven by physics and economics: telephone-grade copper (unshielded, thin gauge) hits hard limits on speed and distance, while modern Ethernet cables (shielded, twisted pairs) and especially fibre optic cables can carry gigabits or terabits of data reliably. Maintaining separate networks for voice, TV, and data no longer makes sense when a single fibre can handle everything.

Note that a side effect of reversing the trend (from *hijacking* phone and TV lines for internet access to running voice and TV over purpose-built data networks) is the corresponding shift from circuit-switched to packet-switched systems for all communications, including legacy voice and broadcast services.

A single LAN can, in principle, use a combination[25] of layer 1 and 2 standards (as long as the switch managing the LAN supports the technologies in question). This is how you can connect both your mobile phone (via Wi-Fi) and your PC (via Ethernet cable or Wi-Fi) to the internet through your home router.

> In the early stages of the internet, existing infrastructure like phone lines was *hijacked* to transport its data. Now the internet has a dedicated infrastructure of its own, and the opposite is happening—phone calls, TV etc. are increasingly using the infrastructure created for the internet.

VLANs

It's not uncommon for an organization to use a single switch (or combination thereof) to create multiple LANs. Each of these smaller LANs is then called a *VLAN (Virtual LAN)*. It's important to note, however, that each such VLAN is no different to a LAN created with its own separate switch to start with, from the point of view of the interfaces on the VLAN[26]. A VLAN is itself a (new) LAN and the original LAN then no longer *exists* in the sense that each VLAN has its own separate broadcast domain independent of the others. The advantage of dividing up a single (original) LAN like this, as opposed to creating them with separate switches to start with, is improved flexibility and performance.[27]

> *Ethernet* (IEEE 802.3) and *Wi-Fi* (IEEE 802.11) are official *standards* developed by *IEEE (Institute of Electrical and Electronics Engineers)*, while Cellular standards such as 3G, 4G/LTE, 5G (and 6G) are developed by *3GPP (3rd Generation Partnership Project)*. All three govern all aspects of both layer 1 and layer 2 (see *Official Standards*). Furthermore, the standards for *Layer 3* and above are developed by *IETF (Internet Engineering Task Force)*. While distinct in their primary focus, the IEEE, IETF and 3GPP work closely together.

Twisted-pair copper cables, such as *Cat6* or *Cat7*, are also simply known as *Ethernet cables* — since they were originally the only kind supported by layer 2 Ethernet. However, layer 2 Ethernet was later generalized to support other cable types, including fibre optic, as illustrated in Figure 8. So, it's not always clear from the context whether *Ethernet cable* is referring specifically to the (traditional) copper cables or Ethernet cables in general.

Limitations

Several shortcomings become apparent when considering scaling a layer 2 network to include more interfaces distributed more widely (let alone across the whole planet).

MAC addresses are inflexible

The MAC addresses used at layer 2 are permanent — the address of a given interface can never be changed. They burned into the hardware (e.g. NIC) during assembly, before it is even sold (let alone its usage determined). When you replace an interface (even using a NIC that is the same model from the same manufacturer), the address changes, requiring all other nodes on the network to relearn it

It's not possible to group interfaces in any sensible way by address. The addresses are effectively *random numbers*. For example, there's no inherent way to identify addresses by **role** (e.g. *the printers*) or **region** (e.g. *in our office*). Any address could belong to any device or location.

No Address Discovery

There's no built-in way for an interface to ask *who's there?* (i.e., discover the addresses of other listening interfaces). The nodes have to *somehow* figure out what other interfaces are connected and with which addresses, and/or be manually configured (and updated) by *someone* with the information.

Limits of a Single Switch

A single LAN can grow using a single switch (or multiple switches, with one being the primary switch *in charge* of the others), and such a switch can handle many (1000+) interfaces well, but every switch reaches its limit at some stage. Even with multiple switches servicing a single LAN, coordination overhead grows with the number of interfaces.

Limits of Multiple Combined Switches

Instead of growing a single big LAN with a single (primary) switch, one could try letting separate (smaller) LANs communicate by enabling switches to send packets to each other.

One could envisage a switch theoretically forwarding a packet (arriving from an external switch) to the destination interface, if the interface in question is in the LAN managed by the recipient switch. And if it's not, forwarding the packet instead further along, one switch at a time, until it ultimately arrives at the intended destination LAN, and the switch that manages the destination interface.

This might seem feasible when the number of switches involved, and the number of paths connecting them, is small. But imagine a global collection of switches, all connected directly or indirectly in a maze of complicated paths. A big challenge would then be determining the *best path* for a packet to take across multiple switches. And how would the switches communicate these paths to each other? See Figure 9 below.

Since MAC addresses are *random*, a switch would need to store the chosen path (or at least the next *hop* along that path) for every possible destination, which scales very poorly (linearly with the number of connected interfaces).

Packets would need to include a further address (in addition to the ultimate destination)—that of the next switch on the path to this destination. This is not something switches, and layer 2 in general, were designed to accommodate, and it's not clear how to *extend* them to do so.

Security

Layer 2 traffic is generally insecure. There is no default encryption of Layer 2 packets or way for interfaces to verify (*authenticate*) each other. Switches just *learn* which interfaces are connected to what port, by *observing the source* addresses of packets they forward to the intended recipient. Any interface can *pretend* to have any address (so-called *MAC spoofing*) by simply writing a different source address into the header of outgoing packets.

An interface could be replaced by a malicious one at any time (without the switch or other interfaces being aware), potentially *intercepting packets* intended for the original device.[28] Chapter 5. Security, will go into more details.

These vulnerabilities highlight why using public Wi-Fi is fundamentally insecure. On any network you join, all devices connected can communicate at Layer 2 with your device, exposing it to potential attacks such as *MAC spoofing* or *packet interception*. Using a VPN, for example, will encrypt traffic at higher layers but doesn't directly address layer 2 vulnerabilities.

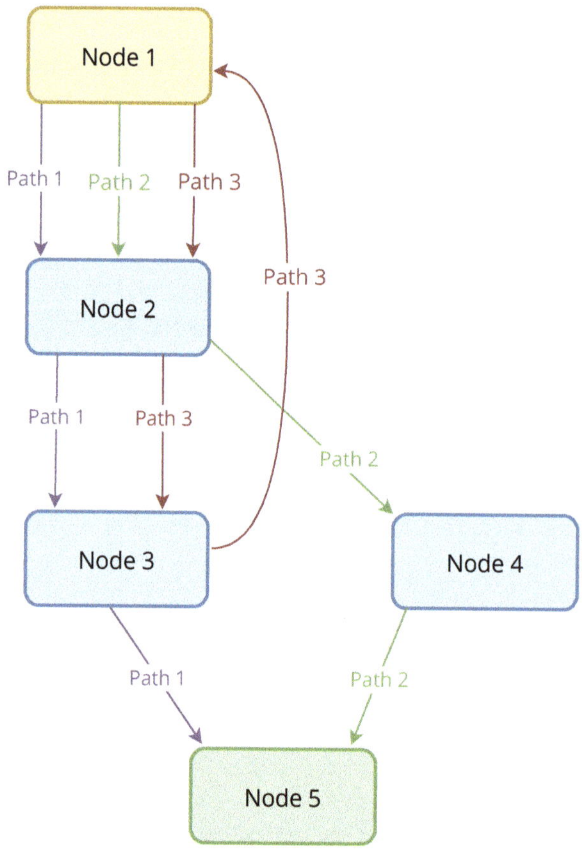

Figure 9. **Best Path Problem.** *A web of nodes (labelled Node 1-5), and some possible paths connecting even this small number of nodes. Note that some paths (e.g. Path 3) from the initial source (Node 1) may never lead to the final intended destination (Node 5), but instead to a (possibly endless) loop. Somehow, for each packet from a given initial source to a final destination node, the best of many possible paths needs to be determined, and each node on this path needs to know to which of the nodes connected to it, it should forward the packet in question to next.*[29]

Summary

- Layer 1 is concerned with the transmission of electromagnetic waves, as well as their conversion to and from a stream of bits.
- Layer 1 service nodes do not change the values of the bits or in any way make logical decisions based on these values.
- Layer 1 networks form a single collision domain, which is identical to its single broadcast domain.
- This single collision domain places severe restrictions on the size of Layer 1 networks, which is typically limited to a few interfaces.

- Layer 2 is concerned with *packets* (which in the context of layer 2 are often also referred to as *frames*) as well as their conversion to and from a stream of bits.
- A packet is the smallest independent chunk data gets handled as, before it's disassembled into a sequence of bits for layer 1 to transmit, or after it's assembled from a sequence of bits layer 1 has transmitted.
- Packet is structured as a payload, together with a header and a trailer.
- The payload is the actual data the sender wants to send.
- The header and trailer contain fields containing extra information used to help deliver the payload reliably.
- The source address identifies which interface sent the packet. The destination address identifies which interface(s) should receive the packet.
- Unlike nodes which only operate at layer 1, layer 2 service nodes can (and often do) actively interpret the incoming bit patterns, and make logical decisions about how to behave, based on these values.
- A switch is the most important layer 2 service node.
- It can efficiently connect a very large number of interfaces into a reliable layer 2 network, frequently called a LAN.
- Ethernet, Wi-Fi and Cellular are technologies commonly used at both layer 1 and 2. Fibre Optics are commonly used (only) at layer 1. Each are governed by official standards to ensure reliable quality and interoperability for everyone involved.

- Despite the huge improvements over layer 1, layer 2 networks still have their limits.
- A layer 2 network can contain thousands of interfaces, but this falls far short of what's needed to connect something as large as the whole internet.
- One of the challenges faced when trying to combine multiple layer 2 networks, is finding the best path through them for any given packet.

Conclusion

You now understand how the lower layers form the foundation of network communication. Layer 1 handles the transmission of bits as electromagnetic signals across copper, fibre, or wireless media, while layer 2 packages these bits into frames and manages delivery between directly connected devices using MAC addresses.

While these layers excel at local communication within small to medium-sized LANs, they face critical limitations. The inflexible hardware-bound addressing, limited error recovery, and minimal security make it impossible to scale LANs to anything approaching internet scale.

Chapter 3 introduces layers 3 and 4, which overcome these constraints. Layer 3 enables us to join multiple LANs into interconnected networks that can scale globally — forming the basis for the internet itself. You'll discover how IP addresses provide the flexible, hierarchical addressing scheme that makes this possible, allowing packets to be routed across countless intermediate networks to reach any destination worldwide.

Layer 4 adds interface sharing through port numbers. While layer 3 delivers packets between network interfaces (like delivering mail between buildings), layer 4 lets multiple applications share the same interface—adding apartment numbers to our postal analogy. This enables a single device to run hundreds of network services simultaneously. You'll also explore how TCP, one specific layer 4 protocol, adds reliability and connection management on top of this basic multiplexing function, while UDP provides a simpler alternative when these features aren't needed.

[1] While virtual networks and software-defined systems can operate without traditional layer 1 connections, understanding layer 1 remains fundamental to grasping how most real-world networks function.

[2] more accurately, any space, including one filled by a vacuum, can act as a medium for electromagnetic waves - see also Electromagnetic Waves and the Role of Media

[3] readers with a background in physics may feel tempted to appeal to the principle of wave-particle duality [en.wikipedia.org/wiki/Wave%E2%80%93particle_duality] here, the photon being the particle counterpart to the wave, but further elaboration would probably be better left to a book on quantum physics. Note also that the illustration of the wave shown (like a standing wave on a guitar string) is not very accurate. The actual wave is much more complicated and is generally composed of a base wave (the 'carrier') on top of which multiple other waves of different wavelengths are superimposed. The exact wavelengths and amplitudes involved and the way they are superimposed are what encodes the information carried by the complete wave.

[4] The physical media (part of Layer 1) represents a complex engineering domain where multiple challenges must be solved simultaneously — much like road construction. Roads must be smooth, weather-resistant, and support bridges. Similarly, network media must handle electrical interference, signal degradation over distance, physical durability, and bandwidth requirements. Not all media solutions are created equal: Cat5e cable (*think*: a local road) supports 1 Gbps up to 100 meters, while Cat6 (*think*: a highway) handles 10 Gbps but only up to 55 meters at that speed. Cat6a extends this to 100 meters but requires thicker, less flexible cables. Fiber optic cables (*think*: high-speed rail lines) can carry signals for kilometers without degradation but require specialized, expensive termination equipment. Each medium represents different trade-offs between cost, performance, distance limitations, and installation complexity — choosing the right one requires understanding both current needs and future growth, just as city planners must decide whether to build a two-lane road or a six-lane highway.

[5] imagine an electron oscillating to and from the end of a conductor in the direction of the cable. As it gets closer to the end of the wire, the repulsive Coulomb force on the free electrons at the end of the wire increases, nudging them down the wire a little. In turn, this increases the repulsive force on the electrons a little further down, and so on. When the first electron moves away from the start of the wire the opposite happens — this is very much like pushing and pulling the end of a spring causing compression waves to propagate down it. And just as no part of the spring moves very far, none of the free electrons in the wire move very far — they just oscillate back and forth harmonically like the first electron. The wavelike electromagnetic propagation *in* the conductor is not normally called an electromagnetic wave, but it is an electromagnetic field propagating as a wave. The magnitude of the field inside the conductor decreases fast — with the square of distance from the source — which is why neighbouring free electrons are needed to sustain it. This very same oscillation of the electron also causes an *independent* electromagnetic wave to be emitted perpendicular to the length of the conductor. Unlike the wave *in* the conductor, it needs no medium with free electrons to propagate it — no neighbouring electrons to feel repelled, and pass on this repulsive force. This wave, outside the conductor and moving axially away from it, is what's normally called an electromagnetic wave (or far-field radiation) and its magnitude decreases linearly in proportion to its distance from the source — here the oscillating electron. The total electromagnetic field generated by a moving charge is called a Liénard-Wiechert Field. Interested readers familiar with Python may wish to have a look at the wonderful simulations by Matthew Filipovich as part of his pycharge [github.com/MatthewFilipovich/pycharge] project available at github.com/MatthewFilipovich/pycharge.

[6] Broadcast and Collision Domains defines the collision/broadcast domain of an individual port. The collision/broadcast domain of the whole network can then be understood to be the union of the set of collision/broadcast domains of the individual ports in the network.

[7] This book shall tend to prefer the general term "*packet*" unless using different context-specific terms for a single concept adds clarity. Another common general term for packet is "*Protocol Data Unit (PDU)*". The reader is advised that when other sources refer to "frames" they are simply referring to packets (or PDUs) of layer 2

[8] Switches are layer 2 infrastructure nodes, so their ports are *not* called interfaces. Routers (though layer 3 infrastructure) are not layer 2 infrastructure nodes — their ports *are* referred to as interfaces. Layers 1 and 2 will be covered in 2. Lower Layers—physical networks and LANs. Only interfaces can serve as original sources or final destinations of layer 2 packages

[9] Strictly speaking, a hash is more complicated to calculate than a checksum, and produces a longer value. As a result, it's much more certain to be unique (*think*: much higher resolution fingerprint) - the *effective* and *almost always* qualifiers above are much more likely to be superfluous.

[10] Note that some fields are omitted, which I feel are details that distract more from a fundamental understanding of the concepts presented here, than add to it. And Wi-Fi defines/uses more such fields than Ethernet, in particular because in the case of Wi-Fi, the media are much less reliable, and thus need more checking. Ethernet cables, for example, are well shielded and much less susceptible to interference or loss than a Wi-Fi signal. Most of these additional fields are part of what's shown as "Other Meta Information"

[11] not necessarily uniquely - see Destination Address Types

[12] What fields are available depends on what layer 2 standard (e.g. *Ethernet*, *Wi-Fi* or *Fibre Optics*) is used

[13] may have padding added to meet minimum packet size requirements

[14] the sender calculates a checksum based on the contents of (the rest of) the packet it's sending, and appends this value to the packet. The receiver performs the same calculation based on the contents of (the rest of) the packet it receives. If the value calculated by the receiver is equal to the value calculated and appended by the sender, it is presumed that the packet contents are equal, since any change (no matter how slight) in packet content would lead to a different checksum value. If not, the frame is discarded by the receiver as invalid. Higher layers e.g. TCP in Layer 4—may then request the frame to be resent

[15] A *MAC (media access control)* address is usually represented as six groups of two hexadecimal digits, separated by colons (:) or hyphens (-). For example: `00:1A:2B:3C:4D:5E` or `00-1A-2B-3C-4D-5E`

[16] Each manufacturer is typically allocated a range of addresses by the *IEEE (Institute of Electrical and Electronics Engineers)*, the first 24 (of 48) bits of which identify the manufacturer itself. In Virtual Devices and Interfaces we'll discuss virtual/software interfaces. While there's no physical *burning* involved for these, they still have MAC addresses, and changing them is conceptually equivalent to replacing the interface. Note that while software can be used to make an interface *appear* to use a different MAC address (called *MAC spoofing*), this doesn't actually change it.

[17] For layer 2 service nodes, *dropping* and *forwarding* are the only two options, since service nodes are never the intended final destination for layer 2 packets. However, if this were not a service node but rather an user node, it could instead *consume* the packet (if the interface was its intended final destination) — meaning it would process the packet's contents for its own use. To the outside world, consuming looks the same as dropping: the packet isn't forwarded anywhere else.

[18] See, for example, Overlay Networks

[19] a specific value (usually all **0s**) is reserved to mean *invalid* or *address unknown*. It is, however, rarely needed

[20] technically, a switch must be (and most modern switches are) capable of so-called *IGMP snooping* to handle multicast correctly. Other less capable switches treat multicast packets as broadcast

[21] The cellular standard is specified by an organization called *3GPP (3rd Generation Partnership Project)*. Like Wi-Fi, it has progressed through various generations, e.g *3G → 4G (LTE)→ 5G →* the emerging *6G*. And like Wi-Fi it covers all aspects of layer 1 and 2. 3GPP subdivides layer 2 into three separate sublayers (called *MAC, RLC, PDCP*), and defines protocols for each.

[22] 1). Ethernet is defined by IEEE 802.3; it specifies both the physical wiring/signals (Layer 1) and link sharing/MAC addressing (Layer 2). Common types: 10/100/1G/2.5G/5G/10G/800G/1.6TBASE-T (twisted-pair copper cables, e.g., Cat5e, Cat6, Cat7) and 1000BASE-LX/10GBASE-LR (fibre); VLANs via IEEE 802.1Q. 2). Wi-Fi is defined by IEEE 802.11. Versions include: 802.11a, 802.11b, 802.11g, 802.11n (Wi-Fi 4), 802.11ac (Wi-Fi 5), 802.11ax (Wi-Fi 6/6E), and 802.11be (Wi-Fi 7), operating in 2.4, 5 and 6 GHz frequency bands. Lower frequency bands have better range, but less bandwidth (more congested). Wi-Fi security is defined by WPA2/WPA3, which is independent of the Wi-Fi version used—you can use WPA3 on older Wi-Fi standards if the hardware supports it, and newer Wi-Fi versions maintain backward compatibility with older security protocols for legacy device support. 5). Between cell towers and beyond (called the *backhaul*), cellular networks switch to Ethernet at layer 2 6). DSL uses copper phone

lines. Speeds up to 1Gbps+ with ADSL/VDSL2/G.fast. Layer 2 runs PPPoE, PPPoA, ATM, or plain Ethernet. 7). Cable internet uses coaxial cables with DOCSIS 3.1/4.0 at layer 2. Your modem outputs Ethernet. 8). Fibre to the home (FTTH) uses GPON/XGS-PON/50G-PON standards. The ONT box in your home converts fibre signals to Ethernet. 9). Satellite internet uses radio waves in Ku-band (12-18 GHz) or Ka-band (26-40 GHz). Layer 2 runs DVB-S2/S2X/RCS2 or proprietary protocols like Starlink. Your satellite modem outputs Ethernet. 10). *Power Line Communication (PLC)* allows data transmission over electric power lines. It's primarily used in home automation systems (like smart meters) and as an alternative to Wi-Fi for extending network coverage within buildings. While convenient for certain use cases, its adoption remains limited compared to dedicated networking technologies.

[23] Note that the marketing emphasis the "digitalization" of internet access—it was only the circuitry in the (modem) devices themselves that made a jump from analogue to digital with ISDN and DSL—before and after layer 1 remained purely analogue (think: electromagnetic waves), and layer 2 purely digital (think: packets of bits)

[24] Circuit-switching creates a dedicated, fixed-bandwidth path between endpoints (like a traditional phone call, where the line is reserved even during silence, wasting resources). *Think*: you get a road to yourself. Packet-switching breaks data into small packets sent independently over shared paths, reassembled at the destination — more efficient, flexible, and scalable for mixed media, but can introduce minor delays or jitter if not managed well. *Think*: you get a car to yourself on a road you share with other cars. You have no control over traffic conditions. This reversal enables unified IP-based networks handling everything from calls (VoIP) to streaming TV.

[25] A typical *home router* used to connect your home to the internet through your Internet Service Provider(ISP) actually a combined *switch* and *router* in a single device. Each are not nearly as high-powered as those designed to handle heavy enterprise loads, but are more than capable of handling the traffic for a small to medium-sized home. It generally supports a combination of Ethernet, Wi-Fi and whatever technology is used to connect your home to the ISP — often DSL or, increasingly common nowadays, Fibre Optic

[26] Strictly speaking this is only true at layer 2. As we will see in the next chapter, so-called *multilayer switches* can also operate at layer 3 and route layer 3 packets between VLANs—but only between those VLANs it manages. *VLAN trunking* allows a single physical connection to carry packets for multiple VLANs. It's typically necessary since packets from different VLANs often need to share the same cables. *VLAN tagging* adds an identifier to each frame so the receiving device knows which VLAN it belongs to and can deliver it correctly. Without tagging, there would be no way to distinguish which VLAN each frame came from once they're combined on the trunk link. In this book, wherever you see "*(V)LAN*" read "*LAN or VLAN*"—used in order to emphasise that what's being discussed applies equally well to both.

[27] Flexibility: in the sense that it's much easier to change VLANs than LANs—the former requires reconfiguring a single switch using software, the latter requires adding/removing whole switches as well as reconnecting individual interfaces, including any cables. Performance: in the sense that an organization can invest in a single high-performance switch which can apply its processing power intelligently to whatever VLANs currently have the most traffic, rather than multiple less capable separate switches, some of which may be idle while others are maxed out with current traffic.

[28] *WPA3*, the latest wireless security technology, significantly improves security on Wi-Fi networks, with encryption and stronger authentication. It's, however, still quite recent and adoption remains limited. WPA3-Enhanced Open, used in some public Wi-Fi, encrypts traffic without authentication, while WPA3-Enterprise, common in corporate settings, offers robust authentication but is rarely used in public networks due to complex setup and compatibility needs.

[29] as we will see in later chapters, the solution to this problem, as to several others, involves a new layer (layer 3) and new class of device called a *router* that plays as important a role there, as the switch does in modern layer 2 networks

3. Middle Layers — encapsulation, logical addressing, routing and conversations

This chapter explores layers 3 and 4 — the critical middle layers that transform isolated LANs into the global internet, enabling packets to flow using logical addressing and routing protocols. These layers solve the fundamental limitations of hardware-bound communication constraining individual LANs.

Layer 3 introduces IP addresses and packet encapsulation. You'll discover the central role played by routers, and how they enable a packet of data to travel from a source interface on one LAN to a destination interface on another. This doesn't just connect two LANs — it can span the entire world, forming the fundamental basis of the internet, enabling packets to traverse dozens of routers, each making independent forwarding decisions based on IP addresses. Layer 4 enables port-based interface sharing, with a choice of protocols such as TCP that ensures reliable in-order delivery, or UDP providing a lightweight alternative.

We'll examine the structure of the internet from two perspectives. Firstly, using a simplified tree-like model that reveals the core concepts of hierarchical routing, address ranges, and packet forwarding. Then, how the messy reality of different systems and economic relationships cause deviations from this model — and how model and reality combine to shape actual internet traffic flow. This dual approach ensures you grasp both the elegant theory and practical complexities of the internet.

We begin with a brief fictional narrative (*Metropolea*) that provides an intuitive metaphor for the technical concepts that follow.

Metropolea

The people of Metropolea were proud of their transport system. Each capsule could comfortably hold about 6 individuals, gliding almost friction-free through invisible electromagnetic tunnels from one station to the next. But impressive as the technology behind the capsules themselves and the details of their locomotion was, what invariably impressed visitors from other parts of Aetheria the most, was the vast and intricate web of routes between the countless stations. Stations which could appear overnight, and disappear even faster.

Aetheria discovered early in its development that solid objects are an illusion. The experience of touching another object is a result of interaction between the electromagnetic field of one object (even your body) and that of the other object. An interaction at a distance. All objects, no matter how solid they seem, are, in fact, primarily composed of empty space, and any touching that might be considered to take place (an overlap of these spaces) is prevented by the mutual repulsion of the electron clouds shrouding the objects. A repulsion, the strength of which increases exponentially as the objects in question near each other. Their mastery of electromagnetism, one of the four fundamental forces of nature, was a key to their technological advancement, and why so much of it is holography-based — what others might call virtual reality. The electromagnetic guides for the capsules, and the ability to make not only stations, but also whole local neighbourhoods serviced by them, appear and disappear overnight, bore testament to this.

Between (almost) every pair of cities was a single, direct, high-speed multi-capsule highway. These inter-city connections formed a mesh that could only be described as a translucent blur, along which the capsules sped in the blink of an eye. The inter-city station of each city was a correspondingly busy and highly secured (virtual) hub. In the rare cases where such a link broke (it generally did so only due to natural disasters, like the solar flares on Alpha-Proxima), it was no longer possible to travel directly from one city to the other. The inter-city mesh was, however, so complete that an alternative indirect route, through one or more intermediary cities, could still be found and used, while the direct link was repaired.

Within each city in the land of Metropolea, the stations were (originally) planned like a tree, the trunk of which sprang from the inter-city station. At each bifurcation of the tree was a new station, and each new station name was logically derived from its parent station. A city was typically divided into 4 zones (north, south, east and west), each of which was directly reachable by capsule from the inter-city hub. Each zone was subdivided into districts, numbered or named uniquely, each of which was further subdivided as necessary. Most (but not all) homes were in the suburbs (close to the stations forming the leafs of the tree). This was a very logical and easy to navigate system. Take, for example, a traveller in (or close to), station luna-east-12 (i.e. district 12 of the east zone of the city of luna), who wished to travel to luna-west-5 (i.e. district 5 of the west zone of the same city). See Figure 10. They first needed to get a capsule to luna-east station, from there another to luna hub (the inter-city station of the city of luna, and ultimate parent station of all other stations in luna), from there to luna-west station, and finally from there to luna-west-5.

The beauty of this system was its simplicity, and it worked impeccably—most of the time. But some routes became much more popular than others, putting a strain on this system. And since many travellers lived (in suburbs) near leaf stations, they typically had to travel all the way up and down the respective branches, to visit family or friends in a different suburb.

Shortcuts began to emerge, often run (or at least sponsored) by private real-estate companies, with a strong vested interest in the areas connected. These shortcut lines offered direct connections between a pair of stations that were not parent-child in the tree structure. They also, however, made the originally clear hierarchical tree structure more mesh-like. One could no longer discern what stations to travel through, in which order, based solely on their names.

One result of this was the transition of the role of station master from almost superfluous to crucial. Understanding and using the prefixes (city, zone, district etc) was still a good first guess, but now, to be able to calculate the best path for capsules to their intended destination stations, they needed to include the ever-changing shortcut lines. But there was no centrally managed, up-to-date list of these shortcuts, that they could query. The only ones who directly observed a shortcut connection joining or leaving the capsule network were the station masters in the stations the new line provided a shortcut between. So the station masters invented a new router protocol to pass on this information to station masters in other stations directly connected to them, and they in turn to those a step further away. So, up-to-date news of the locations and capacities (not all stations could handle the same amount of traffic) spread like a wave through the transport network. The elegance of this router protocol wave was second only to that which the station masters used to incorporate it into split second decisions, to determine which was the best track on which to send each waiting capsule on the next step of its (quickest possible) journey to its final destination station. All the while, the average passenger in the capsule remained oblivious to the complexity of the network it was navigating or the fact that they were even passing through stations along the way.

The invisible network that carried Metropoleans through their daily lives had evolved from a simple, predictable tree into something far more organic — a system that adapted moment by moment to the needs of its users. Like the neural pathways of a brain or the hidden root systems of an ancient forest, the transport network's true complexity remained hidden from those who relied upon it most. As travellers stepped into their capsules each morning, inputting their destinations with casual ease, they remained blissfully unaware of the symphony of split-second decisions. The constant flow of routing information, and the elegant dance of electromagnetic forces, would carry them safely to their destination. Perhaps this was the greatest achievement of Metropolea's transport system: not that it worked so well, but that its users never needed to understand how.

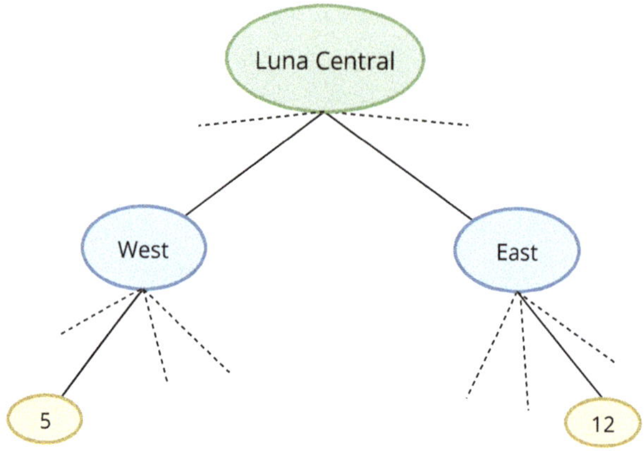

Figure 10. A hypothetical hierarchical connection between station luna-east-12 (i.e. district 12 of the east zone of the city of luna), and luna-west-5 (i.e. district 5 of the west zone of the same city) in Metropolea, before shortcuts became prevalent.

Layer 3

We saw in Layer 2 Limitations various limits one encounters when trying to scale a LAN to include more interfaces. Layer 2 networks (LANs) can't *simply be extended* to overcome these limitations, without introducing new problems. So instead, a new layer — Layer 3 — was built on top of Layer 2, allowing multiple LANs to be connected together.[1] A key technique enabling this is Packet Encapsulation — a clever trick used throughout networking, at various layers, as we'll repeatedly see in the coming chapters.

Logical Addressing

A single switch can handle thousands of interfaces, but this is still far too few to connect something nearly as large as the internet. The best hope is to *divide and conquer* by somehow connecting multiple switches together, each of which manages a subset of the interfaces. Each connected switch can *hide* the details of what port each interface it manages is connected to, saving all the other switches from the burden of having to do so. But the other switches still have to keep a record of all the interfaces managed by every switch—remember the (hardware) addresses are effectively *random numbers*—it would be great if there were a way of *summarizing* concisely which interfaces are managed by any given switch. For example, instead of having to maintain a list of 1000 (or more) entries, each of which is the (*effectively random*) numerical address of an interface managed by a given (other) switch, it would be great if the addresses in question *happened* to be 1000 *consecutive* numbers. Other switches would then only have to *maintain* a list of 2 numbers instead of 1000—the first address, and the last address[2]. See *IP Address Ranges* below.

To achieve just this, each interface is assigned an additional *logical address* in addition to the MAC address the manufacturer burned into it. The switch[3] in any given LAN *knows* both the logical and the MAC address of each interface in the LAN. But the *world outside* (the LAN managed by the switch) need only concern itself with the (convenient) logical addresses of the interfaces within. Whenever a packet enters or leaves the LAN, the switch *translates* the logical addresses to the MAC addresses and vice versa to make this work. Not only does this make it possible to **scale** multiple connected LANs to a network of many more (total) interfaces than would otherwise be possible, it also makes the resulting network much more **flexible** (interfaces may be grouped by role, region etc.). If, for some reason, a node, or interface needs to be replaced for some reason (*think*: replace a printer by a new one), the new interface(s) can be assigned the same logical addresses as before—so outside the LAN where all nodes were using only the logical addresses anyway, no change is *noticed*. One is reminded here of a famous quote, often referred to as the *Fundamental Theorem of Software Engineering*.

Consider by analogy cars, each of which get a globally unique *Vehicle Identification Number (VIN)* burned into it by the manufacturer. Each VIN is a 17-character code like *1HGBH41JXMN109186* that permanently identifies that specific vehicle worldwide. The VIN encodes details about the manufacturer, plant location, model year, and a sequential production number, but from the perspective of a car owner or local authorities, VINs are essentially random numbers. You cannot tell from a VIN alone whether a car is registered in Dublin or Berlin, who owns it, or what it's being used for. The VIN stays with the car forever—if the vehicle is sold, moves across the country, or changes hands multiple times, the VIN remains unchanged. While VINs are essential for manufacturers to track recalls and for investigators to identify stolen vehicles, they provide no organizational convenience for day-to-day vehicle management.

Licence plates provide a logical addressing system layered on top of VINs. Unlike the permanent VIN, licence plates are assigned by local authorities and can be grouped geographically and organizationally. A plate like *IRL 252-D-12345* immediately tells you this vehicle is registered in Dublin, while *D B-AB 1234* indicates registration in Berlin. This geographic grouping provides enormous convenience—when authorities need to search for vehicles in a specific state or city, they can immediately identify candidates by their licence plate format, rather than having to cross-reference millions of random VINs against registration databases. Crucially, licence plates are dynamic and transferable. When you sell your car, the new owner typically gets a new licence plate that reflects their location and registration preferences. The same physical vehicle (same VIN) might have a Texas plate when owned by someone in Dallas, then get a Colorado plate when sold to someone in Denver. This flexibility means the logical addressing system can adapt to how and where the vehicle is actually being used, regardless of where or when it was manufactured.

Network interfaces use this same two-tier addressing approach. Each interface gets a permanent MAC address burned in by the manufacturer (analogous to VIN)—a seemingly random number that stays with the hardware forever. But each interface also gets assigned a logical IP address (analogous to a licence plate) that can be grouped by network location, department, or function. Just as licence plates let authorities easily identify *all California vehicles* or *all vehicles in this city*, IP addresses let network administrators easily identify *all devices in the accounting department* or *all devices in the Paris office*. And just like licence plates, IP addresses are dynamic—when you replace a broken printer, the new device gets a different MAC address but can be assigned the same IP address, so everyone who was printing to that logical address continues to work seamlessly.

> The word *logical* in *logical addressing* can be a bit misleading, as it perhaps conveys mathematical connotations, which are not intended in this context. When you read *"logical"* here, think instead *"convenient and flexible (from the perspective of how they are used)"*. [4]

Fundamental Theorem of Software Engineering

We can solve any problem by introducing an extra level of indirection.[5]

— Andrew Koenig

Packet Encapsulation

Packet encapsulation is the insertion of a new type of packet (used by a higher layer) into the *payload within* an existing (lower-layer) packet. See *Figure 11*.

Imagine a large company with branches in different cities, each with numerous internal departments. An employee at one branch wants to send a packet to an employee in a specific department at another branch, using an external courier. Two options exist. First, the sender could write all address details – including the company internal department – on the packet, hoping the courier ignores or isn't confused by the unfamiliar company-specific info. This mirrors trying to extend Layer 2.

The second option – packet encapsulation – is smarter: The employee places the packet with internal details inside an outer packet. The outer packet is addressed only with the info the courier expects. The courier, unaware of the inner packet's special contents, delivers it to the destination branch without issue. There, a recipient familiar with the company internal *protocol* opens the outer packet and processes the inner one according to its instructions.

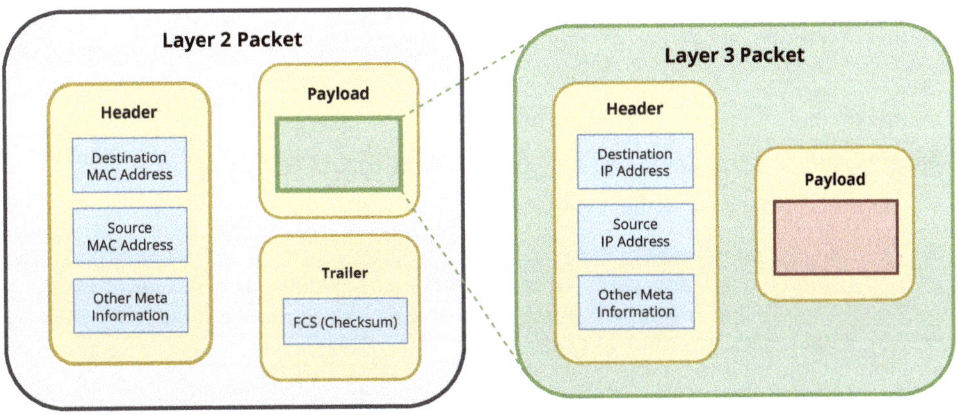

Figure 11. **Layer 3 packet encapsulated** *as the payload of a layer 2 packet. The layer 3 packet contains the logical (IP) address, whereas the layer 2 packet contains the hardware (MAC) address of the destination and source interfaces, respectively. The payload of the layer 3 packet contains the actual data the source is sending to the destination.*[6]

Protocols

A protocol is a set of rules that defines how different parties should behave when they need to accomplish something together. Protocols exist everywhere in human society – they're the agreed-upon ways of doing things that ensure everyone knows what to expect and how to participate. At its core, every protocol specifies:

- Who the participants are and their roles
- What information needs to be exchanged
- What format that information exchanged should take
- What order things should happen in
- How to behave in different situations

Take, for example, when an ambassador is newly appointed, and needs to formally establish their role in a foreign country. The ambassador must request an audience with the local Head of State, dress in specific formal attire, follow a pre-determined procession route, present their credentials (formal letters from their own Head of State) in a specific manner, and exchange greetings using predefined phrases (*Your Excellency, Mr. President*). There are strict rules about who speaks, for how long, and what they should say.

In the world of digital communications, protocols serve the same fundamental purpose — they're the agreed-upon rules that allow different systems to work together effectively. A network protocol specifically defines how information should be exchanged between systems, including:

- *Structure*: The exact layout of *packages* exchanged, including which fields (pieces of information) can be present and where each field is positioned
- *Semantics*: What each field means and how it should be interpreted
- *Timing*: When messages should be sent and how long to wait for responses
- *Error handling*: What to do when things go wrong

At layers 1 and 2 one speaks of *standards* (which *both* define protocols *and* specify hardware). At Layers 3 and above there is no (new) hardware to specify, so one speaks there only of *protocols*.

Layer 3 packets and protocols

Layer 3 packets are often called *IP packets*, and the most fundamental layer 3 protocol is called the *Internet Protocol (IP)*, the most commonly used versions of which are 4 and 6. The main function of the IP protocol is to define a standard structure and semantics of the IP packets — the most important of which are the *IP Addresses*. There are other layer 3 protocols, which we will meet in the course of the chapter, each of which has a specific purpose, but every other (modern) layer 3 protocol relies directly or indirectly on the IP protocol.[7] *Think:* IP is like the postmen who actually deliver packets, while other layer 3 protocols are used to keep that delivery system running (fixing delivery trucks, updating maps, reporting incorrect addresses).

Protocol Layering

Packet Encapsulation facilitates *protocol layering*—a new protocol is layered *on top* of an existing one (recall Layers of Abstraction), which involves embedding a new *packet* type *inside* (as the payload of) an existing one, as illustrated in Figure 12. The lower layer protocol doesn't need to understand what's inside its payload – it just treats the inner packet as data to be transported. *Think*: Russian dolls, where the *inner* doll shells correspond to *higher* (more abstract) protocol layers. And true to the Russian doll analogy, as we will see in later chapters, the inner (higher-layer) packets can themselves in turn contain (even higher-layer) packets, and so on, recursively.

The header of the new layer 3 packet is where the new logical addresses (namely that of the sender and intended final destination of the packets), as well as any other meta information the new layer 3 protocol needs, is stored. Each layer handles its own specific job (like addressing, routing, or error detection) while carrying the complete messages from the layer above it. It's like putting a diplomatic pouch (one protocol) inside a shipping container (another protocol) – the shipping company doesn't need to know about diplomatic procedures to transport the pouch correctly.

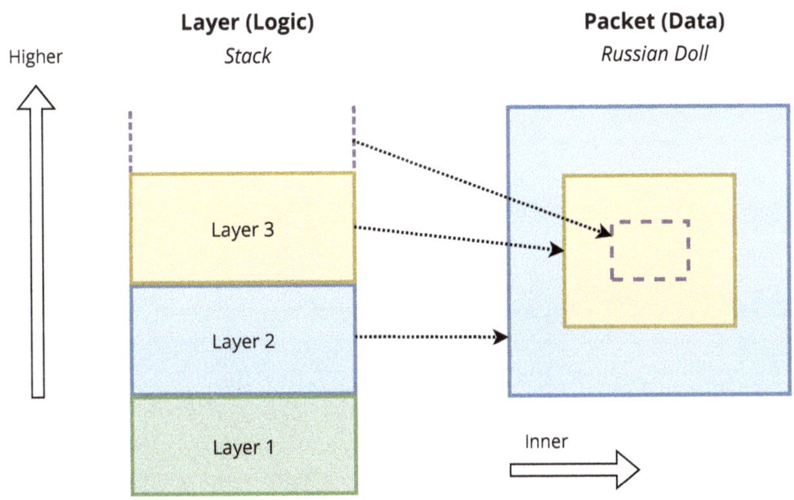

Figure 12. **Protocol Layering** *and* **Packet Encapsulation**. *The extra information in inner packets is "hidden" from lower layers that might be "confused" by it. Higher layers correspond to processing logic that understand and expect this extra information, and know explicitly where, i.e. in what doll shell, to look for it. Layer 1 is an exception in that it does not work with packets of data, but rather streams of bits (and electromagnetic waves).*

The order of packet creation at the source and processing of the logic associated with each layer happens in top-down order, as illustrated in Figure 13. *Think*: When you start planning your next holiday, you first start off with high level considerations like the time of year, and whether you would like to be near a beach or mountains to climb. Only after this has been clarified, do you look into more low level details like flights on suitable dates, or specific train connections to the airport. This higher layer first aligns with packet encapsulation order shown in Figure 12—you need to create an inner packet before you can encapsulate it in an outer one. On the receiving end, the order is reversed. *Think*: Your plane first has to touch down, and you have to figure out the details of train connection from the airport to your hotel, before you can start to enjoy a swim at that beach or a hike up that mountain.

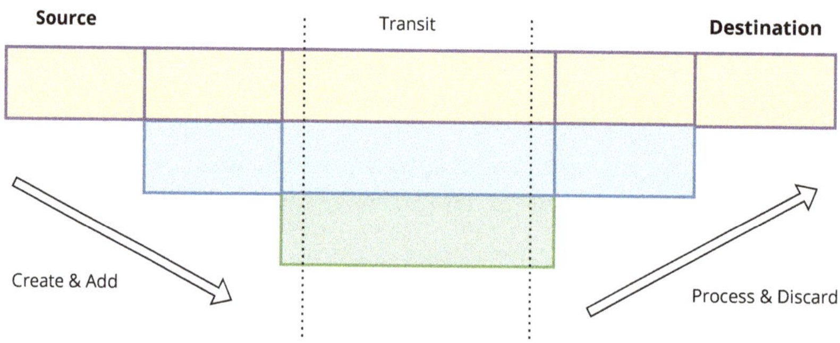

Figure 13. **Layer Lifecycles.** *At the source, the packet for each layer is created, and the layer logic applied, in top-down order. At the destination, the packet for each layer is read, and the layer logic applied, in the reverse order.*

IP

IP (Internet Protocol) is the most important layer 3 protocol. It has evolved over the years into successive standard *versions.*[8] Version 4 of the IP protocol, abbreviated to *IPv4*, has been the predominant version in use since 1981. It is, however, currently being transitioned to version 6, initially released in 1998, and abbreviated to IPv6, which is designed to address IPv4's limitations, especially the much more limited number of IP addresses it allows. However, the transition is happening relatively slowly, and will presumably take several years to complete, as, in order for a packet to be transmitted successfully form its source to final destination using v6, *all* (of the possibly very numerous) nodes the packet passes through, must fully support v6. There are still quite a significant number of legacy nodes that relay internet traffic, that support only v4, and any one of them receiving a packet using IPv6 causes the transmission as a whole to fail—the packet will not reach its final destination. Until all such legacy nodes have been replaced or updated to support v6, all other nodes continue to support both v4 *and* v6 simultaneously. A source node that receives an error message saying that transmission of an IPv6 packet failed due to lack of IPv6 supported along the way, has no choice but to give up or send with v4 instead. As a result, it's not uncommon for many nodes to just use IPv4 from the start. And herein lies both the strength and weakness of the transition - its strength is its flexibility in allowing nodes to continue to (successfully) use IPv4, but the weakness is the lack of sufficient *incentive* for them to update to IPv6, a version of the protocol standardized almost half a century ago, so all nodes can benefit from its improvements.

Rather than dryly list all the differences between v4 and v6 here (and risk corresponding chicken-egg complications), each difference shall be presented as it becomes relevant during the course of the rest of the chapter. See also the chapter *summary* for a more concise presentation.

Decimal, Binary, and Hexadecimal

The system we usually use for numbers is called the decimal system. It uses the digits 0-9, and we say its *base* is 10. A number is an abstract concept, linguistically called a *quantifier*—there is no such thing as a number *on its own*. There is for example no *2* in itself, but only *2 of* something else, e.g. *2 apples*. A number expressed in decimal format is what many of us intuitively consider to *be* a number. However, there is nothing more special or fundamental about the decimal number system than many others. In fact, if humans had evolved with say 8 or 12 fingers,[9] then we would almost certainly be using a number system based on 8 or 12, rather than 10. (The word *digit* comes from the Latin *digitus* which means *finger*).

The *simplest* and most *natural* numbers system for a (digital) computer is binary, which uses just 2 digits: 0 and 1, as mentioned already in *Bits and Bitstreams*. And any number (we express as a series of decimal digits) can also be expressed as a (longer) sequence of binary digits. For example: The number expressed in decimal as 192, can also be expressed in binary as 11000000. It's the same number, just a different way of writing it. Binary is more natural for expressing numbers used by digital computers, since a digital computer works internally with 2 values (which map directly to two hardware *states* in a transistor, often called *on/off* or *high /low*, and the corresponding *bits* in software).

When discussing number systems, it's more accurate to use the term *symbol* than *digit*, since in general any symbol from the set may be used (not only the digits 0-9) in the sequence representing a number. Decimal expresses numbers as a sequence of the *set of symbols* 0-9, and binary from the set of symbols 0,1. Using decimal to express a number is more compact, in that it generally requires a shorter sequence of symbols (from a larger set) than does binary. A number system which strikes a good balance between compactness (it's 4 times more compact than binary, and about 1.2[10] times more compact than decimal) and which has a natural mapping to the internal processing of numbers in digital computers is *hexadecimal*. The *hexadecimal* system uses the symbol set 0-9 together with A-F, i.e. it adds 6 more symbols to those used by decimal. It maps easily (low cognitive load) to binary because each possible sequence of 4 binary symbols corresponds to exactly one hexadecimal symbol. For these reasons, it is often used when dealing with computers and in particular long IP addresses, such as those used in IPv6.[11]

IP Addresses

IP addresses are really just numbers from 0 to some maximum value. How large this maximum value is, is one of the most significant differences between IPv4 and IPv6. In IPv6, this maximum value is much larger, meaning the total number of addresses available is much larger than in IPv4. Each unique value of the number between 0 and the maximum value, corresponds to a unique address—think a street with numbers for the houses[12]—each number can be given to only one house, and if the maximum house number possible is larger, then you can have more (*uniquely numbered*) houses on a single street.

IPv4

An IPv4 address is a **32-bit** number, which means it can represent 2^{32} (about 4.3 billion) unique addresses. Rather than writing this as one (possibly enormous) decimal number, it's usual to divide it into four equally sized, 8-bit sections (octets) and represent each in decimal. For example:

```
192.168.1.1
```

This so-called *dotted decimal* notation is simply a human-friendly[13] way to express the underlying 32-bit number: `11000000.10101000.00000001.00000001`. Which is equivalent to the single very large decimal value: `3,232,235,777`.

IPv6

An IPv6 address is a **128-bit** number, allowing for 2^{128} (an almost inconceivably large number) unique addresses. To represent these efficiently, we use hexadecimal notation (base 16), and group bits into *eight* 16-bit sections separated by colons. For example:

```
2001:0db8:0000:0000:0000:8a2e:0370:7334
```

There are two shorthand *tricks* that can be used when writing such numbers (without causing ambiguity)

- Leading zeros within a group can be removed. e.g. `0db8` can be replaced with `db8`
- One (and only one) sequence of *consecutive* `0000` *groups* can be replaced with `::`
  The double colon can appear *at most once* in an address. If used twice, the address would be ambiguous, as we wouldn't know how many zeros each :: represents. Effectively, wherever you see :: you can mentally replace it with as many groups of *0000* as are necessary to fill out the eight 16-bit sections.

  So, the address `2001:db8:0000:0000:0000:8a2e:0370:7334` can be rewritten in the shorter (but equally unambiguous) form `2001:db8::8a2e:370:7334`

What happened to IPv5

You may be wondering why v6 is the successor to v4 instead of v5. There was, in fact, a version 5 of the IP protocol, which was designed to support real-time traffic, like voice and video. It, however, was not fully standardized for general internet use, before it became apparent that the shortage of IPv4 addresses was a more pressing problem than streaming media efficiently. Work on standardizing v5 was effectively abandoned (streaming support is now the purview of higher layers, which later became apparent are better suited to handling it—we'll see more about this in later chapters).

It's common to specify a particular version of the fundamental protocol of layer 3 by adding a suffix (e.g. v4 or v6) to the base name (IP) as in IPv4 and IPv6. Some of the non-fundamental layer 3 protocols follow this pattern, e.g. ICMPv4 and ICMPv6. Whereas others have entirely different names depending on whether they are designed to work with IPv4 (e.g. ARP) or IPv6 (e.g. NDP).

Subnets

A subnet is a LAN where the interfaces involved are layer 3 (enabled). By this is meant that they understand and participate in communication using the protocols of layer 3 (in particular the *IP protocol*). Recall from *Layer-Specific Devices* that this implicitly means that they are both layer 2 and layer 3 enabled. When a node wants to send an IP packet to a different interface on the same subnet, it encapsulates the layer 3 packet in the payload of a layer 2 packet, as described in *Packet Encapsulation*. The header of the layer 3 packet includes the (logical) IP address of both the sending and receiving interfaces. The layer 2 packet (also known as a *frame*) gets sent like all other layer 2 packets, and arrives as such at the intended destination interface, corresponding to the destination address in the layer 2 header. The recipient (which, like the sender, must be layer 3 enabled—in particular to be able to *understand* the IP protocol) extracts the layer 3 packet from the payload of the layer 2 packet, a process also called *decapsulation*, and processes the rest of the IP packet accordingly.

IP Address Ranges

In theory, a subnet could use any unique IP addresses for its interfaces, and these interfaces could communicate with one another at layer 3 using them. However, in order to be able to communicate with interfaces beyond (which is one of the main motivations for using layer 3 in the first place), a subnet must assign IP addresses to its interfaces from a valid *range*. In general (see *Subnet — reserved addresses*), the first and last possible addresses in the range are reserved, leaving two fewer usable addresses which can be assigned to actual interfaces.

Additionally, as mentioned in *Logical Addressing*, one of the big motivations for using logical addresses is that related[14] interfaces can get assigned (consecutive) addresses from a single *address range*. This has the big advantage that referring to all such related interfaces requires (remembering and) referencing only the range of the addresses (e.g. start and end address), rather than every individual address involved (which would be necessary if the addresses involved were not consecutive).

Imagine by analogy[15] a large storage warehouse with *10 floors*, numbered 0-9. Each floor in turn has space for *1000 units*—individual containment units, each of which can potentially be rented out to a different customer to store their personal property. One could encode the *location* of any individual containment unit using a combination of *1 (0-9) + 3 (0-999) = 4 decimal digits*. However, on each floor, units ending in 000 and 999 are reserved for administrative purposes (*think*: an office for the floor manager and a supplies room)[16], leaving units 001-998 (998 units) available for customer rental on each floor[17]. For example, *7456* might identify the unit 456 on floor 7. Similarly, *7000/1* could identify the range of all units on floor 7. And *7456/1* would identify the same specific unit (456 on floor 7), but additionally signify that the floor has *space* for at total of 998 customer units).

CIDR

CIDR (Classless Inter-Domain Routing) notation is a way of specifying an IP address together with a suffix, that conveys information about an associated address range, as illustrated in *Figure 14*. It's the standard way to specify the address range that defines a subnet. The suffix specifies the *prefix length*,[18] which defines how many left-most bits in the (binary notation of the) IP address are fixed for all addresses in the range (and thus defines all possible values in the range). These left-most bits are often called the *network prefix*. The bits to the right of the network prefix are often called the *host bits*. If the host bits are all 0, then the address is taken to identify the range as a whole (and cannot be assigned to any individual interface). If the host bits are not all 0[19], then the address can be assigned to an individual interface, and the suffix just adds the additional (context) information as to what range this IP address is a *member of*.

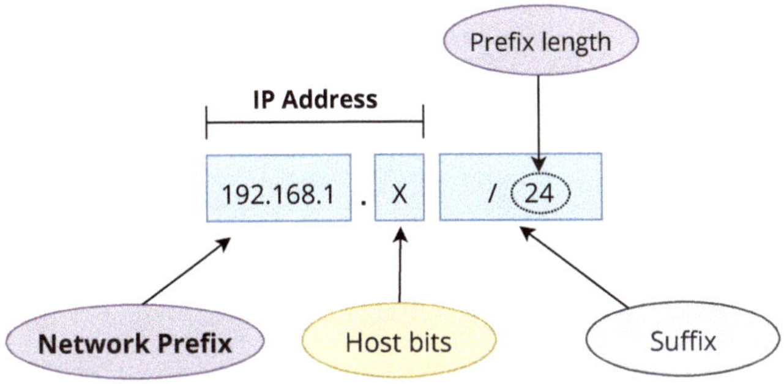

Figure 14. **CIDR** *example specifying an IP address and a suffix. The number in the suffix is called the "prefix length" and can be used to separate the IP address into two parts—that on the left is called the "network prefix" (which defines an address range, and contains as many bits as the value in the suffix) and that on the right is called the "host bits" (or "host identifier"), which defines a specific address in this range. The larger the prefix length, the more digits in the network prefix, and correspondingly fewer host bits (and vice versa, since the sum of both is constant). If the address in question defines a subnet, then the network prefix is also known as a "subnet prefix".*

For example, *192.168.1.0/24* means the range of IPv4 addresses: *192.168.1.0*, *192.168.1.1*, ... *192.168.1.255*. The first 24 bits (192.168.1) identify a range of IP addresses, and the remaining 8 bits, are in principle[20], available for specifying a particular IP address within that range. This range contains $2^{(32-24)} = 2^8 = 256$ IP addresses, and thus can, in principle, contain 256 interfaces. *192.168.1.1/24*, on the other hand (where the host bits are 00000001), specifies the single IPv4 address *192.168.1.1* as a member of the range *192.168.1.[0-255]* (or more accurately, *1-254*, after accounting for reserved addresses).

When using CIDR notation to specify IP address ranges, an important constraint emerges: the ranges cannot be completely arbitrary but must have a start and end which can be expressed as powers of 2—one speaks of the ranges being *aligned on boundaries that are powers of 2*. This is the trade-off for using a single number (the prefix length) to specify a range, rather than explicitly providing both start and end addresses. For example, if you want to create a subnet with 256 addresses (a /24 network), it must start at an address where the last 8 bits are all zeros—such as 192.168.1.0, 192.168.2.0, or 192.168.3.0, but not 192.168.1.50 or 192.168.1.128. This boundary alignment is a natural consequence of using a single number to represent the range, but it also enables routing tables to efficiently represent and process subnet information using simple bit-masking operations[21]. See *Figure 15* and *Figure 20*.

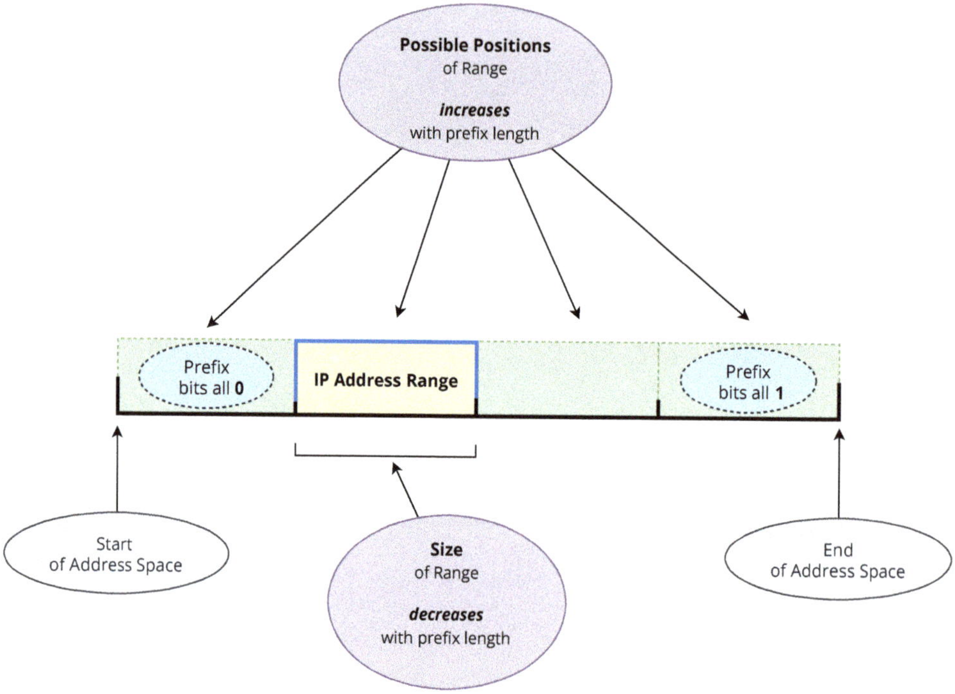

Figure 15. **Visualization of CIDR** *IP Address Range as a rectangular block*[22] *the width of which (and thus the number of addresses it contains) increases with the number of host bits. This, in turn, decreases with the length of the network prefix. The rectangular block can only be located such that its start/end aligns exactly with the start/end of the complete address space, or some position in between that is an integer multiple of the block's size. Note how the larger the block size, the less the number of available positions and vice versa. The address space starts at 0, and end at* 2^{32} *(for IPv4) or* 2^{128} *(for IPv6).*

A *subnet* is always defined by a *single IP address range*, from which its interfaces are assigned addresses.

Multilayer Switches

As we learned in VLANs, a switch can be used to divide a single LAN into multiple so-called VLANs. If the switch in question is a so-called *multilayer switch*, this means it is not only layer 2 enabled, but also layer 3 enabled. Such switches can be used, for example, to connect interfaces on different VLANs only at layer 3 (and above). That is to say, the multilayer switch can be configured to allow those (and only those) layer 2 packets to pass from one VLAN to another, where the payloads of the layer 2 packets are layer 3 packets. Being able to determine this is why the switch needs to be layer 3 enabled—it needs to read the payloads and recognize if they are layer 3 packets. A subnet (layer 3) always corresponds precisely to a single underlying layer 2 (V)LAN—they both contain exactly the same interfaces. So all switches can segregate a LAN into multiple VLANs, but a multilayer switch additionally can do the opposite —to *join* VLANs (and thus the corresponding subnets), at layer 3.[23]

When a CIDR suffix is used after an IP address, one might expect the whole thing (shown for example in Figure 14) to have a simple name such as *CIDR address*. Unfortunately, no such satisfactory name is commonly used. Furthermore, what exactly is meant (i.e. a complete IP address range, or just a single IP address in that range), depends on whether or not the host bits (those not *left-masked* by the CIDR suffix) are all 0. For example:

- *192.168.1.1/24* (host bits are not all 0), means the specific interface IP address 192.168.1.1, seen as one address in the range *192.168.1.[0-255]*
- *192.168.1.0/24* (host bits are all 0), means the IP address range *192.168.1.[0-255]*, also known as the *network address*. Such an address is never used as a source or destination address in an IP packet, but is used in routing tables (see Routing Table example). If this range defines a subnet, then it's also called the *subnet address*.

In a CIDR example like *192.168.1.0/24*, the *24* is sometimes referred to as a *subnet prefix*. This may lead to confusion since it's neither a prefix, nor does it have to define a (single) subnet. It's the size (in bits, of the binary representation) of an address range. Only when this range is used to define a subnet (it may simply be used to define a set of addresses that are not associated with any subnet, or aggregated from multiple subnets) is *192.168.1.0/24* referred to as the *subnet address* and 24 represents *the number of leftmost bits that prefix* every address in the subnet.

Neighbour Discovery (*IP-to-MAC address*)

The above procedure described how an interface can send an IP packet to another *in the same subnet*, using its logical IP address. To do so, however, it must somehow be able to *discover* what (currently) is the MAC address of the destination interface, corresponding to this IP address. One option would be to require user nodes of the network to be manually configured with this mapping. This would, however, offset the benefit in terms of flexibility of using such logical addresses in the first place. All nodes on the network would need to tediously update their mapping, every time even a single interface (MAC address) changes. A better option is to enable nodes to *automatically* discover which MAC addresses corresponding to IP addresses in the same Subnet. This process is called *neighbour discovery*, and the details vary somewhat depending on whether IPv4 or IPv6 is being used as the fundamental layer 3 protocol.

IPv4

Address Resolution Protocol (ARP) is used to map IPv4 addresses to MAC addresses. When a node needs to find the MAC address of another node on the same subnet

- It sends an ARP request broadcast. That is to say, it puts the special *broadcast address* (usually all 1s — see Destination Address Types) into the destination field of the header, and a special payload in a format standardized for ARP requests — which is tantamount to the sender asking *"who has this IP address — respond with your MAC address, please"*.
- The node with the matching IP address responds with an ARP reply, which includes its MAC address. That is to say, it sends a layer 2 packet with the layer 2 address in the header, and with a special payload in a format standardized for ARP requests — which is tantamount to the sender replying *"I have this IP address — and here's my MAC address. Please make a note of it for future use"*.
- The original node then caches this IP-to-MAC mapping for future use, in its so-called *ARP table*, the entries of will expire after a set time.

IPv6

Neighbour Discovery Protocol (NDP) is used to map IPv6 addresses to MAC addresses. When a node needs to find the MAC address of another node on the same subnet using IPv6, the process is similar to IPv4's ARP but with a few key differences:

- *Payload Format:* The request and response payload format is standardized by the NDP protocol, which IPv6 uses, instead of ARP used by IPv4. This ensures consistent and efficient information exchange.
- *Multicast Request*: The initial request is a multicast, not a broadcast. This means interfaces that wish to receive such requests must have previously joined a designated multicast group. (*Think*: *"Please subscribe to our newsletter"*).[24]

NDP is a more reliable and efficient protocol than ARP for neighbour discovery. It also provides additional features like *Neighbour Unreachability Detection* (which helps nodes keep their mapping caches up-to-date, especially when other interfaces become temporarily unavailable or leave the network) and *Router Discovery* (which allows nodes to automatically find the IP/MAC address of connected routers — see Routers).

Routers

Routers are the rock star devices of layer 3, just as switches are at layer 2. A router is the only device capable of connecting subnets — through a router is the only way an interface in one LAN (i.e. subnet) can communicate with an interface in another. This may not seem such an extraordinary function, but what's impressive and valuable is not so much the service any single router provides, but the way they work together. Not unlike ants in a colony, routers across the world work together to form the backbone of an emergent phenomenon — the internet.

When an interface in a subnet wants to send a packet to another interface in the same subnet, it sends a layer 2 packet (encapsulating the layer 3 packet) to the hardware (MAC) address of the recipient. If it doesn't yet know the MAC address of the recipient, it must first determine it via neighbour discovery, which itself is a layer 2 functionality, available only inside a single LAN or subnet. So, what if any interface wants to send a packet to an interface outside its subnet? The short answer is that it can't — at least not directly. And even if it could, it couldn't find the MAC address, since neighbour discovery is limited to the scope of a single subnet. A router interface must be added to each subnet that should be connected to *the outside world*. Other interfaces of the same router can then be added to other subnets, in effect connecting the subnets through the router, which acts as a gateway between the subnets connected by it. Each router can also be connected directly to other routers as illustrated in Figure 16, and each such router-router connection forms its own two-interface subnet.

If the destination is remote (i.e. in a different subnet), the interface knows it needs help from its default gateway router. It encapsulates the IP packet in a layer 2 packet as usual, but, instead of addressing the layer 2 packet to the destination interface, it addresses it to the gateway router's interface (which, being an interface on the same LAN, also has a MAC address the sender can find via neighbour discovery), and sends it. The router on receiving the layer 2 packet (see Figure 17) looks at the layer 3 packet encapsulated as its payload. It sees that, even though the MAC address in the layer 2 packet was the layer 2 address of its own interface, the IP address in the layer 3 packet is *not* that of its own interface.

It then discards the outer layer 2 packet and encapsulates the layer 3 packet in a new layer 2 packet, which it in turn sends out of (a different) one of its interfaces. And this process of figuring out which *next-hop* to send a particular packet along, in such a way that the packet arrives efficiently at its intended destination, rather than zigzagging around the internet (possibly indefinitely) like the *Flying Dutchman*,[25] is where the *magic* of routers lies. Central to this ability are routing tables and routing protocols.

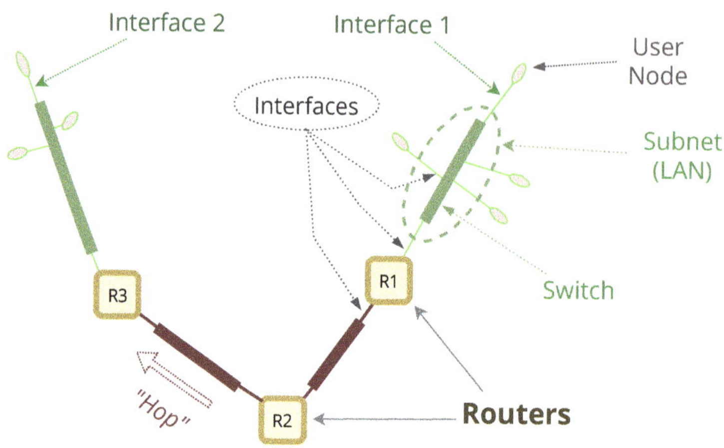

Figure 16. **Routers** *can connect subnets when they have an interface in each. Routers can also be connected to other routers (typically via point-to-point connections), and the traversal of a packet from one router to another is often referred to as a "hop". When Interface 1 wants to send a layer 3 packet to Interface 2, it must first pass it to R1, the gateway router for its subnet. R1 forwards to R2, which in turn forwards to R3, the gateway router for the subnet of the ultimate destination, Interface 2. Note that the layer 3 packet is always sent as the payload of a layer 2 packet, as shown in Figure 11. Each router along the way, however, repackages this payload as illustrated in Figure 17.*

Caching

Caching is the practice of temporarily storing copies of information locally to avoid repeatedly fetching it from the original source. This fundamental technique is used throughout computing systems to improve performance and reduce load on resources.

Think of caching like keeping a phone number written on a notepad by your desk. The first time you need to call the pizza place, you look it up in the phone book (slow). But you write it down on your notepad. The next time you want pizza, you just glance at your notepad (instant) rather than digging out the phone book again. You don't write down every phone number you ever call — that would clutter your desk with numbers you rarely need. You keep the ones you use frequently. And occasionally, you need to erase old numbers because the pizza place changed its number, or to make room for new ones you're calling more often now.

On the web, this happens constantly: images, stylesheets, and other content get stored locally after the first download, so returning to a site loads much faster the second time. Like your notepad, the cache has limited space and stored items can become outdated, so systems must decide what to keep and when to refresh it.

Gateway Routers

A *subnet gateway* is a router[26] that IP packets must traverse to enter or leave a particular subnet. A subnet gateway *originates* prefixes for subnets that it is directly connected to, and may *advertise* prefixes for all subnets it knows how to get a packet closer to (including those it originates).

Interfaces in a subnet[27] must be configured with a *default gateway* where they send packets destined for interfaces outside the subnet. It's possible for a single router to serve as a gateway for multiple subnets (if the router has an interface in each subnet).

Multiple routers may together form a so-called routing domain, which requires packets to pass through a *domain gateway (router)* before entering or leaving the domain as a whole. (A domain gateway may also be called an *edge router* or *border router*). A domain gateway is thus a particular kind of subnet gateway.

It's possible for multiple routers to serve as (redundant) gateways for subnets or domains.

Routing Tables

A routing table is basically a list of entries that tell the router how to reach different IP address ranges—specifying which interface to use, which directly connected router this will forward a packet to (if any), and the so-called *cost* of each path. So when a packet with a particular destination IP address arrives at the router, the router looks up its routing table to figure out which connected router is best suited to getting the packet closer to its intended destination. It then sends the packet in question to the other router on the interface that router is connected at. The other router then in turn looks up its routing table and figures out which is the next (*hop*) router to send the packet to next. And so on until the packet gets to the router that is the gateway for the subnet of the destination interface, and this gateway router passes the packet on to its final destination interface.

Note that if, for example, the second router were to *think* (i.e. its routing table would contain information that leads to this conclusion) that the first router were closer to the final destination, then the packet would bounce back and forth between them indefinitely. Not only would the packet not get delivered, but the routers would be wasting resources sending it back and forth, possibly delaying other packets waiting to be forwarded. This shows how important it is that routers keep their routing tables up to date and in sync with one another. They do so using so-called *routing protocols*, which we will read more about in Routing Protocols.

Routing Table example

```
IP Address Range    Interface    Next-Hop IP Address    Cost
----------------    ---------    -------------------    ----
127.0.0.1/32        lo           127.0.0.1              0
0.0.0.0/0           eth0         192.168.1.1            10
192.168.0.0/16      eth0         192.168.0.1            5
192.168.1.0/24      eth0         192.168.1.1            7
192.168.2.0/24      eth0         0.0.0.0                0
```

- **IP Address Range**: The address range that can be reached, expressed in CIDR notation (see *CIDR*). A special value like `0.0.0.0/0` indicates the *default route* - to be used when no other entry in the table matches the destination address.
  For each specific IP address range (e.g. *192.168.0.0/16*) there may be at most one entry in a routing table (the *preferred path*), but this range may be a subset of an aggregate range (e.g. *192.168.1.0/24*) which also has its own specific entry, i.e. *multiple entries for a given range are not allowed, but separate entries for overlapping ranges are.* In forwarding mode (see *Router Modes*) the longest matching (i.e. most specific) prefix is used.
- **Interface**: The router's interface that can be used to reach an interface in this IP Address Range (e.g. *lo* the so-called *loopback interface*)[28]
- **Next Hop IP Address**: The IP address of the next(-hop) interface, on the path to this IP Address range. (If the router's interface is itself in the IP Address range, then this column contains a special value like `0.0.0.0`). Its IP address is (only) needed to determine the MAC address of the next-hop interface in question—which must be entered as the destination MAC address of the layer 2 packet. The destination IP address of the IP packet is never that of an intermediate next-hop router, but that of the (ultimate) recipient interface.
- **Cost**: A numerical metric indicating the preference of this path. A lower cost means a more preferred path. This value is used *only when updating the table* (never when making forwarding decisions) - if multiple paths to a given prefix are available (which is not possible in a purely tree-like topology), only the one with the lowest cost gets written into the table (overwriting any existing higher cost entry previously present).

Regular (non-router) nodes also use routing tables. However, they are much simpler and generally only contain two main entries—one for directly attached subnets (generally connected to a switch that manages the LAN), and one for the default gateway (to which all packets are sent that are addresses outside the local subnet).[29]

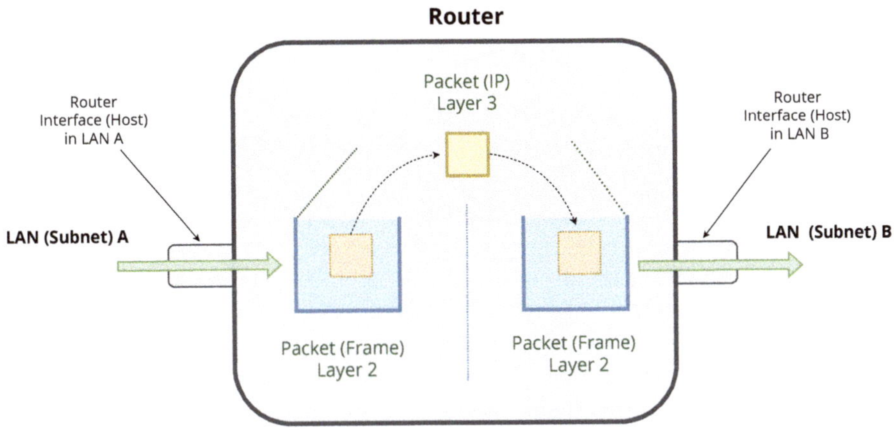

Figure 17. **Router Repackaging**. *When a layer 3 packet (also called an IP packet) arrives at an interface, the router extracts it from the encapsulating layer 2 packet (also called a Frame), which has the MAC address of the router's (incoming) interface as the destination. The router discards this layer 2 packet, and creates a new one. It writes the MAC address of its (outgoing) interface as the source of this new layer 2 packet and encapsulates the (original) layer 3 packet in it. The new layer 2 packet is sent out the appropriate (outgoing) router interface, bringing it a step closer to the interface corresponding to the (ultimate) destination IP address specified in the layer 3 packet. The routing table plays a key role in figuring out which outgoing interface to choose, and which MAC address to enter for the destination in the layer 2 packet.*

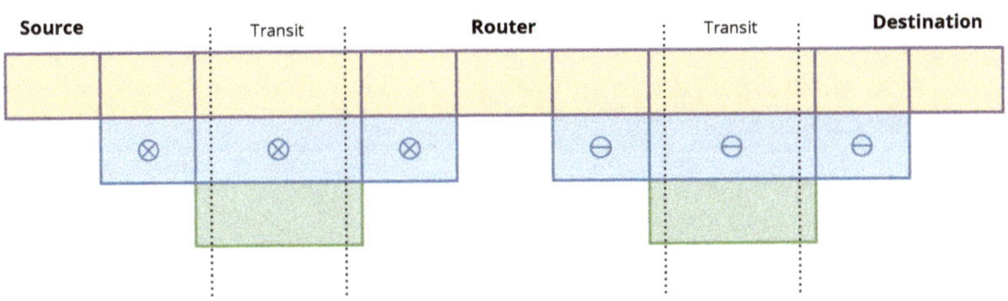

Figure 18. **Layer Lifecycles** *view of source—router—destination journey. Layer 3 packets are preserved on their journey from source to destination, even when they pass through a router. Layer 2 packets are not. The layer 2 packet leaving the router is not the same one that arrived. The layer 3 packet gets "repackaged" into a new layer 2 packet before being forwarded, as illustrated in Figure 17. Compare also Figure 13.*

Router Modes

Routers can be perceived[30] as functioning in exactly one of 2 modes: *updating* their routing table, and *forwarding* packets based on this table.

- **Table Update**: Routers learn the available paths to (ideally all) network prefixes, from directly connected routers (and through them, from indirectly connected routers), from information exchanged efficiently using routing protocols. In a pure tree-like topology, there will be exactly one path to each network prefix (see also *Figure 20*). Deviations from this tree-like topology may introduce alternate paths to a given prefix, in which case the ***lowest cost path*** is chosen.
- **Packet Forwarding**: If any *routing policy* is configured on the router (see *Routing Domains*) with specific instructions that apply to the packet in question, they will be followed. Otherwise (as is usually the case), *prefix-matching* is performed based on the current state of the table, to decide how to forward a packet: Prefixes matching the IP address of the packet are searched for in the routing table. Multiple entries may match, but they will all have different prefix lengths (corresponding to more or less specific address ranges—see also *Figure 20*). The cost plays no role. The ***longest matching prefix (LMP)***—i.e. the most specific matching prefix range—is chosen.

Cost is a value assigned by routing protocols to each possible path, based on factors like distance (number of routers to cross), speed (how fast data travels on the links), reliability (how often the path stays working), or even manual preferences set by network admins. A path gets a lower cost if it's shorter, faster, more dependable, or prioritized —- making it the preferred choice to avoid delays, data loss, or inefficiency.[31]

Routers attempt[32] to forward each packet to whichever neighbouring[33] router advertises it's able to get a packet to the smallest (most specific) IP address range, containing the destination IP address of the packet in question. In the case of a tie, it picks the neighbouring router that does so with the lowest cost[34].

A typical *home router* is used to connect a typical family home to the internet through an Internet Service Provider (ISP). It is actually a combination of a simple *switch* and *router* in a single device, both usually of very modest capacity. The dedicated routers that form the backbone of the internet, and the switches used in production LANs, are vastly more performant (and expensive).

The Internet (Simplified)

This section presents a simplified view of the structure and principles of the internet, without getting bogged down with all the details. You can think of it as a high-level view designed to give you a decent overall impression of the big picture. In *The Internet (Realistic)* we will descend to get a more detailed realistic view, and it is hoped that after having first gotten a bird's-eye perspective, the details of the latter will be easier to see in context and less overwhelming. After all, the internet is possibly one of the most complicated things mankind has ever created.

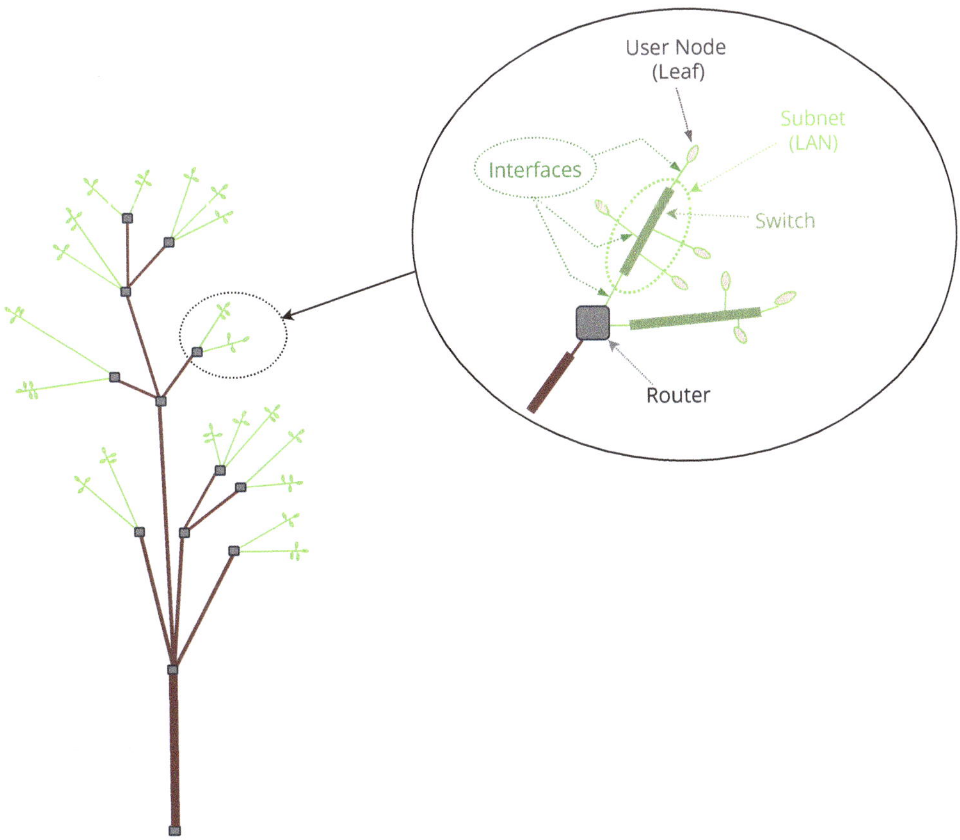

Figure 19. **Internet (simplified) as a single tree.** *Routers connect subnets in which they have an interface. An example subnet is highlighted, as well as some example interfaces within. Each subnet is also a LAN, and the interfaces are usually connected by a switch (shown as thicker line). The routers are generally connected via point-to-point connections with each other (each such connection also forming a subnet containing 2 interfaces).*

One can envision the internet at this high level as a single tree (see *Figure 19*). The trunk of the tree branches out at bifurcation points, each branch in turn further branching etc. Branches that no longer split to form sub-branches, we will call *extremity sub-branches*, and these contain the leaves of the tree. Think of the extremity sub-branches as subnets, and the leaves on them as the interfaces of user nodes. Consider how water from the ground would flow up the trunk of the tree, out through the branches and to the leaves—we will call this direction *downstream*, and the opposite direction *upstream*.

One can envision routers to be located at the bifurcation points, and together with the trunk and branches, they form the infrastructure of the tree, that leaves use to send packets to one another. A leaf can send a packet directly to another packet if it's on the same extremity sub-branch (i.e. they are in the same LAN and can thus communicate at layer 2). But if a leaf wants to send a packet to a leaf in any other extremity sub-branch, it has to send it *upstream*, through as many bifurcation points (routers) as necessary until it reaches the closest (upstream) bifurcation point common to both of the leaves in question. From there, it's passed downstream again along the other (sub) branch until it finally reaches the destination leaf.

Not only do the leaves have interfaces, but the routers at the bifurcation points do as well. In fact, each router has an interface for every branch entering and an interface for every branch leaving the bifurcation point at which it's located. And each of these interfaces has an IP address.

The internet begins with a finite pool of IP addresses—think of this as the entire *address space* available for the whole tree, with the trunk representing this complete address space. Just as the tree trunk carries all the water that will eventually reach every leaf, this total address space must be systematically divided and allocated as it flows downstream through each bifurcation point. As the tree branches out from the trunk, large ranges (also known as blocks) are progressively subdivided into smaller, more specific ranges. Each bifurcation point (router) acts as both a division point for address space and a routing decision point for packets.

So each router sits between a larger upstream address range and multiple sub-ranges that are subdivisions of this larger range—each sub-range *reachable* through a corresponding downstream interface of the router. The router effectively serves as a gateway between the larger upstream address range and the component sub-ranges downstream, and vice versa. The router saves in its routing table all the information it needs to distinguish these ranges (both upstream and downstream), and which are connected to which interface. (Because of the strict hierarchical structure of tree and IP address range division, each interface will be connected to exactly one range, and the totality of all downstream ranges will equal the single upstream range). When a packet arrives at a router (bifurcation point), the router examines the packet's destination IP address and compares it against all the IP address ranges directly connected to its interfaces, as listed in its routing table, and picks the *best match*.[35]

Subnet — reserved addresses

When an IP Address range is used to define a subnet, the first and last addresses in the range, cannot (generally) be assigned to any specific interface in the subnet. The first address (host bits all 0's) is the so-called *subnet address*, and the last address (host bits all 1's) forms the so-called *subnet broadcast address*.

The subnet broadcast address may appear as the destination address in IP packets (*think*: *to all interfaces which can hear me*), but never as the source.

The subnet address is never used as source or destination address in an IP packet, but is used to identify IP address ranges (for individual and aggregate subnets) in routing tables.

An exception is when a range of size 2[36] is used. Such subnets are free to assign both addresses in the range to individual interfaces. These subnets are typical of point-to-point connections between routers, and have the CIDR suffix */31*

Advertising

One says a router *advertises* (via routing protocols) routes for all IP address ranges it's able to reach. If one of the ranges defines a subnet in which the router has an interface — i.e. the router is directly connected to the subnet, one says the router (also) *originates* this IP address range.

One may feel it would be more natural to omit the CIDR prefix and trailing 0s, simply using *192.168.1* instead of *192.168.1.0/24* to refer to the subnet as a whole. After all, the */24* effectively says, *"ignore the 0"*. Then *192.168.1.0/24 would* be available as an IP address for an individual interface. The IP standard mandates, however, that all available bits (32 for IPv4) must be specified even when designating an address range (and 0 is the value the *unused* bits must be given). This has the disadvantage of wasting an address per subnet, but makes parsing and other handling of IP addresses standardized and thus simpler and more reliable, especially in routers. The software knows it can always expect a fixed number of bits in a known format.

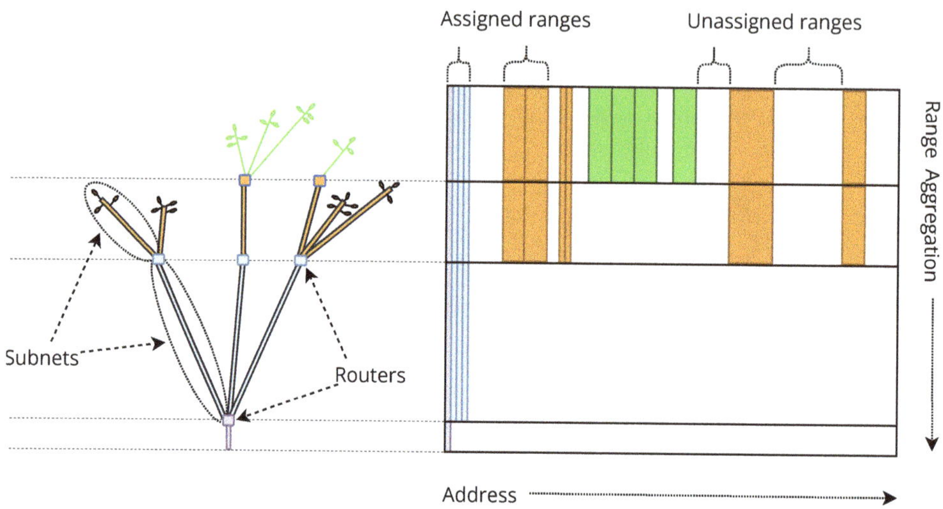

Figure 20. **IP address (range) distribution** *example in a tree-like network, such as our simplified model of the internet. One can observe, from bottom to top, that the complete IP address space is divided successively into smaller (more specific) ranges. And equivalently, when viewed from top to bottom, smaller IP address ranges combine into larger aggregates, recursively. Each router in such a purely tree-like model is the single gateway between any upstream (toward the trunk) address and any downstream (away from the trunk) address range. An IP address in any range may or may not be assigned to an interface[37]. Note how all address ranges (both assigned and unassigned) adhere to power-of-2 boundary alignment, a fundamental constraint of CIDR. See also Subnet — reserved addresses.*

The Internet (Realistic)

The single tree model from *The Internet (Simplified)* provides a helpful foundation for understanding the structure of the internet and routing, but the real internet is considerably more complex. The internet is not a single tree, but a forest of trees, connected to each other in a non-hierarchial fashion (there's no *tree of trees*). Furthermore, inside each tree, there are also *shortcut connections* between different branches. These and other complications, which are discussed further below, make internet routing both more complex and powerful.

1). Autonomous Systems — Complexity of a Forest

Rather than one unified tree, the internet is actually a forest of over 130,000 interconnected trees, each representing what's called an *Autonomous System (AS)*, each with a unique *Autonomous System Number (ASN)*. Unlike our idealized single tree where the complete address space flowed from one trunk, each AS tree is allocated its own separate IP address ranges from the complete address space, by *Regional Internet Registries (RIRs)* such as *ARIN* in North America or *RIPE* in Europe.

The trees are not completely isolated—they connect to each other, but *only* at their bases (trunks). Each AS has *border routers* (also called *edge routers*) that serve as the connection points between trees. These gateways form a partial mesh network, meaning each AS connects directly to only some other ASs, not all of them. When a packet needs to travel from a leaf in one tree to a leaf in another tree, it must first travel upstream within its origin tree to reach that tree's border routers, then hop across one or more AS connections through the forest, and finally travel downstream within the destination tree to reach its target leaf.

Each AS *advertises* its IP ranges to other ASes using the *external Border Gateway Protocol (eBGP)*. This creates a global routing table that allows any AS to know which other AS can reach any given IP address range. The beauty of this system is that each AS can manage its internal structure independently while participating in the global internet. An AS might reorganize its internal tree structure, add new branches, or change its internal routing, but as long as it continues to advertise the same IP ranges to the outside world, other ASs don't need to know or care about these internal changes.

2). Complexity within each Tree

Even within individual AS trees, the real-world deviates from our idealized model in several important ways:

- **Shortcut (Mesh-like) Connections.** Rather than a pure tree structure, routers within an AS often have *shortcut* connections between different branches. These cross-connections create mesh-like topologies that provide redundancy, improve performance, and enable load balancing. When a packet travels within an AS, it might take a shortcut directly between two branch points rather than going all the way upstream to their common ancestor and then back downstream, as would be the case in our simple tree model above.
- **Internal Routing Complexity.** These internal shortcuts, combined with the need to distribute external routing information learned from other ASs, require sophisticated internal Routing Protocols. Each AS typically uses an *Interior Gateway Protocol (IGP)* like *OSPF* or *IS-IS* for internal routing decisions, combined with *internal BGP (iBGP)* to distribute external routing information throughout the AS.

4). Non-contiguous IP Allocation

Organizations may acquire IP address blocks through mergers, acquisitions, or transfers, meaning that nearby IP addresses might actually be allocated to nodes in entirely different places of the world. This breaks the assumption that IP address proximity corresponds to network proximity.

4). Routing Domains

A group of routers under the control of a single organization may form a so-called routing domain. Autonomous Systems (ASs) are the most prominent examples of routing domains. However, smaller organizations may also establish routing domains for internal network management. Any packet entering or leaving a routing domain must pass through one of its *domain gateway routers*. These *gateway routers* are generally configured by the controlling body to follow *routing policies* of their choosing.

- **Routing Policies.** A routing policy is a set of rules for how a (gateway) router should deviate from the standard *prefer the lowest cost path* criterion, when forwarding a packet, i.e. choosing a next-hop. For example:
    - Prefer next-hops through certain partners, or avoid those through competitors
    - Implement traffic engineering to balance loads across multiple next-hops
    - Prioritize traffic from paying customers, or certain types of traffic (VoIP) over others
    - Block traffic from certain countries/regions, or reject next-hops in ASes they don't trust
- **Private Addresses.** Routing domains can also internally use so-called *private IP addresses.*[38] IP packets with such addresses may only be sent (unchanged) between interfaces located inside the routing domain. The gateway routers of the routing domain may, however, perform *NAT (Network Address Translation)* on such packets — rewriting the source and/or destination address (and sometimes port numbers) so that they can cross the routing domain boundary.[39] An address is considered private if it falls within one of the standard IP ranges:
    - **IPv4**
        - *10.0.0.0/8*
        - *172.16.0.0/12*
        - *192.168.0.0/16*
    - **IPv6**
        - *fc00::/7* [40]

5). Anycast

Some IP addresses are intentionally assigned to multiple interfaces in different geographical locations for redundancy and performance. When you connect to a service that uses anycast, you are typically steered to the closest interface.[41]

Despite these complications, the core tree-like structure within each AS and the hierarchical nature of IP address allocation still provide the fundamental organizing principles that make internet routing tractable. The routing protocols and mesh connections add robustness and efficiency, while the forest-of-trees model enables the internet to scale to billions of devices across tens of thousands of independently managed networks. Understanding this progression from the simplified single tree to the complex forest of interconnected trees helps explain why internet routing requires such sophisticated protocols and why routing tables can become quite large — each router must not only understand its local tree structure but also maintain information about how to reach the many other trees in the forest.

Hosts — layer 3 interfaces

Interfaces (on nodes) which are layer 3 enabled are often called *hosts*. Each host can be assigned one or more IP addresses, in addition to the single MAC address the manufacturer burns into it. Just as a **subnet** can be seen as the layer 3 equivalent of a **LAN**, a host can be seen as the layer 3 equivalent of an interface. See also *host* component of a URL.

Beware, that it is not uncommon to find the term host used *incorrectly*, for example to mean the whole node in question (which may, in fact, contain multiple interfaces, and thus multiple hosts). When we later discuss layer 4, we will see that a single host can be subdivided into multiple *endpoints* (see *Port Numbers — interface sharing and network endpoints*). And again, it's unfortunately not uncommon to find the terms host and endpoint confused.

Routing Protocols

The complexity of this forest structure makes routing protocols absolutely critical. In our simplified single tree model, routing decisions were straightforward — packets simply followed the tree structure up to the common ancestor and then down to the destination. In the real internet, routers must constantly exchange information such as:

- Which IP ranges are reachable through which paths.
- The cost or preference of different routes.
- Changes in network topology as connections come and go.
- Traffic engineering policies that might override the *shortest* path.

Different kinds of routing protocols are used in different situations:

- *eBGP (external Border Gateway Protocol)* handles communication between *ASes (Autonomous Systems)*, allowing them to advertise their IP ranges and learn about routes to external destinations.[42]
- *iBGP (internal BGP)* distributes this external routing information within an AS
- *IGPs (Interior Gateway Protocols)* handle the detailed internal routing within each AS.[43]

BGP is an umbrella term for *eBGP* and *iBGP*.

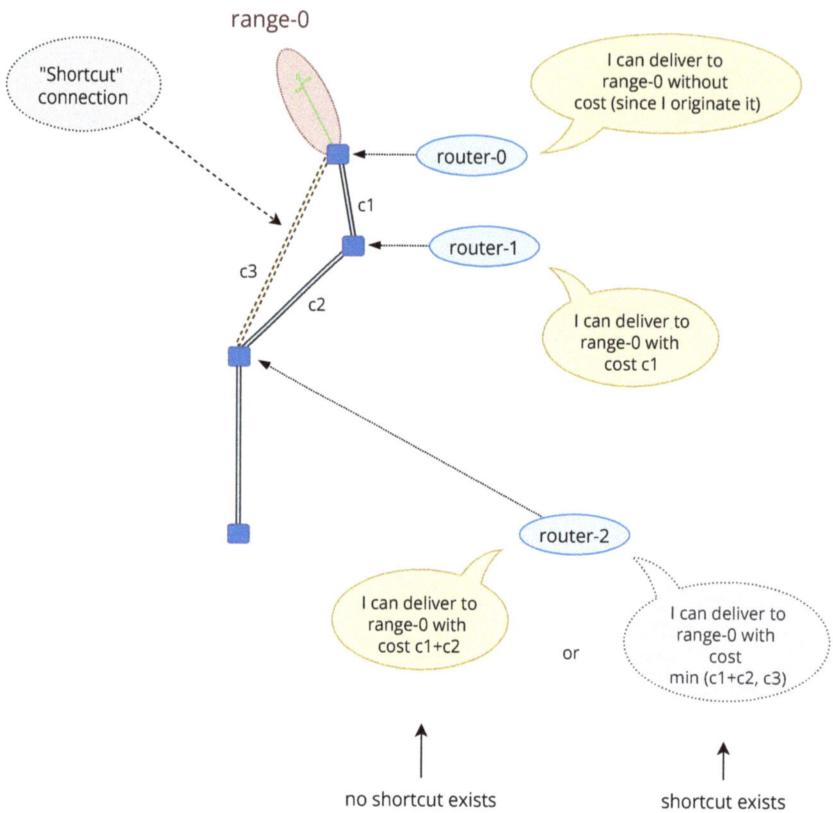

Figure 21. **Route Advertisement and Cost Accumulation.** *router-0 can deliver packets to the subnet with IP address range-0. It can do so without any cost since it's directly connected to (or "originates") the subnet. router-1 can deliver packets to router-0 with cost c1*[44]*, and router-2 can deliver packets to router-1 with cost c2. Costs accumulate additively, so a packet delivered from router-2 to router-0 via router-1 incurs a total cost of c1 + c2. The addition of a "shortcut" connection would cause a deviation from the otherwise pure tree-like structure (in which every packet has at most one possible path to its destination. This shortcut presents a new path, which will be chosen by router-2 for delivery to range-0 if (and only if) its cost, c3, is less than the total cost for the other path (i.e. c1 + c2)*

Packet Fragmentation

Packet fragmentation occurs when a packet is too large to traverse a network link in its current form. Think of it like trying to move a large piece of furniture through a narrow doorway — you either need to break it down into smaller pieces that fit, or find a different route with wider doorways. Every individual network link has a *Maximum Transmission Unit (MTU)* — the largest packet size it can handle. When a packet exceeds this limit, something must be done to make it deliverable. However, IPv4 and IPv6 handle this challenge very differently.

IPv4 (The Helpful Router Approach)

IPv4 routers act like helpful movers who will disassemble your furniture if it doesn't fit through the door. When an IPv4 router encounters a packet that's too large for the next link, it automatically fragments the packet into smaller pieces, each fitting within the MTU limit. Each fragment gets its own IP header and is sent independently to the destination, where the receiving host reassembles them into the original packet. However, the sender can opt out of this service by setting the *Don't Fragment (DF)* field in the packet header — essentially saying *don't break this up automatically, send it back to me if it's too big, and I'll figure out an alternative myself.* When a router encounters such a packet that's too large, it sends back an ICMP *Fragmentation Needed* packet to the source and discards the packet.

IPv6 (The Strict Policy Approach)

IPv6 takes a completely different philosophy: routers never fragment packets, period. If a packet is too large, the router sends an *Packet Too Big* packet back to the source and drops the packet. This forces the sender to deal with the problem. The sender must then discover the *Path Maximum Transmission Unit (PMTU)* — the largest packet size that can traverse the entire path to the destination. This is done through a process similar to a game of *how low can you go?*. The sender tries progressively smaller packet sizes until it finds one that doesn't trigger PTB responses. If the discovered PMTU isn't sufficient for the application's needs, the IPv6 source must perform fragmentation itself before (re)sending packets.

Why the Different Approaches? IPv4's router-based fragmentation seemed helpful but created problems: fragmented packets consume more router resources, increase the chance of packet loss (losing any fragment means losing the entire original packet), and complicate network troubleshooting. IPv6's approach pushes this complexity to the network edges, where it can be better managed, keeping the core network infrastructure simpler and more efficient.

While the IP protocol covers the general mechanics of how (and where) fragmentation should be handled, the *ICMP* protocol covers the structure and semantics of the packets that embody the error messages. Some overly restrictive firewalls mistakenly block all ICMP traffic (often in misguided attempts at "security" or to prevent ping floods), including these essential fragmentation messages. This creates *PMTU black holes* where transports mysteriously fail for larger packets — small emails go through but attachments fail, web pages load but file downloads stall, or VPN connections work initially then hang.

ICMP (Diagnostics)

Complex systems like networks need ways to report problems and verify that everything is working correctly. At layer 3, this is primarily handled by the *Internet Control Message Protocol (ICMP)* — think of it as the network's built-in messaging system for *status updates* and *error reports*, on *individual packets*. ICMP acts like a helpful postal service worker who not only delivers letters, but also reports back when deliveries fail. When routers encounter problems with packet delivery, they use ICMP to send informative messages back to the source, explaining what went wrong and why. ICMP uses IP - the messages are in the form of IP packets. The particular combination of standard values, specified by the ICMP protocol, set for specific header fields in the header (see in *Other Meta Information* in Figure 11), is what distinguishes an ICMP packet from a generic IP packet, and the different ICMP packet types from one another. The most common ICMP packet types are:

Destination Unreachable

This is ICMP's way of saying *I can't deliver this package*. It's sent when a router cannot forward a packet to its intended destination. The message includes specific *subcodes* that explain why — e.g. *fragmentation is needed*, or the *destination network doesn't exist*, the *target host is down*, or a *firewall is blocking the connection*. It's like a postal worker returning mail with a note explaining *address unknown* or *access denied*.

Time Exceeded

Sometimes packets get lost in routing loops or take too long to reach their destination. Every IP packet has a *Time To Live (TTL)* counter (see *Other Meta Information* in Figure 11) in their header, that decreases at each router hop. When this counter reaches zero, the router discards the packet and sends a *Time Exceeded* message back to the source. This prevents packets from circulating endlessly in the network, like having a postal service that stops forwarding mail after it's been passed between too many offices.

Fragmentation Needed

When an IPv4 packet that is too large for the next-hop router also has the *Don't Fragment (DF)* field in its header set, the current router drops the packet and sends this message back.[45]

Packet Too Big (PTB)

The IPv6 equivalent of *Fragmentation Needed*. When an IPv6 packet is too large for the next-hop router, the current router drops the packet and sends this message back.[46]

Echo Request and Echo Reply

These are ICMP's equivalent of "*Can you hear me*"? The *Echo Request* asks a remote host to simply echo back the same data it received (*think*: "*yes, I heard you say....*"). If successful, the host responds with an *Echo Reply* containing the identical data (*think*: "*And, I heard you say, that I said....*"). This simple exchange verifies that the network path is working and measures round-trip time. The *ping* [47] command is essentially a user-friendly wrapper around these ICMP Echo messages.

ICMP is used with both IPv4 and IPv6, but ICMPv6 adds some extra functionality specific to IPv6's needs. Both versions act as the network's diagnostic and status reporting system, essential for network troubleshooting and automated error handling.[48]

Layer 4

While layer 3 handles getting individual packets from one interface to another, layer 4 builds on this by adding *interface sharing*. Think of Layer 3 as a postal service that can bring individual letters from one building to another. Each building has a single outbox and single inbox, and no way of distinguishing *who* in the building wrote the outgoing letter or should receive an incoming letter. The source and destination IP addresses are analogous to the addresses of the *whole building*. Layer 4 adds the ability to be more specific.

The protocols of layer 4 are often called *transport protocols*. The two main ones are *UDP* and *TCP*, and they offer vastly different service levels. UDP provides adding port numbers and little else. TCP also adds extensive reliability features: guaranteed delivery, automatic retransmission of lost packets, and preservation of packet ordering. So UDP is barely more than *IP with port numbers*, but this minimalism makes it very efficient. TCP is very reliable, but at the cost of additional complexity and latency. The choice is a trade-off that must be made on an application-by-application basis.

Port Numbers — interface sharing and network endpoints

Layer 4 combines an IP address with a so-called *port number*, each pair uniquely identifying a so-called *network endpoint*. An endpoint can be thought of as an individual software program[49] running on the node that can share access to a single interface (and IP address) on the node, with other software programs. This way, multiple programs on your PC can access the internet simultaneously, even though you may have just one Wi-Fi antenna or Ethernet cable.

> Do not confuse *port number* (a software concept defined and used in layer 4) with *port* (a hardware-level entry/exit point on a node in layers 1 and 2, of which an interface is an example — see Nodes and Ports).

> Cloud *"Subnets"* (e.g. *Azure VNets* and *AWS VPCs*) are not actually subnets, but constructs[50] similar to routing domains. Each interface in the *cloud subnet* is effectively connected directly to (and only to) a (software defined) router that routes to other interfaces in the same *cloud subnet*. Effectively, each interface is in a LAN together only with a (software defined) router. These constructs, are confusingly called *subnets* by the cloud providers, but subnets they are not. Subnets, by definition, don't require a router. These constructs would merit a name of their own, but in classic *Humpty Dumpty* style, an existing name, meaning something else, gets overloaded.

Packet Encapsulation

Continuing in Russian doll fashion, layer 4 packets are embedded as the payload of layer 3 packets, which in turn are embedded as the payload of layer 2 packets. See *Figure 22*.

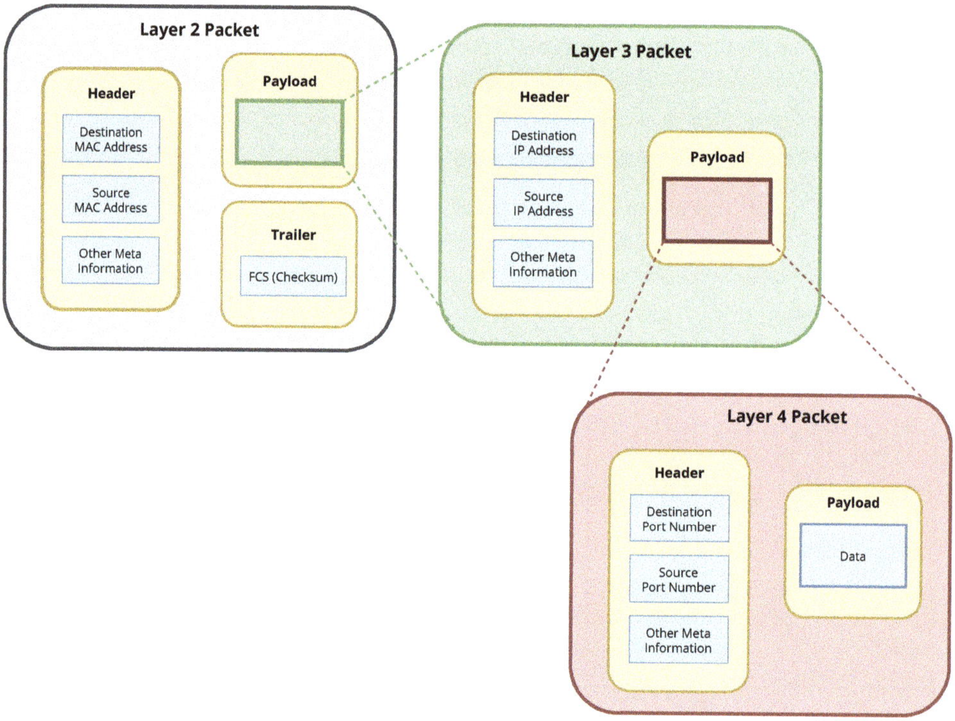

Figure 22. **Layer 4 packet encapsulated** *as the payload of a layer 3 packet. The layer 4 packet contains the Port Number, whereas the layer 3 packet the contains the layer 3 (IP) address, of the destination and source respectively. The payload of the layer 4 packet contains the actual data the source is sending to the destination.*[51]*. The layer 3 packet is in turn encapsulated as the payload of a corresponding layer 2 packet.*

Packet Delivery—order and reliability

When a single source sends a series of packets (e.g. as part of a conversation) to a single destination, it's not certain that all the packets will travel along exactly the same path on the way to their destination (see also *The Internet (Realistic)*). Various factors, including current congestion, load balancing etc come into play when a router decides which *next-hop* to send a packet along. And it may send one packet of the series to one next-hop router, and the next to another. The same applies to all subsequent routers in the chain. Thus, it may happen that a packet that was sent later than another, arrives at its destination before the other. It may, in rare cases, even happen that some packets do not arrive at the intended destination at all (e.g. if a router on one path breaks down) even though the others did. There are two standard layer 4 protocols: UDP and TCP. And how exactly this challenge is (or isn't) dealt with, is the main difference between them.

UDP - the minimalist approach

UDP (User Datagram Protocol) is the simpler of the two main Layer 4 protocols. It doesn't see the challenge of reliable, in-order packet delivery as its problem. The upside is that it's faster and more efficient, since it avoids any overhead involved in the extra processing it would take to meet the challenge. It's basically layer 3 packets with port numbers, and not a lot else.

TCP — the reliable conversation manager

TCP (Transmission Control Protocol) adds port numbers just as UDP does. Additionally, however, it creates clearly defined *connections* in order to meet the challenge of *reliable, in-order packet delivery*.

Connection Management

This is like formally beginning and ending a phone call, so both parties know when the other is ready to begin. Before any data flows, TCP establishes a connection through a so-called *three-way handshake. Think*:

- *"Can we talk?"*
- *"Yes, let's talk"*
- *"Great, let's begin"*

When the conversation ends, TCP properly closes the connection with a *graceful teardown. Think*:

- *"I'd like to end the call now. Goodbye"*
- *"Ok, goodbye"*

Reliable Delivery

TCP uses *acknowledgments (ACKs)* and *retransmissions* to ensure data arrives. When the receiver gets a packet, it sends back an ACK saying *"got it"*. If the sender doesn't receive an ACK within a reasonable time, it assumes the packet was lost and sends it again. It's like requiring a *message received* confirmation for every important communication.

In-Order Delivery

TCP assigns *sequence numbers* to packets, allowing the receiver to reassemble them in the correct order, even if they arrive jumbled. Think of numbering the pages of a multi-page letter — even if the postal service delivers page 3 before page 1, the recipient can still read them in the intended sequence. All of these TCP features operate independently of the underlying IP layer, which continues to provide its best-effort packet delivery service. TCP builds reliability on top of IP's unreliable foundation, creating a dependable communication channel from unreliable components.

Choosing between TCP and UDP

UDP is often used when speed and efficiency matter more than perfect delivery, i.e. getting as many packets as quickly and efficiently as possible is more important than ensuring none of them get *lost* or *swapped*.

For example, in a real-time application like a phone conversation: if a packet containing a couple of syllables gets lost, you'll barely notice a brief glitch. But if the call stalled every time a packet went missing — buffering while waiting for retransmission — the conversation would become unusable. For live communication, it's better to skip the missing syllables and keep the conversation flowing.

TCP is essential when data integrity matters more than speed. Typical use cases include file transfers, emails, and any application where corruption would be unacceptable. When you email your boss a spreadsheet with the company's monthly sales figures, even a single byte out of place could scramble the numbers or corrupt the file entirely. You need every byte to arrive correctly and in sequence — TCP guarantees this happens, even if it means waiting a bit longer for retransmissions.

The fundamental trade-off is : UDP says *"Give me what you can, as fast as you can"*, while TCP says *"Give me everything, in perfect order, no matter how long it takes"*.

There are some new higher level protocols, like *HTTP/3 and QUIC*, which have recently been developed, that try to combine the best of both approaches. These are finding increasing use, for example, in high performance, media streaming (e.g. Netflix and co.). More on this in the planned follow-up volume *(Modern Networking - Software and Techniques)*.

Endpoint on its own, is confusingly used to mean both a *network endpoint* (as defined here), and an *API endpoint*, which is usually a *URL*.[52]

Summary

- Packet *encapsulation* is the process whereby a packet of one type is embedded as the payload of a different packet type. It's a clever technique often used to help cleanly implement layering of a higher layer protocol on top of a lower one, with the *higher* layer protocol using the *inner* packet.
- The (outer) lower layer packet can be processed as usual at layer 2, by any network components enabled at this lower layer (or above).
- The (inner) higher layer packet can (also) be examined and processed by any network components (also) enabled at this higher layer. Thus, new higher layer functionality can be introduced without the risk of *breaking* or *complicating* the lower layer functionality in any way.
- *Logical addressing* is the assignment of an additional (logical) address to interfaces, in addition to the MAC address each was manufactured with.
- Using logical addresses allows a *natural* grouping of interfaces, allocating addresses based on how/where the interfaces are used, rather than who manufactured them, and when.
- Layer 3 uses exclusively logical addresses, which are commonly referred to as *IP addresses*.
- A *Host* is a layer 3 Interface.
- A *Subnet* is a layer 3 LAN.
- A subnet is allocated a single *IP address range* (sometimes called the *subnet address*), from which its individual interfaces can be assigned individual IP addresses.
- CIDR is a notation which appends a suffix like */24* to an IP address. This can be used to indicate an IP address range (and optionally also a specific address in the range). It does so indirectly, by specifying how many (left-most) bits of the address do not vary between addresses in the range.
- Interfaces within a subnet can communicate using IP addresses, but behind the scenes, they *know* (or can find out) the permanent MAC addresses of the other interfaces in the subnet, and use these MAC addresses, to deliver the packets to destinations in the subnet directly, themselves.
- In order to get packets to/from interfaces outside the subnet, however, a *router* is required. The router can be configured as the *default gateway* for the subnet, so that interfaces use it by default for delivering packets to interfaces outside their own subnet (of which they have no knowledge, or means to discover, the MAC addresses themselves).
- The router may be directly connected with the destination subnet. In this case, it has one of its interfaces in the same subnet as the source interface, and a second interface in the same subnet as the destination interface.
- Or, it may not be directly connected with the destination subnet. In this case, it needs to pass on the packet to an intermediary router, which in turn may have to pass on the packet to a further router, etc. This is essentially how packets get from one computer on the internet to

another in some other part of the world.

- Layer 3 enables packets to be sent anywhere in the world—this is the internet's primary function. Higher layers add useful functionality on top of this core capability of global packet delivery.
- Generally, each router is connected to not one, but many other routers, forming a mesh-like web. Figuring out which router to pass which packet on to is the *magic sauce* of routers. They make these decisions using information stored in their *routing tables*, and keep these tables up to date by regularly syncing with nearby routers via so-called *routing protocols*.
- The standard (routing) behaviour for a router is to pick the next router, based on a single metric called *cost*, which is calculated based on how fast and reliably the packet should reach its destination as a result.
- Groups of routers can be combined to form *routing domains*, that are configured with *routing policies* that cause the routers to deviate from this standard routing behaviour, in specific ways decided upon by the organization responsible for the routing domain.
- As a first approximation, the internet can be seen as a single tree, with routers at the bifurcation points, and regular (non-router) hosts as leaves on the tree. As the trunk divides into branches, which in turn subdivide into sub-branches etc, the IP range of the whole tree, gets progressively subdivided.
- A more realistic model, is a forest of trees, interconnected only at their trunks. And within each tree, there are additional *shortcut* connections between routers. This makes routing much more complex.
- A network *protocol* defines how information should be exchanged between systems, including the structure of the packets (which fields are where) exchanged, as well as their semantics (what each field represents).
- Layer 3 is concerned with getting an individual packet from one interface to another using logical (IP) addressing. The most fundamental layer 3 protocol is *IP*. It currently exists in both versions 4 and 6. Other layer 3 protocols also exist, but nearly all extend or rely upon IP.
- Layer 4 adds the ability for a software program on the node to share an interface with other programs on that node. It uses *port numbers* to do so. Thus, you can watch a film, while your email program checks for new mail in the background, and your operating system checks for important updates, simultaneously, without the data for each getting *mixed up*.
- The two main protocols of layer 4 are TCP and UDP. TCP provides reliable, in-order delivery of packets. UDP doesn't, but the packets it does deliver arrive more efficiently, and consume less processing resources in the process. Each has uses cases for which it tends to be more suitable.

Conclusion

You've successfully navigated the middle layers of the networking stack — the layers that transform isolated LANs into a global communication system. You now understand how IP addresses provide location-independent identity, how routers make forwarding decisions to move packets across LAN boundaries, and how they keep each other updated on the state of a constantly evolving network. Furthermore, you've learned how layer 4 protocols like TCP and UDP use port numbers to enable multiple applications to share network interfaces while meeting different reliability needs.

It's worth dwelling on the significance of layer 3 for a moment—it's what enables packets to traverse the entire planet — this is the internet's primary function. The higher layers we encounter more about in the coming chapters essentially add functionality and features on top of this core capability of worldwide packet delivery. So just as one can consider layers 1 and 2 making networks possible, one can consider layer 3 as that which makes the internet possible.

These aren't just abstract concepts any more. You can trace a packet's journey from source to destination, understanding each encapsulation step, every routing decision, and how port numbers can be used to deliver data to the different applications sharing a single interface. You've seen both the elegant hierarchical theory and the messier reality influenced by routing policies and economic relationships.

With this foundation firmly in place, you're ready to explore how applications actually harness these capabilities. Chapter 4 shifts focus upward to the protocols and services that make the internet useful to humans — transforming raw packet delivery into web pages, file transfers, and the countless applications we interact with daily.

[1] Various terms such as MAN (Metropolitan Area Network) and WAN (Wide Area Networks) are sometimes used as terms for collections of multiple LANs of various *sizes*. Unlike LANs, however, these terms are not clearly defined, and as such will be avoided in this book.

[2] or equivalently the number of addresses

[3] and the nodes on which the interfaces reside

[4] logical addresses are, in fact, a layer of abstraction on top of the underlying (hardware) addresses

[5] ...except for the problem of too many levels of indirection. The *theorem* does not describe an actual theorem that can be proven, but rather, is a general principle for managing complexity through abstraction. The humorously intended exception highlights what seems to be an even more fundamental theorem: "There's no such thing as a free lunch", also familiar to physicists in the forms of the *laws of conservation of energy/momentum*, and the *first/second laws of thermodynamics*

[6] Note that some fields are omitted, which, I feel, are details that distract more from a fundamental understanding of the concepts presented here. These additional fields are shown for simplicity as "Other Meta Information"

[7] And since higher layers rely on those below, this effectively means layer 3 and all layers above rely on the IP protocol

[8] similar to other evolving protocols such as USB, with each new version aiming to improve performance, stability, or address shortcomings discovered after the release of a previous version.

[9] I'm using the term *fingers* to include *thumbs*

[10] `log10(16) ≈ 1.204`. The number of digits needed to represent a number N in decimal is $\log_{10}(N)$, rounded up to the nearest integer. For example, representing 1000 requires 4 decimal digits. $\log_{10}(1000) = 3$, and 3 rounded up to the next integer is 4. This principle applies to any base B using log_B(N). The relative compactness is the ratio of these logarithms: binary takes $\log_{10}(N)/\log_2(N) = \log_{10}(2) \approx 3.32\times$ more digits than decimal, while hexadecimal takes $\log_{10}(N)/\log_{16}(N) = \log_{10}(16) \approx 1.204\times$ fewer digits than decimal.

[11] In binary each symbol represents a power of 2, starting from the right at 2^0. For example, the binary number 10110101 is equivalent to $1\times2^7 + 0\times2^6 + 1\times2^5 + 1\times2^4 + 0\times2^3 + 1\times2^2 + 0\times2^1 + 1\times2^0 = 128 + 32 + 16 + 4 + 1 = 181$ (decimal). To convert to hexadecimal, group the bits into sets of 4 from right to left (1011 0101), then convert each group: 1011 = B and 0101 = 5, giving B5 in hex.

[12] notwithstanding the fact that house numbers usually start with 1 instead of 0 - a classic example of an *off by one* error that seems to strike street planners as wilfully as software developers. Actually, 0 and the maximum value are special *reserved* addresses in networking, so you could consider my analogy to be *off by two* :-)

[13] the dots (`.`) are both visual and group separators. This grouping has a saving in apparent *size* of the numbers due to the ability to omit leading zero digits, without which we would otherwise have to write `192.168.001.001`. But more importantly, the heavy cognitive load of translating a single big decimal number (to binary) is reduced to 4 smaller cognitive loads—one per group. The latter advantage being especially apparent in this example in the rightmost groups (those containing `1`). *Think*: calculating `14 + 25 = 39` is a higher cognitive load than grouping into *tens* and *ones*, and individually calculating `1 + 2 = 3` (*tens*) and `4 + 5 = 9` (*ones*).

[14] It's at the discretion of whoever is assigning the IP addresses to decide what interfaces are *related* and why this definition of related is useful. But a common choice is considering the interfaces closely related if they are physically close together or in the same LAN. And the decision is dynamic in that should one interface be later *moved* (e.g. into a different LAN) thereby affecting its *closeness* to the others, then the IP addresses can be updated accordingly. Unlike the case with MAC addresses, which can never change.

[15] using decimal rather than the networking standard of binary or hexadecimal, to keep the example simpler

[16] the network and broadcast addresses

[17] to be very precise, a further 2 units need to be reserved to connect floor with the building as a whole—*think*: elevator. These 2 IP addresses are used for the interfaces connecting the routers

[18] A *subnet mask* is an alternative way of expressing the same information as the CIDR suffix. Instead of writing "/24", you could write the subnet mask "255.255.255.0". The mask shows which bits are fixed (the 255 parts, or all 1s in binary) versus which bits can vary (the 0 parts). Both notations tell you which addresses belong to the same subnet, but CIDR notation is more compact and is the modern standard.

[19] and also not all 1 — see *Subnet — reserved addresses*

[20] notwithstanding the first and last addresses in the range being reserved, as mentioned above

[21] The network prefix acts as a binary mask, allowing routers to quickly determine whether a destination IP address belongs to a particular subnet by performing a bitwise AND operation.

[22] Even though it's only the value of the single horizontal dimension that's relevant, visualization is often easier if we do so as a block (with an arbitrary height), the width of which is $2^{\text{number of host bits}}$

[23] (and above). Note that the source still needs to *know* the hardware (MAC) address of the destination interface. Surmounting this limitation requires a router — see *Routers*

[24] In general, all Layer 3 enabled interfaces in a subnet will want to join this multicast group, as not doing so would prevent them from communicating with other interfaces via IP. There may be specific exceptions, such as security reasons or resource limitations in IoT devices. Therefore, the multicast approach in NDP is primarily about efficiency and flexibility, rather than a mere technicality.

[25] As an additional safeguard, IP packets include a *TTL (Time to Live)* field (as part of *Other Meta Information* in *Figure 11*) in their header. This field is initialized at the source router to an integer — often 64 or 128 — which represents a reasonable limit for how often a packet can be forwarded before it should be presumed something is amiss. Every time a router forwards the packet, it also decrements the TTL. When the TTL reaches 0 the router in question presumes the packet is not deliverable and drops it

[26] It's possible for a router not to be connected to multiple LANs, in which case it would not be functioning as a *gateway*. However, this is very uncommon, as connecting multiple LANs is the primary *raison d'être* of a router. So *gateway* and *router* are effectively synonymous. However, whether the router joins subnets on different sides of a routing domain determines whether it's a domain gateway or *just* a subnet gateway.

[27] Each interface in a subnet needs to have its default gateway configured individually. It's technically possible for different interfaces in a subnet to have different routers configured as their default gateway (if the subnet has multiple routers available). However, it's more common for all interfaces in a single subnet to be configured with the same default gateway, in which case one speaks of the *subnet default gateway*.

[28] This is a virtual interface that exists on every device. This means it is solely a software construct, and does not have a corresponding (physical) *port*. As a result it cannot be used to communicate with anything outside the device itself. It uses the special IP address `127.0.0.1` (or `::1` for IPv6) and allows a device to send network packets to itself. Unlike physical interfaces, the loopback interface is always up and reachable as long as the device's networking stack is functioning. It's commonly used for testing network software without requiring actual network hardware, and for inter-process communication on the same machine. The entire `127.0.0.0/8` range is reserved for loopback, though `127.0.0.1` is most commonly used. `localhost` is often used instead, since *DNS* resolves this to the IP address *127.0.0.1* (or *::1* for IPv6)

[29] The routing tables of routers are generally much longer than the above example, and often contain many hundreds (or even thousands) of lines and must be updated regularly via routing protocols.

[30] even though technically, they may be doing both simultaneously — updating a copy of the table, while using an earlier copy for forwarding

[31] In a simplified tree-like model, as discussed in *The Internet (Simplified)*, *cost* does/can not factor into routing decisions, since there is only a single path between any two interfaces in such a model. The *cost* associated may not be uninteresting, but the next-hop gets chosen independently of it — it's the only next hop that gets the packet closer to its ultimate intended destination.

[32] Exceptions are: 1) when routing policies (see *4). Routing Domains* are configured that specify deviations from this standard behaviour. 2) when the router itself is directly connected to the subnet containing the destination, in

which case it can deliver the packet directly. 3) When no neighbouring router advertises it can deliver the package to any address range, in which case it forwards the packet to the neighbouring router that has been configured as its *default route*

[33] i.e. directly connected to it - so that both routers have an interface in a common subnet

[34] This tie-breaking happens implicitly since only the lowest cost option for any given address range is kept in the routing table, and thus only this can be chosen from. The others aren't necessarily discarded, but may be cached in secondary data structures in the router's memory, as a failover in case the path in the routing table becomes (temporarily) unavailable.

[35] There's only one path joining any two interfaces in a tree-like model. The routing table, however, may or may not *know about* it. More specifically, when a router receives a packet, one can distinguish two separate cases, according to the direction of packet motion: (1) moving upstream—in which case 1 or 0 matches can be found—corresponding to the routing table *knowing about* the path and not, respectively. The match happens when the IP address is within the router's (direct) upstream range. The router forwards the packet to its upstream router in both cases. (2) moving downstream—in which case 2 or 0 matches should be found. The matches happen when the IP address is within a downstream sub-range (which automatically means it must be within the upstream range, since this range is included in the upstream range). The router forwards the packet to the downstream router corresponding to the matched range. Note: one could also say the router prefers the *most specific* range or *smallest matching* range — which is another way of saying it prefers the *longest matching prefix*. This last statement holds in general, including for The Internet (Realistic) model also.

[36] or less. A range of size 1 (which has the CIDR suffix */32*) is sometimes used for so-called *loopback* interfaces — which will be discussed further in the planned follow-up volume *(Modern Networking - Software and Techniques)*. Ranges are defined in binary as *powers of 2* i.e. *{1, 2, 4, 8, ...}*

[37] not to be confused *allocated* which may be when a person or body has been given the authority to decide how to assign a given IP address or address range.

[38] The need for private addresses is often justified by two arguments: *scarcity* (valid only for IPv4 with its 4.3 billion address limit; irrelevant for IPv6's 340 undecillion) and *security* (overstated for both—hiding behind private addresses is just obscurity, not actual security, which (additionally) requires proper firewalls and access controls).

[39] More accurately, a routing domain can group the ranges of private addresses it uses into one or more private *address realms*. Such realms can be thought of as independent addressing *scopes* within each of which the private addresses used are unique and meaningful. Each realm has one or more dedicated gateway routers. Only between interfaces within any single such realm may the private IP addresses of the realm be freely used for packets. Packets can cross a realm boundary only if their source/destination addresses are meaningful on the other side. For example, forwarding packets from a private address realm to where globally routable (public) addresses are used (e.g. the public Internet) typically requires SNAT (private→public *source*), and traffic forwarded in the opposite direction typically requires DNAT (public→private *destination*). Different realms may (re)use the same address ranges (for different purposes), which is harmless since realms are thus isolated—packets can't pass between them without appropriate address translation. The use of private addresses is much more common with IPv4, with its limited number of addresses, than with IPv6, where address number limitations are no longer a concern. *Private Subnet* is a term used mainly in cloud networks, to mean a subnet whose interfaces are (to some degree) restricted from communication with interfaces outside, and/or vice versa. The exact form and degree of this restriction is a matter of policy, and is strictly speaking independent of whether the interfaces in such subnets use private addresses or not (though it's often implemented using them). The gateway routers for such a private subnet may be configured with various *isolation policies* (e.g. through firewalls), such as *'no packets may enter or leave'*, or *'(HTTP) requests may pass outward only (and responses to them back in)'*. *Link-Local Addresses* are a special class of IP address that are effectively even *more private than "private addresses"*, in the sense that their visibility is even more restricted—to a single subnet rather than to a single private address realm (which may, and typically does, encompass multiple subnets). Link-Local addresses are *never forwarded by a router*—not even between subnets inside the same routing domain—making them inherently isolated. (Private addresses, by contrast, may be

forwarded between subnets in the same address realm). Unfortunately, as previously noted, the term *link* is overloaded, but is used here to mean a *subnet* (and not, for example, just a single segment thereof). Link-local addresses are always in the range *169.254.0.0/16* (IPv4) or *fe80::/10* (IPv6). Note that private and link-local addresses provide binary isolation (*think*: road closed), whereas private subnets and firewalls provide graduated control (*think*: police checkpoint allowing selective passage).

[40] Typically, just the subset *fd00::/8* is used in practice

[41] More precisely, the same IP address prefixes are *advertised* from (the interfaces of) multiple routers at different locations. The individual locations are often called *Points of Presence (PoPs)*, and you are typically routed to the one which is *topologically closest*. Often, but not always, this is also the one which is geographically closest. Anycast is one of the main features offered by *CDNs (Content Delivery Networks)* like *Cloudflare*.

[42] more accurately, each router learns what IP ranges are advertised by each router directly connected to it (i.e. those it can choose as a next-hop for *packet forwarding*). But since this happens recursively, i.e. each of these routers in turn do the same, the original router learns what IP ranges it can ultimately reach through each directly connected router (even if possibly multiple hops thereafter are necessary). The same applies to all routing protocols, including iBGP and IGP.

[43] *OSPF* and *IS-IS* are examples of *IGPs*. AS subdivisions are often called *areas* in *OSPF* and *levels* in *IS-IS*

[44] the cost of a link is direction-dependent, so each link has a (possibly) different cost for a packet delivered in one direction to the other direction. This duality reflects the fact that just because a router has a certain measure of trust in the information provided by router b, does not necessarily mean that b trusts a equally so.

[45] It includes the MTU of that outgoing connection, enabling the sender to discover the *Path MTU* — the largest packet size that works for the entire path. If DF is not set, the router fragments the packet itself and forwards the fragments.

[46] Since IPv6 routers never fragment packets, any packet that exceeds the MTU of the outgoing connection to the next router triggers this message. The PTB message contains that next-hop connection's MTU. This is the only way IPv6 senders can discover the Path MTU, making these messages essential for IPv6 operation

[47] which will be discussed further in the planned follow-up volume *(Modern Networking - Software and Techniques)*

[48] While ICMP is essential for network diagnostics, excessive ICMP traffic (sometimes called *ICMP storms*) can overwhelm network resources. Network providers often implement *rate limiting* on ICMP messages (allowing only a certain number per second) to prevent abuse while maintaining essential diagnostic capabilities. Complete blocking is rare as it would break critical network functions.

[49] more specifically this is generally an *operating system socket* opened by a *process*, running in an operating system, which controls access to all fundamental network software and hardware (including the interface in question) on the node, as well as the port numbers available. This will be discussed further in a follow-up book *Modern Networking - Software and Techniques*

[50] Their implementation is an example of multiple, same-layer encapsulation - something which will be looked at more closely in a planned follow-up volume *(Modern Networking - Software and Techniques)* to this book. The cloud provider's layer 2 (used to implement the cloud provider's own physical infrastructure) encapsulates the cloud provider's layer 3 packets, which in turn encapsulate the cloud user's layer 2 packets, which in turn encapsulate the cloud user's layer 3 packets. It's only the innermost layer 2 and layer 3 packets which users of the cloud actually *see* when they *create* and *use* such *subnets* via the cloud provider's web interface or SDK.

[51] Note that some fields are omitted, which, I feel, are details that distract more from a fundamental understanding of the concepts presented here. These additional fields are shown for simplicity as "Other Meta Information". UPD and TCP define different fields here

[52] at least in the context of web-based APIs, like *REST* and GraphQL

4. Upper Layers and Applications

This chapter explores the upper layers where the packet delivery mechanisms from the previous chapter becomes the platform on which human-friendly applications and services can be created. These new layers build on the addressing, routing, and transport protocols introduced in the previous chapter, adding the abstractions that make networked computing accessible and powerful.

The journey begins with DNS — the system that lets us use memorable names like *"example.com"* instead of memorizing IP addresses. You'll see how this distributed database works, how caching speeds lookups, and how your computer automatically obtains its network configuration through DHCP. From there, we explore HTTP — the protocol powering the web. You'll understand how URLs map to remote resources or function calls, how REST principles shape modern APIs, and how various protocols build on the TCP and UDP foundation to serve different application needs. The chapter concludes by revealing how these fundamental layers enable software-defined networks and virtual overlays — showing that the layered model isn't just descriptive but generative, spawning new forms of networking that transcend physical infrastructure.

By chapter's end, you'll understand the complete stack from physical signals to user applications — possessing the conceptual foundation needed to approach any networking challenge, whether that's designing new systems, troubleshooting existing ones, or innovating beyond current limitations.

Layer 5+

DNS - FQDNs (dotted strings) for IP addresses

DNS (Domain Name System) is a system for allowing humans to use easier to remember *dotted strings* (like *example.com*) to specify an interface in lieu of an IP address (like *93.184.216.34*). The technical name for such a dotted string is an *FQDN (Fully Qualified Domain Name)*. Without DNS, users would need to memorize numerical IP addresses for every website they visit. This also provides flexibility: you can change the IP address (for example, when switching hosting providers) without visitors noticing any change, since they only remember and use *example.com* (which recalls to mind once more the *Fundamental Theorem of Software Engineering*). Every FQDN maps to at least one IP address[1]. The process of using a DNS lookup to find the IP address in question is called resolving the FQDN or DNS resolution — see Figure 23.

Figure 23. **DNS Resolution.** *An FQDN is a 'dotted string", such as www.three.two.com, that can be used as an easy to remember alternative to an IP address. This is especially useful in URLs. Every FQDN should correspond to (at least one) IP address, and the process of using DNS to find the IP address(es) in question is called "resolving the FQDN". Going the other way around i.e. IP → FQDN, is called "reverse lookup" or "reverse resolution".*

The structure of an FQDN is illustrated in Figure 24, with the individual *words* corresponding to names in a tree-like hierarchy illustrated in Figure 25. The highest level of this name hierarchy is called a (top level) *domain (name)*, then *subdomain (names)* of successively lower levels. An FQDN must be composed of a top-level domain and at least one subdomain. Further subdomain prefixes can be prepended, in order, on the left. This process may be repeated recursively. An optional *hostname* may be prepended as the final, left-most word.[2]

The information about which FQDN corresponds to which IP address isn't stored and managed in a single location for the whole internet. The hierarchical naming structure is mirrored by a corresponding hierarchy of *DNS servers* (also called *nameservers*) which store their data as *records* in so-called *zone files*. The DNS servers (and zone files) are deployed by the organizations involved for storing and replying to requests about the mappings they manage. Each DNS server returns the IP addresses for domains they manage directly, and the IP addresses of the DNS servers for any subdomains they have sub-allocated to other organizations.[3] When you need to look up a domain name, a *DNS resolver* (a service that queries DNS servers on your behalf) asks these servers from the top down, in sequence, until it finds the answer.

So, when a DNS resolution is needed, a DNS resolver traverses the DNS hierarchy - starting with *root DNS servers*, which direct it to the appropriate top level *DNS server* (e.g., the *.com* server), which then directs the query to the *authoritative server* [4] for that specific domain (managed by the domain owner or their DNS provider).

> Don't confuse *FQDN* with URL. An FQDN is the dotted string that often forms part of a URL. But a URL can contain an IP address instead of an FQDN, as illustrated in Figure 27.

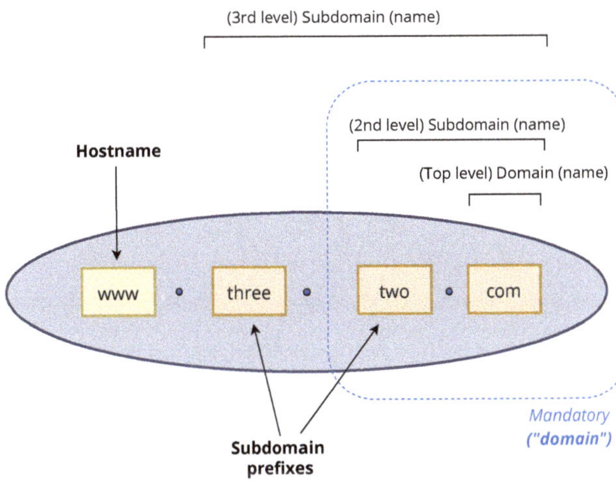

Figure 24. **FQDN.** *Joined by "dots" are individual words, each of which corresponds to a name in a tree-like hierarchy illustrated in Figure 25. The mandatory right-most two names are together sometimes called a "domain".[5] The hostname is optional, and an FQDN without a hostname is sometimes called a "bare FQDN"*

Using FQDNs instead of IP addresses has the double advantage of being:

1. *easier to remember* (*example.com* instead of, say, *93.184.216.34*), and
2. *more flexible*:
   - You can move your website to a different IP address and visitors notice no change.[6]
   - Some *advanced routing* techniques become possible.

It's not uncommon to hear of the mandatory part of an FQDN — i.e. *two.com* in *www.three.two.com* referred to simply as "the *domain*". See also Domains.

It's not clear just by looking at an FQDN (such as *b.a.com*) whether the left-most *word* (here *b*) is a hostname or a subdomain prefix.[7] In *Figure 25*, for example, the *three* in *three.two.com* is a subdomain prefix, but the *hostname1* in *hostname1.two.com* is a hostname. Only DNS resolution — querying the DNS server hierarchy and then examining the DNS records returned — can be used to tell.

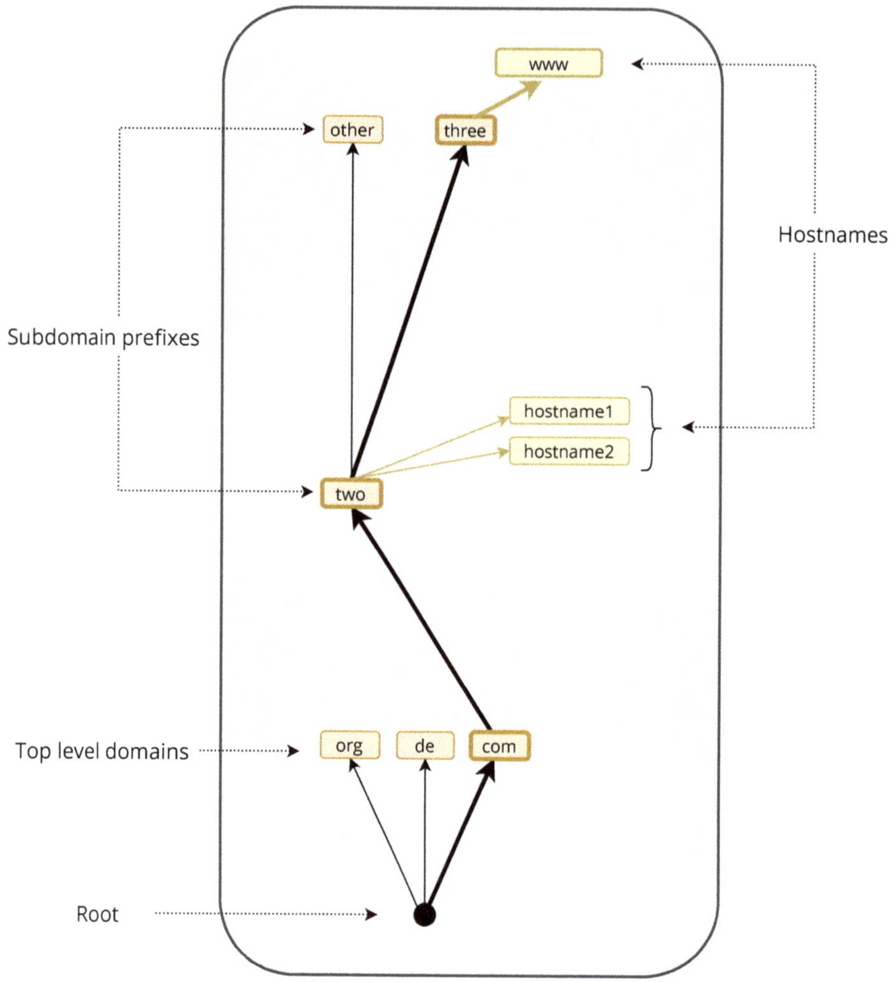

Figure 25. DNS **Name Tree**. *Each word in the "dotted string" of an FQDN, like "www.three.two.com", corresponds to a node in a DNS name tree.*[8] *And the whole dotted string can be seen as encoding a path from the root to a node in the tree. Subdomain prefixes may, but need not, have children. A subdomain prefix without children forms a leaf of the tree. If a subdomain prefix does have children, each child can be another subdomain prefix or a hostname. Hostnames may not have children. Thus hostnames are always leaves of the tree, and can only occur as the left-most word in a dotted string of an FQDN.*

Example DNS resolution — *www.three.two.com*

A *DNS resolver* finds the IP address for *www.three.two.com* by traversing the hierarchy of DNS servers shown in *Figure 26*.

- 1: *Query Root Server*. The resolver contacts a root DNS server at *198.41.0.4*. The root server responds: *"For .com domains, query the server at 192.5.6.30"*
- 2: *Query .com Server*. The resolver queries the .com DNS server at *192.5.6.30*. This server responds: *"For two.com, query the server at 198.51.100.1"*
- 3: *Query two.com Server*. The resolver contacts *198.51.100.1* (the two.com nameserver). This server responds: *"For three.two.com, query the server at 198.51.100.2"*
- 4: *Query three.two.com Server*. The resolver queries *198.51.100.2* (the three.two.com nameserver). This server provides the final answer: *"www.three.two.com is at IP address 203.0.113.66"*

Each response is cached to speed up future lookups.

DNS Resolvers, Non-Authoritative Servers and Caching

Authoritative DNS servers form a clear hierarchy and have direct access to the DNS data in the corresponding zone files, as illustrated in *Figure 26*. *DNS Resolvers* are clients that query authoritative DNS servers, either directly or through other resolvers, to translate domain names into IP addresses. Most resolvers *cache* the results of previous queries to improve performance and reduce load on the DNS system.

Authoritative DNS servers themselves don't cache — they only serve their own zone data. DNS resolvers do, however, rely heavily on caching at every level.[9] Every DNS record includes a *TTL (Time To Live)* value specifying how long resolvers should cache it. Short TTLs (minutes) allow quick changes but increase query load on DNS servers; long TTLs (hours or days) reduce query traffic but delay propagation of changes.

When administrators need to make changes — such as moving a website to a new server (changing its IP address) or switching email providers (updating MX records) — they often temporarily reduce TTLs beforehand. This ensures that when they make the actual change, DNS caches worldwide will expire quickly and fetch the new information, minimizing downtime or misdirected traffic. When a resolver needs to look up a domain name, it first checks its cache. If the answer isn't cached (or has expired based on its TTL), the resolver must obtain it either by querying other resolvers or by traversing the authoritative DNS hierarchy from the root servers downward.

Some resolvers are also called *non-authoritative DNS servers*, but the distinction between these and any other *resolver* is subjective and depends primarily on deployment and accessibility. Both query for DNS data they don't own and cache results. The difference is who can query them:

- *Resolver* (narrow access): Serves specific clients or internal contexts. Examples are a *Browser's DNS cache* (only serves that browser instance), *Operating system resolver* (only serves applications on that computer), or a *corporate DNS resolver* (only serves devices within the company network)
- *Non-authoritative DNS server* (broad access): Accepts queries from many external clients. Examples are *ISP's DNS servers* (serve all the ISP's customers), and *public DNS servers* [10] (serve anyone on the internet)

In practice, these are the same technology — software that performs recursive DNS resolution and caches results. The terminology simply reflects how openly they're deployed. Your ISP's *DNS server* is functionally identical to your OS's *resolver*; the difference is that one accepts queries from thousands of customers while the other only serves your local computer.

When you type a domain name in your browser, the query moves through increasingly broader scopes: *browser cache → OS resolver → ISP's DNS server* (or configured alternative). Each level checks its cache first. Only when none have a cached answer does the final DNS server in the chain perform top-down, recursive resolution, starting from the root servers and working down the authoritative DNS hierarchy.

DNS Record Types

The most important type of information stored in DNS (zone files) is the mapping of FQDN to IP address — so- called *A records* for IPv4 addresses, and *AAAA records* for IPv6 addresses. However, various other record types are also stored, each serving different purposes:

- **A records** — map domain names to IPv4 addresses.
- **AAAA records** — map domain names to IPv6 addresses.
- **CNAME records** — create aliases that allow one domain to *point to* another.
- **MX records** — specify mail servers for a domain.
- **TXT records** — store arbitrary text, often for verification or security policies.
- **NS records** — identify a DNS server for a subdomain. For example, the *.com* DNS server returns NS records pointing to *two.com*'s DNS server, telling resolvers where to find authoritative answers for *two.com*

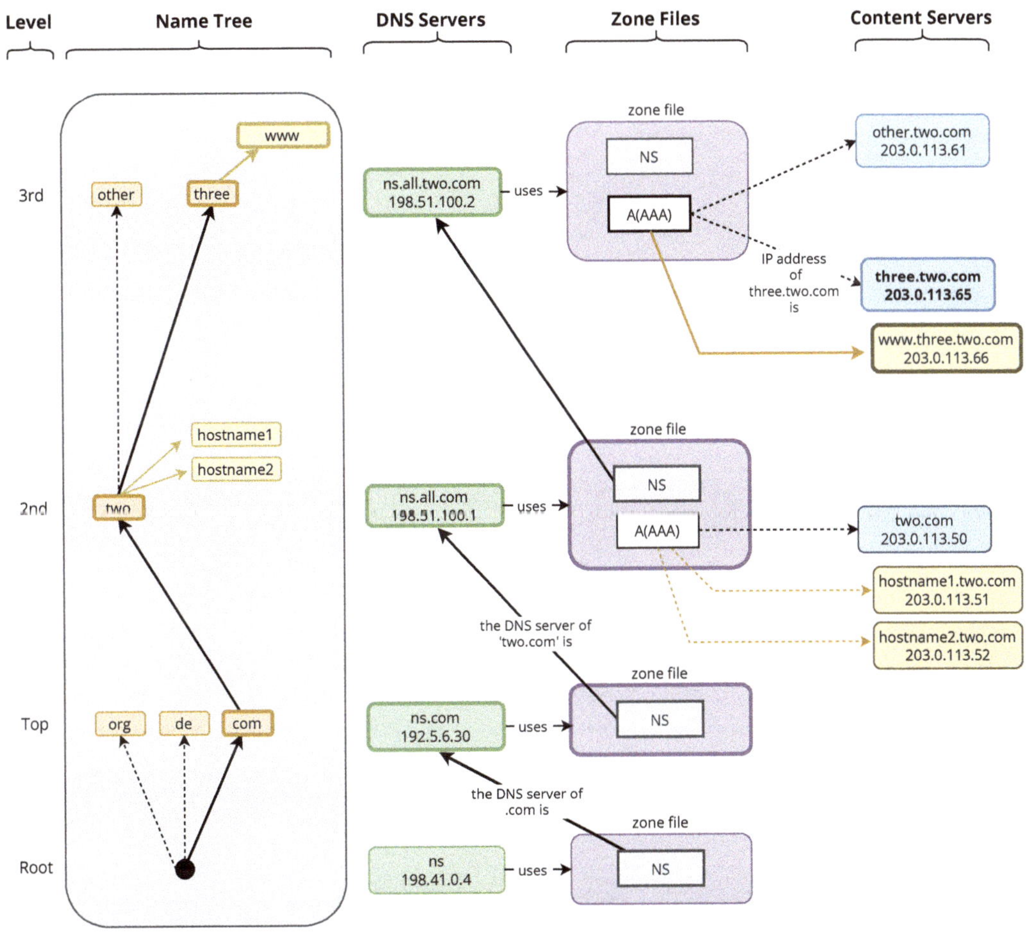

Figure 26. **DNS Architecture** *— A DNS resolver traverses the hierarchy top-down until it finds the IP address for the FQDN it's trying to resolve, as described in the example DNS resolution. The zone file of a parent (e.g. .com) contains an NS entry for the DNS server of each child (e.g. two.com). The zone file of the child contains an A (for IPv4) or AAAA (for IPv6) entry for the "bare" FQDN of itself (e.g. two.com), plus entries for any hostnames prefixed to it (e.g. hostname1.two.com). And so on, recursively. The two highest levels of the tree (Root and Top) have only NS entries (since there are no content servers for root, .com, etc.).*[11]

Dont't confuse DNS and content servers.

- **Content servers**: Deliver actual content (web pages, files, emails, etc.). These are what most people mean when they think of *servers*.
- **DNS servers**: Store and return mapping information (which IP address goes with which FQDN). They help you find the content servers.[12]

Host Configuration

DNS resolution requires hosts to know which DNS servers to use - this is part of the broader host configuration process.

In order to be able to participate in layer 3 communication, each host[13] needs to be configured with essential network information. The most fundamental requirement is an IP address, but hosts also typically need additional configuration such as:

- *Default gateway* — the router to which to send traffic destined for other networks
- *DNS Resolver addresses* — which DNS servers to query for DNS resolution
- *Network mask/prefix length* — to determine which addresses are on the local network
- *Domain name and search domains* — the DNS domain the host belongs to (e.g. if the host is *laptop.company.com*, then *company.com* is its domain), and additional domains to search when resolving short hostnames - typing just *server* (in a browser) might automatically result in trying to resolve *server.company.com*

One option is to statically configure each interface with all this information — the node containing the interface would have the details manually written, e.g. to a configuration file by an administrator. Though possible, this is tedious and error-prone (the person writing the configuration may unintentionally make a mistake, such as using the same address for two different interfaces, or providing incorrect DNS server addresses). A better option is to have the interfaces configured automatically (dynamically), using DHCP.

DHCP

Dynamic Host Configuration Protocol (DHCP) can be used with both the IPv4 and IPv6 protocols to automatically provide all this configuration information. DHCP relies on a central server to hand out addresses from a pool and can also provide the DNS resolver addresses, default gateway, domain name, and other network parameters in a single response. With IPv6 there's an additional option: using *Stateless Address Autoconfiguration (SLAAC)* for IP addresses, combined with other mechanisms like *Router Advertisements* for default gateway discovery and manual or DHCP configuration for DNS resolvers. SLAAC allows devices to essentially pick their own IPv6 address based on network announcements from routers, and effectively use NDP to make sure the address has not already been taken. This makes SLAAC simpler to deploy for basic connectivity, but DHCP more controllable for administrators and more comprehensive for providing all necessary network configuration. Note also that although they are used to perform configuration of layer 3 (they interact with layer 3), SLAAC and DHCP are themselves higher layer protocols.

APIs

An *API (Application Programming Interface)* can be thought of as a contract between two pieces of software that specifies exactly how they can communicate with each other. It's essentially a kind of *standard* for specific software-to-software communication.[14] Knowing what an API is, will be helpful in developing a deeper understanding of *URLs*, an important topic which will be introduced presently.

This contract specifies exactly what each can ask, how to ask it, and how the response will be structured. One speaks of one piece of software *calling an API function* on the other.

It's not unlike ordering food at a restaurant. The menu shows you all the dishes you can order (the available *functions* in the API). When you place an order, you specify details like whether you want rice or potatoes, or if you have allergies (these are function *parameters*). The waiter takes your specific request to the kitchen, and the kitchen sends back exactly what you ordered in a predictable format - your meal on a plate.

Similarly, when one piece of software calls an API function on another, it chooses from available functions and includes specific parameters, and *calls the function with these parameters*. The other piece of software is the receiver of this function call. It processes this function call and answers by returning data in a structured, predictable format that the calling software knows how to handle.

This standardization means developers of such pieces of software don't need to understand the details of how the other system works internally - they just need to follow the API's documented rules, just like you don't need to know how the kitchen operates to successfully order a meal. Good APIs make different pieces of software interchangeable - you can swap camera lenses without the camera caring whether it's a Canon or Sigma lens, as long as it has the right mount and responds to the right controls.

URLs

URLs (Uniform Resource Locators), as illustrated in *Figure 27*, are traditionally defined as a way to define where to locate and how to retrieve resources on the internet. For example, when you type a URL into a web browser and hit *Enter* or click on a link, you are effectively saying to the web browser *get me the web page identified by this URL*.

The problem with this definition is that it depends on the definition of *resources*, which is typically left vague, at best. I think it's more helpful and generally accurate to think of a URL as a description of a function call, including any specific parameters needed, in a network-based *API*. The resource of the traditional definition can then be seen as the *value* the function returns.[15] URLs, though very commonly used with web browsers, are not restricted solely to *HTTP* (where they often give rise to requests - see *Figure 29*) and the *Web*.

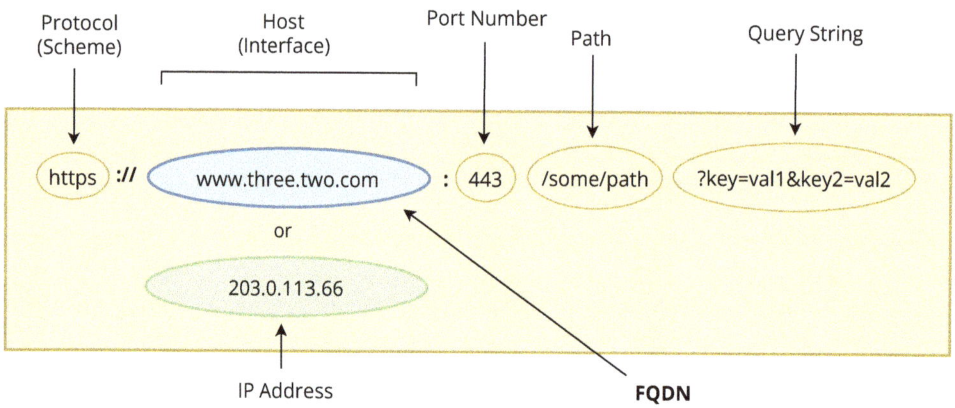

Figure 27. Structure of a **URL**, *as used for example in Web Browsers. DNS is what enables you to write the URL with an FQDN (dotted string) like 'www.three.two.com' instead of an IP address like '203.0.113.66'.*

For example, a URL like *www.drugstore.com:443/medicines/painkillers/ibuprofen?form=liquid&size=200ml* could be seen as encapsulating all the information needed to call a function that places an order and returns a response (corresponding to the item ordered) from an online pharmacy:

- Protocol *(https://)* — *How* you want it sent, e.g., priority registered or regular mail.
- Host *(www.drugstore.com)* — *Where* you want to order from.
- Port Number *(443)* — The specific worker/department you'd like to process the order (e.g., prescription desk vs. general counter).
- Path *(/medicines/painkillers/ibuprofen)* — The specific product you're ordering.

URLs *must* include:

- **Protocol (Scheme)** — which should be used. Common examples are *https*, *scp* and *mailto*.
- **Host** — identifies an interface, specified as either 1) an IP address, or equivalently 2) an *FQDN*. Note that DNS resolves the *entire* Host (including any optional hostname) - not hostname (if present) and domain name individually. See also *Hosts — layer 3 interfaces*.

URLs *may* (optionally) include:

- **Port Number** — If not explicitly specified, a default for the protocol is presumed (e.g., 443 for HTTPS). This is associated with a specific (server) process, running on the remote machine, that handles the remote call.
- **Path** — additional (*hierarchical*) information the server can use to decide what's being requested,[16] e.g. */products/shoes/nike.html*. You can think of it as being like a *name of the remote function* to call.
- **Query String** — additional (*key-value*) information the server can use to decide what's being requested—in practice often used for server-side querying, filtering or searching, e.g. *?color=red&size=10*. You can think of these as being like *arguments for the function* to be called.[17]
- **Fragment** — not shown in the image above, but looks like *#some_link_on_page*. Fragments are NOT sent to the *server*, but may be used by the *client* to process the resource after it's retrieved. For browsers, this is typically scrolling to a corresponding position on the page.

Think of a *URL* as a *description of a function call*, including any specific arguments required, in a network-based *API*.[18]

DNS and URL terminology is rife with potential for confusion:

- *Host* is sometimes confusingly also used to mean *Node*, even though a node can have multiple interfaces, each with (one or more) IP address, and thus multiple hosts
- *Hostname* is not the name of a host (but forms part of it), whereas *domain name* is the name of a domain
- *FQDN (Fully Qualified Domain Name)* - is not a name for a domain, but a name for a combination of *hostname* and *domain name*
- *DNS (Domain Name System)* - is a system for defining and resolving complete FQDNs (not just the *domain name* part thereof)

URIs

URIs (Uniform Resource Identifiers) were introduced alongside URLs as an attempt to separate the *what* (the thing being identified) from the *where and how* (its location and access method). The well-intended motivation was that a URI would identify a resource independently of any particular URL that returns it, allowing the same resource to be referenced in different contexts—such as in databases, citations, or alternative retrieval systems. The choice of *URI* as a new term is somewhat puzzling, since terms like *identifier* or *unique identifier* already existed and would have served the same purpose; the *U* (for *Uniform*) seems added to emphasize a connection to the similarly-named URL.

However, this distinction never proved practically useful. In cases where resources are well-defined and stable (like academic papers with persistent identifiers, books with ISBNs, or XML documents with embedded identification tags), they tend to be self-identifying and don't need separate URIs. In cases where what a URL returns isn't really a stable *thing* at all (like the current time or a random number, or even when a URL returns nothing but *"OK"*), having an identifier separate from the URL is meaningless. For everything in between, people simply use the full URL itself as an identifier when needed.

Moreover, as discussed in the *URLs*, even the *where and how* characterization of URLs is oversimplified — URLs are better understood as function call descriptions rather than *resource* locators. While you could theoretically separate out a *what* component from such a function call, this only makes practical sense when the function returns something stable and meaningfully identifiable — which many URL invocations simply don't.

In practice, URIs have faded from use except as a formal umbrella term in web-related technical specifications.[19]

URL Encoding

URLs traditionally only support ASCII[20] characters. Non-ASCII characters require encoding: domain names use *Punycode* (*münchen.de* becomes *xn—mnchen-3ya.de*), while other URL parts use *percent-encoding* (empty spaces become *%20*, *café* becomes *caf%C3%A9*). Modern browsers handle this encoding automatically, displaying the human-readable form while using the encoded form for actual requests.

Domains

The term *domain* can refer to one of three[21] different things:

Administrative Domain

A set of nodes on a network that are centrally managed by a *domain controller*, which maintains information about *user accounts* and enforces *policies* governing roles and *access controls* for these accounts within the domain. Examples of domain controllers are *Entra ID* on *Microsoft Windows*[22], *Samba* on *Linux*.[23]

DNS Domain

A hierarchical namespace such as *example.com*, managed by a single organization that controls the associated *DNS records* (the mappings of names to IP addresses and other data). These records are stored on *DNS name servers* — specialized servers that answer queries about domain names. The organization designates specific DNS name servers as authoritative for their domain, meaning these servers hold the official, definitive copies of the domain's records that all other DNS servers trust as the source of truth. The organization can create DNS *subdomains* in a given DNS domain (e.g. *mail.example.com*, *www.example.com*) and delegate their management as needed.

Routing Domain

A group of routers under the control of a single organization—see *Routing Domains*.

Though the three are independent, it's not unusual for a given organization to align them for simplicity. For example, a domain controller may often also function as a DNS server, in which case administrative domain and DNS domain coincide. And an organization's routing domain (AS) typically encompasses all the infrastructure for both their administrative domain and DNS domains.

Buying a DNS (Sub)domain

You don't actually *buy* a subdomain (like *example.com*), so much as lease the right to use it, typically for 1-year periods that you must renew. This fee covers two main costs:

1. *Registration*: The administrative overhead of maintaining official records in the global registry, ensuring no one else but you can claim *example.com*, and handling disputes.
2. *DNS hosting*: Someone still needs to run the *authoritative DNS servers* that hold the official records saying which IP addresses your domain points to. This covers the actual operational cost of keeping these servers online to answer queries about your domain.[24]

HTTP

HTTP (Hypertext Transfer Protocol) is the protocol that powers the World Wide Web. It is based on a client-server model. The client (usually a web browser) sends an HTTP request, and the server sends back an HTTP response. Every interaction follows this pattern.[25]

Before diving into HTTP's mechanics, it's worth understanding what it brings to the table. HTTP's primary advantage beyond layer 4 is enabling the advanced routing techniques, which will be discussed in detail in Host Header and Advanced Routing.

HTTP also gives servers fine-grained control over caching — how and when browsers or intermediate proxies store copies of content. Without HTTP's caching headers, every image, stylesheet, or page would need to be downloaded fresh every single time, making the web painfully slow and wasting bandwidth. HTTP solves this with headers like *Cache-Control* and *ETag* that let servers say "keep this for an hour" or "check if this changed before downloading again." A news site can mark its logo as cacheable for days while marking breaking news as "always fetch fresh." This dramatically speeds up browsing and reduces server load — visiting a site the second time loads mostly from your local cache rather than re-downloading everything.

Beyond routing and caching, HTTP provides standardized message *structure and semantics*. Layers 3 and 4 excel at packet delivery — getting data to the right computer and program. But they deliberately don't dictate what goes inside the payload of those packets. This separation is intentional: the delivery system stays simple and universal, while higher layers add meaning. *Think*: the postal service (layers 3-4) delivers any envelope to any address. But imagine if those envelopes only contained random words with no grammar — *"want food you do?"* The postal service still delivers perfectly, but the message lacks clear meaning. HTTP adds the grammar that turns those words into proper sentences and conversations: *"Do you want food?"— "Yes, please send pizza."* HTTP also provides standardized forms and labels. When organizations require specific information, they use forms with labelled fields like those from the tax office. HTTP similarly defines *"shipping labels"* that describe each message: like what type of action is requested, what format the response should be in (e.g. *HTML, JSON*, agreed upon through *content negotiation*), and whether the request succeeded (*200 OK*) or failed (*404 Not Found*).

Without this pre-agreed structure and semantics, a browser could send packets to a web server perfectly e.g via TCP, but neither side would necessarily understand the meaning of the other's messages. HTTP bridges this gap by defining a common language with fixed attributes and predefined values that all web software understands. This enables the rich interactions we expect from the web: requesting specific pages, submitting forms, handling errors, and more.

Packets

A header of a HTTP packet, as illustrated in *Figure 28*, begins with one or more *start line(s)*.[26] For a request, the start line(s) contain the *path*, and *query string* as well as one of several possible predefined strings (e.g. *GET*, *POST*), which the HTTP specification calls *methods*. Every request must specify exactly one method—you can't omit it or use multiple methods.[27]

The HTTP specification places some constraints on which HTTP methods can be used under which circumstances, and how the choice influences what the remainder of the message may look like (in particular whether the packet payload may be non-empty). HTTP methods are only used in requests (never in responses) and it's not unhelpful to think of them intended to describe what *kind* of request is being made. Intentions of this and other kinds (both implicitly and explicitly stated in the official HTTP specifications) are described further in *REST*. For a response, the single start line contains its *status*, which typically summarizes whether the initial request could be successfully fulfilled, and if not, why.

Each HTTP packet has a header composed of one or more start lines, followed by zero or more lines each containing an *attribute* (i.e. a *key: value* pair) lines_. These attribute lines are also, somewhat confusingly, known as *headers*. Most HTTP attributes (both keys and possible values) are defined in HTTP specifications and understood by all web software. These are called standard headers. Applications can add custom headers (traditionally prefixed with `X-` though this is no longer required), but the client and server must be programmed to understand them.[28]

HTTP/1.1 is the original widely deployed version of HTTP, but is now largely legacy. It was superseded by HTTP/2, which remains the dominant version for modern web traffic. *HTTP/3* is the latest version and its adoption is growing steadily.

Clients like web browsers typically use HTTP/2 for the first request to a website. When the server responds, it can include a signal saying *"I also support HTTP/3, the newer faster version."* If the browser understands this signal and supports HTTP/3, it may switch to HTTP/3 for later requests to the same server. This gradual approach ensures the website works for everyone while allowing newer technology when possible.[29]

HTTPS is HTTP secured using *TLS*, to protect the http packets in transit, and confirm the identity of the parties involved. Modern browsers warn users about non-HTTPS sites, and many features only work over HTTPS.

> In requests, HTTP 1 uses a single start line, whereas HTTP 2 and 3 split essentially the same information across multiple separate lines for (parsing) efficiency. For responses, the start line is always a single line.[30]

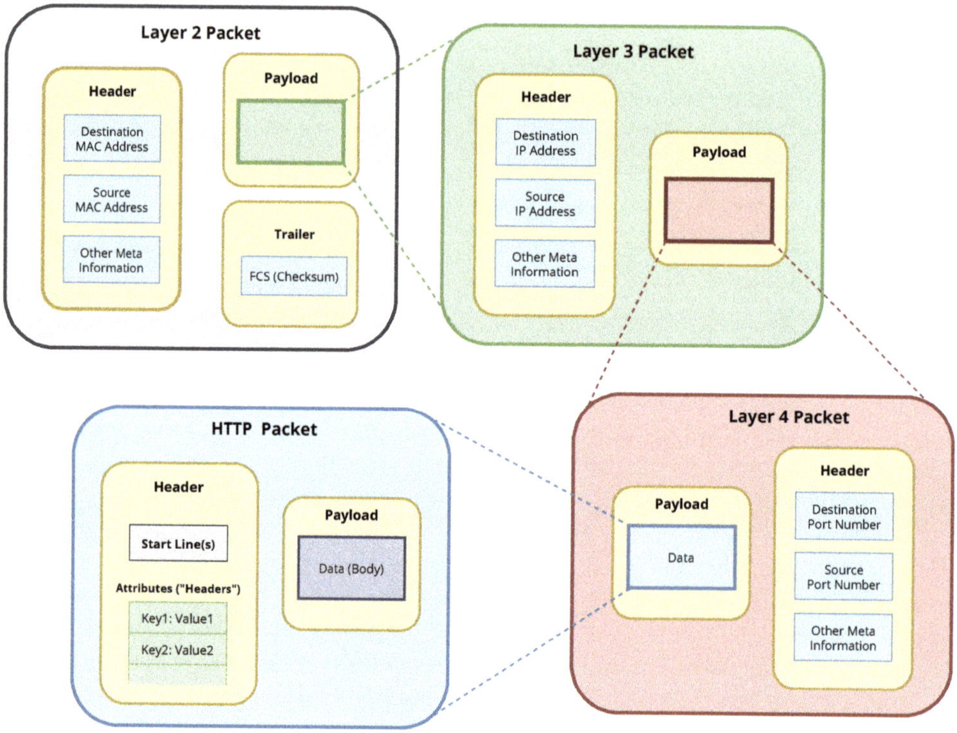

Figure 28. **HTTP Packet** *shown encapsulated as the payload of a layer 4 packet. The header always begins with a single "Start Line" in HTTP/1 and the same information split onto multiple "Start Lines" for HTTP/2 and 3. The start line(s) may be followed by zero or more other lines (confusingly called "HTTP headers") all of which are attributes, i.e. each is a key and an associated value, separated by a colon.*[31]

Request-Response pairs

Since HTTP follows a *client-server* model, messages always come in pairs: a client sends a *request*, and the server sends back a *response*.[32] The structure of the request and response headers depends on the version of HTTP used, and is illustrated in *Figure 29* and *Figure 30*. The payload structure is not prescribed by HTTP and depends entirely on the application, so we focus here on header structure. The *Start Line(s)*, shown in the top half of each, contain the most important information. The *Attributes* (bottom half) provide supplementary details such as the client software being used, size of the HTTP payload in bytes, and content format preferences. An exception is the *Host Header*, which was promoted to the start lines in HTTP 2 and 3 requests to reflect its importance.

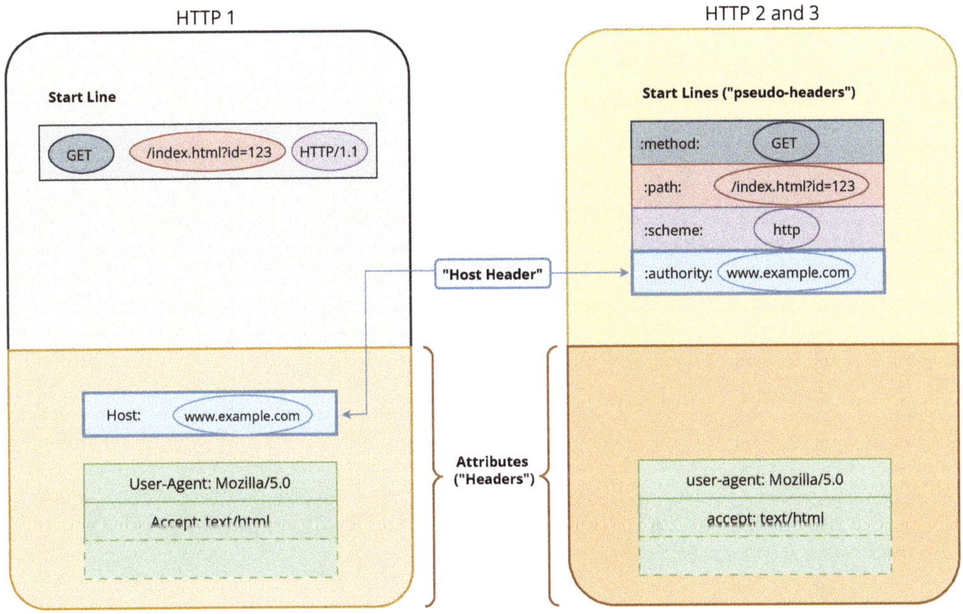

Figure 29. Example **Request** *HTTP Packet* **Header**. *HTTP 1 uses the structure on the left, whereas HTTP 2 and 3 both use that on the right. This request could have been generated from a URL like www.example.com/index.html?id=123 – either by typing it into a browser's address bar or clicking a link that references this URL.*

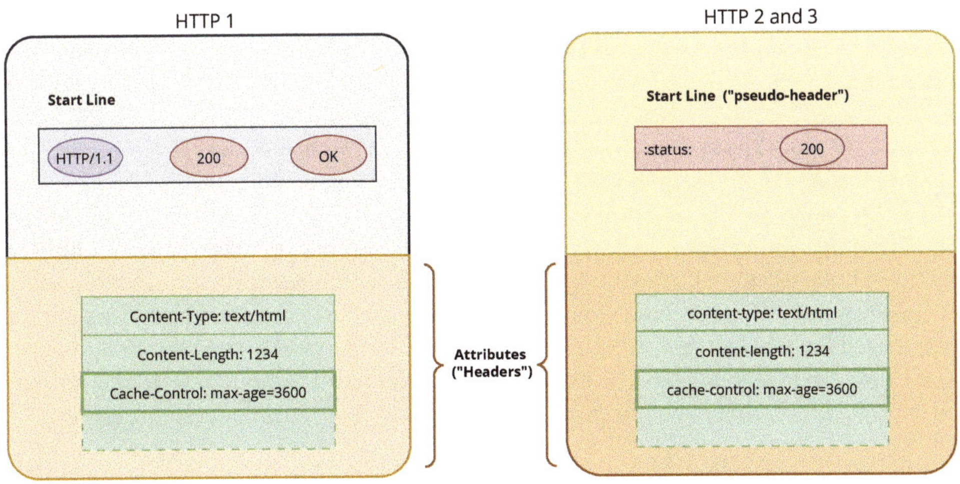

Figure 30. Example **Response** *HTTP Packet* **Header**. *HTTP 1 uses the structure on the left, whereas HTTP 2 and 3 both use that on the right.*

Don't confuse *HTTP "headers"* with the *header of an HTTP packet*. Each HTTP packet has a header composed of one or more start lines, followed by zero or more *attribute* lines. These attribute lines are also commonly referred to as HTTP headers. See *Figure 28*.

Host Header is commonly used as an umbrella term for the `Host` attribute in HTTP/1, and the equivalent `:authority` pseudo-header in HTTP/2 and HTTP/3.

When used with HTTP, a *URL* typically leads to the generation of a *request* like that shown in *Figure 29*, where the URL's components (*path*, *query string*, *host*) map directly to the HTTP packet structure.

Host Header and Advanced Routing

We've already mentioned the *flexibility* gained at a packet source by clients that use FQDNs instead of IP addresses — DNS resolution shields them from any IP address changes. And using FQDNs can (after DNS resolution and the arrival of the packet at the corresponding destination IP address) also make processing at the destination more flexible too.

This is where the HTTP *Host header* comes in. After DNS resolves an FQDN to an IP address, that FQDN is preserved in the Host header of the HTTP request. This means the server at that IP address knows not just that it received a request, but also *which FQDN* the client used to refer to it.[33] When more than one FQDN could resolve to the same IP address, specifying which FQDN was used provides additional information that can be used to tailor the processing of the incoming request.

In particular, the Host header enables two *advanced routing techniques*, which are among the main advantages of using HTTP (as opposed to using only layer 4 and below):

Virtual Hosting is illustrated in *Figure 31*. A shared web server can respond differently to incoming requests based on the value of the host header. Often used when multiple websites use shared hosting (multiple websites running on the same node to reduce costs). This approach is commonly used for cost savings, especially when sites contain mostly static content (unchanging files like HTML pages and images). Static files can be efficiently stored on shared disk space and require minimal processing power to serve, allowing many sites to run on a single server.[34]

Reverse Proxies can use the host header as illustrated in *Figure 32*, to forward the HTTP request (encapsulated in a new layer 3 packet) to an appropriate interface.[35]

Advanced routing techniques such as these will be discussed in more detail in the planned follow-up volume *(Modern Networking - Software and Techniques)* but note that both of these techniques require the HTTP Host Header to use an FQDN (rather than an IP address). Note also that these techniques are independent of *DNS resolution*, which has happened before the HTTP packets even get created.

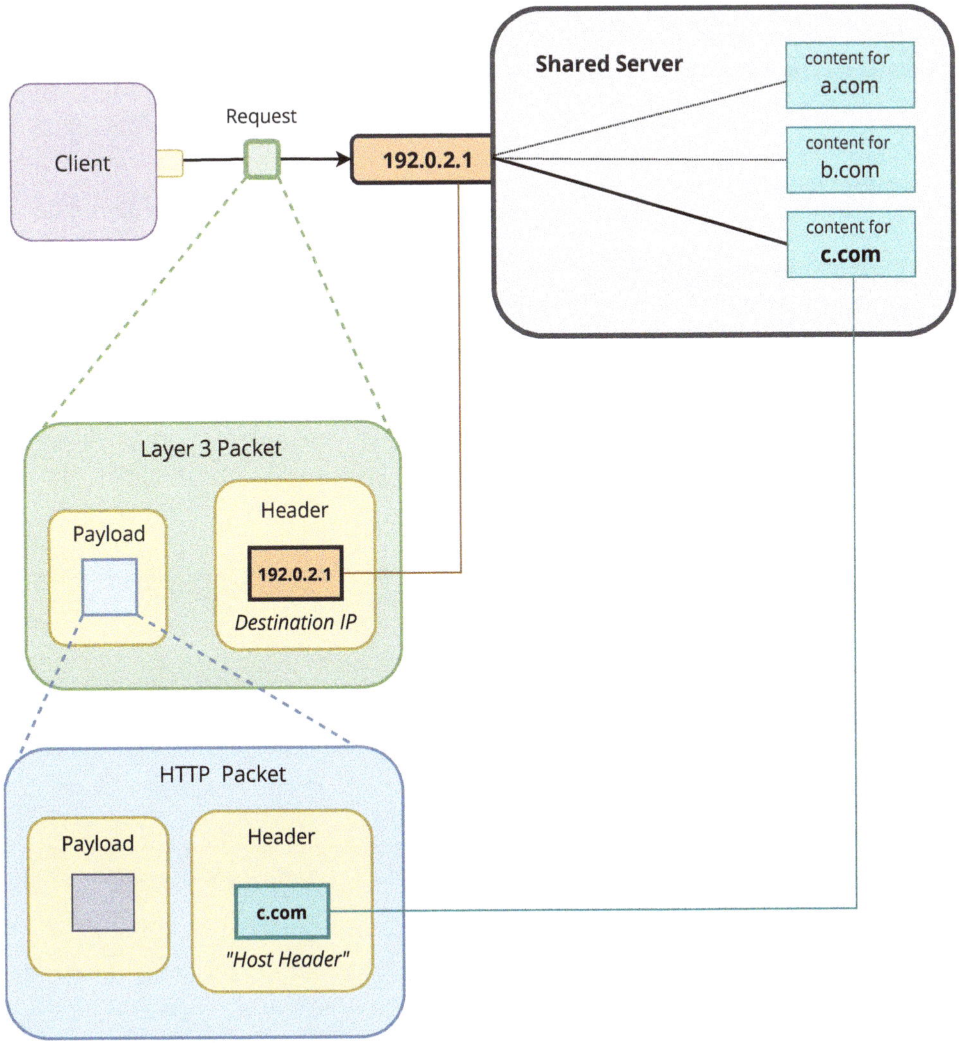

Figure 31. **Virtual Hosting**. *The shared server receives a packet containing a HTTP request on its interface matching the destination IP Address in the layer 3 header. It processes the request itself, using the "Host Header" in the HTTP header to decide how exactly, often using dedicated content for the value in question. Note that for simplicity layer 4 encapsulation has been omitted.*

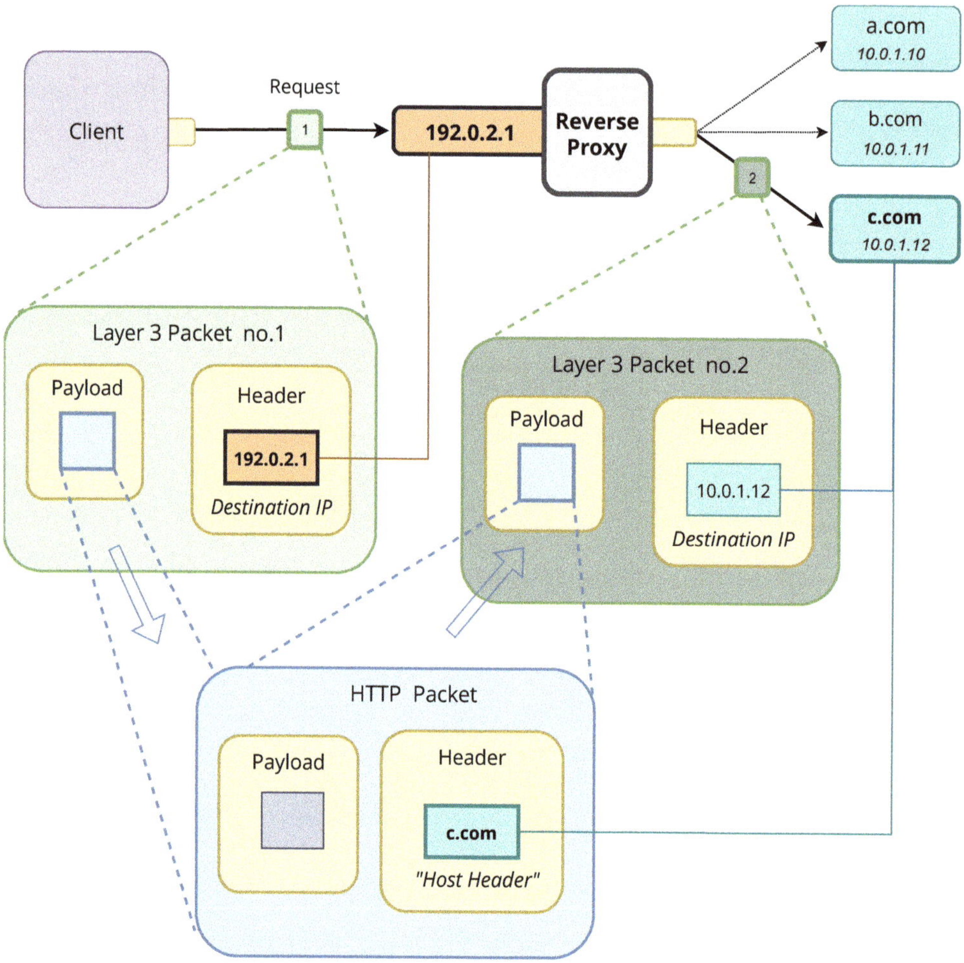

Figure 32. **Reverse Proxy** *receives a packet containing an HTTP request interface matching the destination IP address in the layer 3 header. It does not process the HTTP request itself, but extracts it and repackages it inside a new layer 3 packet. The "Host Header" in the HTTP header determines which new IP address to use, so that the HTTP packet arrives at the appropriate ultimate destination interface, which then does the actual processing. Note that for simplicity layer 4 encapsulation has been omitted*

Advanced routing techniques using the Host header require any intermediate device, such as a reverse proxy, to be HTTP-aware. If *HTTPS* is being used, the Host header (along with the rest of the HTTP packet) is encrypted, so the intermediate device must also be able to decrypt i.e. to perform *TLS Termination*. It can then either forward to backends over plain HTTP, called *TLS Offloading*, or establish a new TLS connection to the chosen backend, called *TLS Bridging*.[36]

REST

Roy Fielding, as part of his 2000 PhD dissertation, performed an analysis on the use of HTTP. He coined the term *REST (Representational State Transfer)* as a general architectural style, the principles of which, he used to *explain* the success of HTTP on the internet. Even though REST was meant to be protocol-agnostic, it's virtually impossible to find a meaningful REST *API* that isn't HTTP. REST emphasized semantic guidelines already present (explicitly or implicitly) in HTTP specifications and mapped them to HTTP methods, as illustrated in *Table 1*.

Table 1. REST semantics for HTTP methods

HTTP *method*	**Semantics**
`GET`	Read/retrieve a resource (safe, idempotent[37]).
`POST`	Create a new resource (neither safe nor idempotent).
`PUT`	Update/replace entire resource (idempotent).
`PATCH`	Partial update of resource (sometimes idempotent).[38]
`DELETE`	Remove a resource (idempotent).

These mappings (as many other principles of REST) aren't enforced by HTTP itself — the protocol doesn't *care* if your *GET* deletes data or your *DELETE* creates resources. Since most methods support request/response bodies and any valid URL, a client and server could technically use any method for any operation. The only *enforcement* comes from intermediaries (e.g., browsers retry *safe* methods, *cache*y store *GET* responses) and conventions, not from the protocol.

When people say *REST API* they generally mean an API using HTTP according to *REST-like principles*—see *REST Principles (Theory vs. Practice)*. Many modern APIs need capabilities (e.g., real-time features, stateful context-awareness), however, that require violating these principles, and many (e.g., *GraphQL*, *gRPC*) deliberately do so. Despite past gospel about *the only good API being a REST API*, it should be seen as an option with pros and cons, whose benefits should be weighed against those of alternatives. Understanding the tradeoffs involved is more important than blindly following the *rules*. For many, a pick-and-mix of REST and other principles may be the right choice for their particular API.[39]

REST Principles (Theory vs. Practice)

The following presents key REST principles as originally conceived, followed by how it works (or doesn't) in real-world implementations.

Client-server architecture

The system is designed to separate the concerns of the client from those of the server.
In practice: Real systems (e.g., microservices) are not always clearly client-server.

Statelessness

Each request from the client to the server contains all the information necessary to complete the request. The server does not store any client state between requests.
In practice: Cookies (and anything that requires authentication) violate this by design.

Cacheability

The system must support *caching* to improve performance, scalability, and reliability.
In practice: Many typical web requests are not cacheable (get current time, value in database that could have changed since last GET).

Uniform interface

The system must use a uniform set of interfaces to enable communication between clients and servers. The uniform interface enables a client to interact with a server in a predictable and consistent way, regardless of the specific implementation details of the server.
In practice: One would expect any good interface to be such - so it's hardly a defining characteristic of REST.

Layered system

The system can be composed of multiple layers, with each layer providing a well-defined interface for the layer above it.
In practice: One would expect any good system to be designed in or viewable as layers - so it's hardly a defining characteristic of REST.

Client-Server and *Peer-to-Peer* models

Networks are often described as being either *Client-Server* or *Peer-to-Peer*. These are not really fundamental fixed properties of the networks themselves, but rather models of message exchange patterns between particular interfaces.

- **Client-server:** One party (the client) initiates the communication with a so-called *request*. Another (the server) waits and *responds*. The roles are defined per exchange — a *web* server is a *server* when handling client requests, but may become a *client* when querying its database or another server. *HTTP*, for example, follows this pattern.

  Think: A market where the stall owners are the servers, who have to set up their stalls and wait patiently for potential clients to come and request their goods.

- **Peer-to-Peer (P2P):** Any party can initiate requests to any other party. All interfaces have equal capability to send and receive. *Microservices* (where a large application is broken into smaller independent services that communicate with each other) follow this pattern — any service can initiate requests to any other service as needed.

  Think: A dairy farmer with surplus butter who goes out to visit a neighbouring wood cutter, who is not awaiting a visitor, to ask if he would like to swap firewood for butter.

The same interfaces can use both patterns at different times. A seller at market can, for example, leave his stall and buy goods from another stall. Or at the weekend, when the market is closed, knock on a neighbour's door and ask him if he wants to exchange goods.[40]

Though the client-server model may be most familiar in the context of HTTP (due to its prevalence in *The Web*), its use isn't restricted to HTTP.[41]

POST Parameters

Web developers may be familiar with so-called *POST parameters*. Despite the name, these are *not an HTTP concept*, but originate from *HTML* forms (or similar client-side constructs such as *APIs*). From HTTP's viewpoint, they're simply part of the request payload—opaque data alongside any other content in the body.[42]

Anatomy of a Browser Request

When an HTTP client like a browser processes a URL such as *www.example.com/index.html?id=123#section*, a typical sequence of events is:

The client:

- Performs DNS lookup to resolve the FQDN (*www.example.com*) to an IP address.
- Sets the *Start Line(s)* of the HTTP packet header to contain the path (*index.html*) and query string (*?id=123*).
- Includes a *Host* header (attribute) containing the exact host from the URL (*www.example.com*).
- Creates an HTTP packet that constitutes an HTTP request, as depicted in Figure 29.
- Encapsulates this HTTP packet inside a layer 4 packet, the header of which is set to contain the port numbers (443 for the destination, since this is the default for HTTPS and no other was explicitly specified in the URL).
- Encapsulates the layer 4 packet in a layer 3 (IP) packet, the IP addresses of which are set to those of source and destination (resolved FQDN).
- Note that it does not send the fragment (*#section* is never sent to the server).
- If the URL starts with *https://*, then TLS is used to encrypt the complete HTTP packet in the layer 4 payload.
- The layer 4 packet containing the HTTP request is sent to the IP address that was resolved.

The server (listening for requests at the IP *address* and *port number* specified):

- Reads the *Host* header, and may use it for advanced routing.
- Whichever interface ultimately processes the request can use the destination port number, and any path and query string passed to decide exactly what response to return.[43]

After the client receives the response, it processes any fragment (*#section*) in the original URL.[44]

HTTP/3 and QUIC

HTTP/3 has identical methods (*GET*, *POST* etc.) and the same request/response model as HTTP/1.1 and HTTP/2. The only difference is the what they use behind the scenes: HTTP 1.1 and 2 use *TCP*, whereas HTTP 3 uses *QUIC* (which in turn uses *UDP*).[45]

Why QUIC exists (the TCP problem)
HTTP 3 runs on QUIC, which uses UDP instead of TCP (which HTTP 1.1 and HTTP 2 use). This might seem odd since HTTP needs reliable, in-order delivery — exactly what TCP provides. However, QUIC's creators were dissatisfied with TCP's implementation, and reimplemented this reliable, in-order delivery more efficiently as part of QUIC itself.

For example, when TCP receives packets out of order, it buffers[46] them until missing packets arrive, then delivers everything in sequence. This is called *head-of-line blocking*. This causes delays even when some data could be processed immediately. QUIC makes this blocking less likely by adding *multiple independent streams*[47] per connection. If packets are lost in one stream, other streams continue processing without waiting. Both TCP and QUIC receivers send acknowledgments to the sender indicating what they've received. The sender can figure out from this which, if any, packets didn't arrive, and retransmits them.[48]

Security approach
For encryption, QUIC takes a hybrid approach with TLS 1.3. Rather than using DTLS (UDP's version of TLS), QUIC runs the TLS 1.3 handshake to negotiate keys and parameters, then handles packet encryption itself. This contrasts with HTTPS, where TLS manages all encryption. QUIC encrypts both headers and data using TLS 1.3-derived keys before sending over UDP.

Performance benefits
QUIC's multiple simultaneous streams with low overhead give each stream reliable, in-order delivery (like TCP) but without cross-stream blocking. This makes HTTP/3 particularly effective for modern web applications transferring many resources simultaneously.

The Web

The *(World Wide) Web* began as a global system of hyper-linked HTML documents. The Web's essence lies in three foundational technologies working in concert: *HTML* documents containing URLs (in the form of *hyperlinks* [49]), the HTTP protocol for retrieving them, and web browsers for viewing them. As such, *the (world wide) web* is a *subset of the internet*. Users *surf* or *browse* this web by following links from one document to another, traversing servers across the globe with simple clicks.

Think: a spider's web — the intersection points of which are the hyperlinks and the path between them travelled by HTTP.

HTML (HyperText Markup Language), is a simple format for documents that could link to other documents through hyperlinks. These links are what make the web a *web* — any document can reference any other document anywhere on the internet using URLs. When Tim Berners-Lee created the first web browser in 1990, he called it *WorldWideWeb* (later renamed Nexus), establishing both the technology and the name we use today.

A web browser's primary function is to retrieve HTML documents via HTTP and render them for human consumption. When a user clicks a hyperlink or enters a URL, the browser sends an HTTP request to the specified web server, receives the HTML document in response, and transforms the markup into the formatted page the user sees.[50] The browser interprets HTML tags to determine structure (headings, paragraphs, lists), follows references to embedded resources (images, videos), and processes hyperlinks that connect to other documents.

Early web pages were so-called *static* HTML documents containing only text, basic formatting, and links. The Web has since expanded far beyond these origins. CSS (Cascading Style Sheets) arrived to separate presentation from content, allowing rich visual designs without cluttering HTML with formatting instructions.[51] JavaScript brought interactivity, transforming static documents into *dynamic* applications that could respond to user actions without reloading the page. Modern web pages often fetch data asynchronously, update content dynamically, and provide experiences that rival desktop applications.

The Web now encompasses various content types beyond HTML documents. Web servers deliver images, videos, PDFs, and arbitrary data formats. APIs use the same HTTP protocol to exchange structured data between applications, not just documents for human readers.[52] Modern browsers execute complex JavaScript applications, render 3D graphics, play multimedia, and even run compiled code through WebAssembly.

Different clients beyond traditional browsers now access the Web. Mobile applications use embedded web views or make HTTP requests directly. Command-line tools like curl retrieve web resources programmatically. Screen readers parse HTML to make web content accessible to visually impaired users. Search engine crawlers follow hyperlinks to index the Web's content.[53]

The newest additions to the web technology family — *WebSockets*, *WebRTC*, and *WebTransport* — extend the Web beyond HTTP and its request-response pattern to enable real-time, bidirectional communication. WebSocket creates a persistent connection between browser and server, allowing both sides to send messages at any time without the overhead of HTTP headers — ideal for chat applications, live notifications, and collaborative editing.[54] WebRTC (Web Real-Time Communication) enables browsers to exchange audio, video, and data directly with each other, bypassing servers entirely for the actual media streams—powering video calls, screen sharing, and peer-to-peer file transfers.[55] WebTransport combines the best of both worlds: the flexibility of WebSocket with the performance of modern transport protocols, supporting both reliable and unreliable data streams over HTTP/3's QUIC foundation.

What unites all web technologies — from basic HTML to WebRTC — is that they are software and data (originally) *designed* to be used in web browsers, using protocols such as HTTP. But a modern definition of what parts of the software of the internet is or isn't part of *the web* is becoming more difficult to give. It seems more appropriate to consider how web-like something is rather than try to make a binary decision whether it is or is not web. At one extreme: HTML documents with hyperlinks, served over HTTP to browsers — the original Web, undeniably *web*. At the other extreme: routing protocols, DNS, Ethernet and Wi-Fi have nothing to do with the Web. The interesting cases lie in between.[56] *Web* only makes sense when talking about layer 5+ technologies — in particular those originally designed to be used as web technologies (HTTP, HTML, WebSockets, Web APIs etc). The more something relies on these technologies, the more it belongs to the Web — a spectrum of *web-likeness* rather than a clear boundary.

Other Protocols

While HTTP and DNS are by far the most important application layer protocols on the modern internet, many other protocols build on the lower layers in similar ways. Each adds its own specialized capabilities for specific use cases.

WebSockets enables persistent, bidirectional communication between browsers and servers — useful for real-time applications like chat systems or live updates. *WebRTC* goes further, allowing direct peer-to-peer communication between browsers for video calls and file sharing. *WebTransport* is a newer protocol providing low-latency, multiplexed connections for gaming and streaming applications.

For file transfer, *SFTP (SSH File Transfer Protocol)* and *SCP (Secure Copy Protocol)* provide encrypted alternatives to the older FTP protocol, each of which runs over an *SSH* connection.

> Don't confuse *SFTP (SSH File Transfer Protocol)*, the modern standard, with *FTPS (FTP Secure)*, which is largely obsolete.[57]

Email relies on a trio of protocols: *SMTP (Simple Mail Transfer Protocol)* handles sending messages between mail servers, while *POP3* and *IMAP* let email clients retrieve messages — with IMAP offering more sophisticated folder synchronization across devices.

SMB (Server Message Block) enables file and printer sharing on local networks (allowing remote directories to be mounted as local drives, and remote printers to be used as if they were directly attached).[58] *RPC (Remote Procedure Call)* protocols allow programs to execute functions on remote systems as if they were local calls — fundamental for distributed computing.

Just as HTTP builds its request-response model atop TCP's reliable streams, each of these protocols leverages the lower layers' guarantees while adding their own abstractions. The planned follow-up volume *(Modern Networking - Software and Techniques)* explores several of these protocols in greater detail, examining their internal mechanisms and practical applications.

Overlay, Virtual, and Software-Defined Networks

Modern networking extends beyond the simple layer models illustrated in *Figure 4* through three prominent constructs: *overlays* (which stack networks on top of each other), *virtual networks* (which eliminate physical transmission), and *software-defined networks* (which centralize control). These aren't mutually exclusive — cloud platforms routinely combine all three to create flexible, scalable network architectures that would be impossible with traditional physical networking alone.

Before we begin discussing these three constructs, and develop a deeper understanding of what they mean, it's helpful to first introduce two additional definitions. Namely, *layer set* and *addressing layer set* which will make the discussion thereafter simpler and hopefully clearer.

> Don't be dismayed if the concepts below take some time to wrap your head around or seem abstract at first—they build directly on the layers you already understand, and concrete examples (and experience with the technologies involved) will make them clearer.

Layer Sets

A *layer set* can be defined as a group of *consecutive* layers designed to work as a unit.[59]

Furthermore, let's define an *addressing layer set* as a layer set whose top layer creates a new addressing scheme. Layer 5+ is not an addressing layer set — even though HTTP, for example, adds deeper packet encapsulation and higher layered logic to layer 4 (as illustrated in *Figure 28*), it reuses the layer 4 addressing scheme (IP addresses and port numbers).[60]

> *Layer Set* and *Addressing Layer Set* are terms I've coined for this book, to make the discussion that follows more coherent.

Virtual Devices and Interfaces

Modern networks often include software-based components that simulate physical hardware, allowing multiple isolated systems to run on the same physical machine. *Machine* is synonymous with *device* or *computer* in this context.

VMs (Virtual machines)

are simulated computers running inside a physical computer — like having multiple separate computers within one actual machine.

Containers

are similar but lighter-weight, sharing more resources with the host computer. *Docker* and *Podman* are systems for creating and running containers on a single node (optionally within a VM), while *Kubernetes* is a system that orchestrates containers across potentially multiple nodes (physical or virtual).[61]

Loopback Interface

is a special virtual interface that even physical nodes can have one of. It has an IP address (usually *127.0.0.1*) that always points back to the same node that sent the request — like mailing a letter to yourself. Packets sent from the loopback interface automatically arrive back at the same interface without going anywhere in between. It operates purely in software at layer 3 and above. Nodes (both physical and virtual nodes like VMs and containers) often use a loopback interface for internal testing.

Virtual (Software) Networks

Virtual networks (also called *software networks*) have layer sets without layer 1 — there is no physical signal transmission between nodes. This happens when the network nodes themselves are also virtual (i.e. VMs or containers) and thus reside within a single physical node. Packets move between them through memory operations, not physical media. There's no conversion to bit streams or electromagnetic waves. Without layer 1 there is also no need for the parts of layer 2 that interface with it — no packet-to-bit-stream conversion or vice versa. *Think*: transferring money between bank accounts by updating database entries, rather than moving physical cash between vaults.[62]

Overlay Networks

Overlay networks are created by stacking one layer set on top of another layer set.[63]

For instance, *VXLAN (Virtual eXtensible Local Area Network)* uses an overlay layer set *{2}* on top of a base layer set *{1–2–3–4}*, effectively creating a LAN that can span the world. This underscores why *local* in LAN is misleading and that proximity is not a defining characteristic of layer 2 networks, but rather that the addressing system (MAC addresses) and protocols used are. Consider two VMs that need to communicate: one running in a data center in Tokyo, another in London. Both VMs believe they're on the same simple LAN—they only see layer 2, using MAC addresses to send frames to each other. But when the Tokyo VM sends a frame, VXLAN wraps it inside a UDP packet (layer 4) and ships it across the internet using regular IP routing. At the London end, VXLAN unwraps the frame and delivers it to the destination VM, which has no idea the internet was involved. The VMs never see or configure IP addresses for this communication—they simply use MAC addresses as if connected to the same physical switch. This is useful for moving VMs between servers without any network reconfiguration, and for applications that discover each other by broadcasting at layer 2 to all devices on the same network. Cloud providers also use VXLAN to create thousands of isolated customer (layer 2) networks.

Similarly, *Kubernetes* uses an overlay layer set *{2-3-4}* on top of a base layer set *{1–2–3–4}*, as illustrated in Figure 33. Kubernetes groups containers into *pods*.[64] Pods and thus the containers withing them, are id_ephemeral: they're constantly being created, destroyed, and moved between nodes or VMs as applications scale or when failures occur. Without an overlay, each time a pod each time a pod moved to a different node or VM, you'd need to reconfigure network routes, firewall rules, and addressing—making the constant churn of pods impractical. The overlay solves this by creating a (private and stable) IP range that's independent of the base network. Each pod gets a (stable) IP address from this range and can reach any other pod using theirs. When a pod sends a layer 4 packet to another pod on a different node, Kubernetes encapsulates as the payload of another (base) layer 4 packet and ships it across the base network using regular routing. At the destination node, Kubernetes unwraps the packet and delivers it to the destination pod, which has no idea the base network (or its IP addresses) was involved. The pods never know or care which VM or node they're on -you can move, scale, and replace them freely without any network reconfiguration.

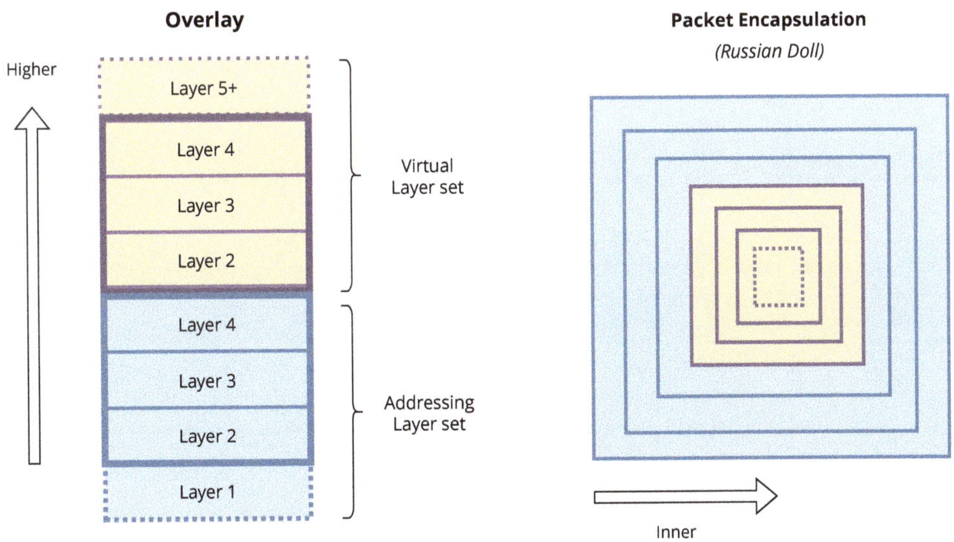

Figure 33. **Overlay** *network as typically used in Kubernetes. One layer set is stacked on top of another to create the (compound) network stack. The lower set must be addressing and may be virtual, i.e. the lower layer 1 may be omitted if the whole stack runs on a single physical node. The upper must be virtual and may be addressing, i.e. the upper layer 5+ is not strictly part of the definition of the overlay but is usually present in actual traffic.*

Software-Defined Networks

Software-defined networks (SDN) are networks where routers/switches do not independently update their routing/CAM tables. The table updates, traditionally handled by each device individually, are instead performed by a central *software controller*. The controller decides what the table entries should be, and programs them.[65] The switches/routers just forward according to these tables. The name is misleading, since all networking above layer 1 involves software; what's actually *software-defined* is the centralized control.

Don't confuse *Software Networks* (which is a synonym for *Virtual Networks*) with *Software-Defined Networks*. The latter would probably be more aptly named *"networks with centrally programmed forwarding tables"* but this name was presumably less catchy.

Network stack is confusingly used to refer to *both* a compound layering of multiple layer sets, *and* to the individual layer sets themselves. Another reason to prefer *layer set* to disambiguate.

Routers, when operating in *table update* mode, actively send routing protocol packets specifically to gather information for updating their routing tables. In *SDNs*, routers never operate in *table update* mode, but only in *packet forwarding* mode. Switches, like routers, perform both table updates and packet forwarding. Unlike routers, however, switches don't have distinct operational *modes*. Instead, they learn passively — updating their CAM tables by examining source MAC addresses of packets they're already forwarding. The learning happens as a side effect of normal forwarding operations, not as a separate activity. This is why SDN's centralized control is particularly notable for switches: it removes even this passive learning from them, making them purely forwarding devices.

Combinations

In practice, these concepts combine in complex ways. When containers on the same physical node communicate (e.g. *Docker or Kubernetes* on a single node), they use a network stack composed of just a single virtual layer set.[66] No layer 1 exists — packets move through kernel memory.

When containers on different nodes need to communicate (e.g. in Kubernetes), this entire layer set becomes an overlay that's the payload of a lower (addressing) layer set.[67] Docker handles only single-node virtual networks. Kubernetes adds the overlay capability for clusters containing multiple physical nodes. The containers running inside these environments don't *know* the difference — Kubernetes[68] transparently chooses between memory operations or UDP encapsulation as needed.

In any case the routers/switches used in the networks in question, may or may not have their tables updated by a separate software controller.

Understanding these distinctions helps decode vendor claims, e.g. *software-defined virtual overlay network* means centralized control (SDN) of a layer set without layer 1 (virtual), that is in turn layered (overlaid) on top of another layer set.

If you're unfamiliar with containers and Kubernetes, don't worry about those specific details — the key point is that the individual concepts like those introduced above (overlays, virtual networks, and software-defined control) can be, and often are, combined in creative ways to build new technologies.

Summary

- *DNS (Domain Name System)* is a system allowing a *dotted string* (like *example.com*) to be used instead of an IP address (like *93.184.216.34*) to identify an interface.
- The technical name for such a dotted string is an *FQDN (Fully Qualified Domain Name).*
- Finding the IP address for a particular FQDN is called *resolving* the IP address or *DNS resolution.*
- A hierarchy of DNS servers can be queried (top down) to resolve an FQDN to its corresponding IP address.
- Each DNS server stores the information it needs as *records* in *zone files.*
- Zone files contain multiple record types, the most important of which are A/AAAA records and NS records.
- A records directly map FQDNs to IPv4 addresses. AAAA records do the same for IPv6 addresses.
- The NS records provide the IP addresses of the DNS server one step lower in the hierarchy, who should be queried next if the current DNS server has no direct mapping, and so on recursively.
- A *URL (Uniform Resource Locator)* is a description of a function call, including any specific parameters required, in a network-based API.
- A crucial part of a URL is the interface (host), which can be specified as an IP address or an FQDN.
- If an FQDN is used, DNS resolution must first be performed, as the HTTP request for the resource in question is embedded in the payload of an IP packet, and IP packets require IP addresses. The FQDN is often still included in the HTTP header. (It can be used to facilitate advanced routing, such as by reverse proxies).
- Any port number, path, and query string also specified in the URL, can be used by the destination interface to process the request.
- HTTP (along with DNS) is probably the most important layer 5+ protocol. It is used to power the (browser centred) World Wide Web.
- HTTP (coupled with DNS) enables some advanced routing techniques like *virtual hosting* and *reverse proxies*, where the HTTP *host header* (containing an FQDN) plays a central role.
- HTTP uses a client-server model.
- HTTP adds structure and semantics to both requests and responses, as well as fine-grained caching control.
- HTTPS is HTTP secured using TLS, to protect the HTTP packets in transit, and confirm the identity of the parties involved.

Conclusion

You've successfully explored the upper layers — the protocols that transform routing and transport capabilities into the applications people actually use. You now understand how DNS provides human-friendly naming for the internet, how HTTP enables the World Wide Web, and how these independent systems work together seamlessly. Furthermore, you've seen how URLs map to resources, how DHCP automatically configures network settings, and how various protocols leverage TCP and UDP to serve different needs.

Through tracing a typical browser request, you've witnessed the elegant Russian doll-like encapsulation that makes the internet work: HTTP messages nested inside Layer 4 packets, in turn wrapped in Layer 3 packets. Each layer is processed independently by different components — routers handle IP addressing, interfaces inspect port numbers,[69] web servers parse HTTP headers — yet they work in harmony. This layered architecture demonstrates the internet's fundamental strength: complex functionality built from simple, modular pieces that can evolve independently.

But these foundational protocols were designed in an era that prioritized openness and functionality over security. DNS queries typically travel unencrypted, revealing which sites users visit. HTTP transmits data in plain text, exposing everything from passwords to personal information. These aren't mere oversights — they reflect the internet's evolution from a trusted research network to today's global platform.

As we'll explore next, security in modern networking requires comprehensive methods to protect our communications, from cryptographic foundations to identity management, transforming these open protocols into secure channels suitable for an increasingly hostile network environment.

[1] This is not always a 1:1 mapping. A single FQDN can resolve to more than one IP address (typically different interfaces on different nodes). This is often done in *load balancing* where multiple nodes share the workload, or for *redundancy* where backup nodes ensure availability if the primary server fails. The converse is also possible — multiple FQDNS may resolve to a single IP address. This is most common for FQDNs which differ only in their hostnames and is typical for *shared web hosting* - see Advanced Routing Techniques. A single process on the node can handle all incoming packets, but it's also possible for the packets for each FQDN to have a distinguishing port number in the layer 4 header. So, separate software processes on the node can handle each FQDN — see Port Numbers — interface sharing and network endpoints

[2] FQDNs technically end with a root "." as in *www.three.two.com.*, but it's usually omitted. Note that DNS resolves the *entire* FQDN — not hostname and domain name individually. The available top-level domains (*.com*, *.org*, *.net*, *.de*) are limited and allocated by *ICANN (Internet Corporation for Assigned Names and Numbers)* to large organizations (or countries). These organizations may in turn allocate subdomains of these top-level domains to smaller organizations by defining names that are placed immediately to the left of an existing domain, separated by dots, to form a longer FQDN. Confusingly there are a few top-level domain names which are themselves a dotted string eg "co.uk"

[3] as we will see in DNS Record Types, the former are stored in A (or AAAA) records, and the later in NS records.

[4] The root servers are managed by ICANN (Internet Corporation for Assigned Names and Numbers). An *authoritative server* contains the official DNS records for its zone (portion of the DNS namespace) and provides definitive answers for that zone. Each such server in the hierarchy is authoritative for its own "region" of the name tree — root servers for the root zone, TLD servers for their top-level domain, domain servers for their specific domains. *Non-authoritative servers* are typically caching resolvers (like your ISP's DNS servers) that store temporary copies of DNS data but don't hold the official records. Note that even though the dotted strings involved may be similar (e.g., *siblings* may differ by just one label from each other or from their *parent*), the IP addresses they resolve to may be completely independent, and the interfaces in question may be in entirely different parts of the world. This is a feature — unrelated IP addresses can be 'grouped' into closely related dotted strings that mirror the semantics or organizational structure of the hosts in question, much as IP addressing can group logically related interfaces whose underlying hardware (MAC) addresses are otherwise unrelated.

[5] Confusingly there are a few top-level domain names which are themselves a dotted string eg "co.uk"

[6] For example, when changing hosting providers, simply update which IP address *example.com* points to. Visitors continue using *example.com* while the DNS system (which works behind the scenes) automatically directs them to the new location. This contrasts with advanced routing techniques, which take effect after DNS resolution—see Host Header and Advanced Routing for more details

[7] at least those composed of more than two words — since top levels domains almost never have hostnames — only subdomains

[8] not to be confused with a node in a network

[9] This granular caching makes the system highly efficient. If a resolver recently looked up any domain ending in *.com*, it will have cached the *.com* nameserver addresses and can skip querying the root servers. Similarly, if it recently looked up *example.com*, it has those nameserver addresses cached and can go directly to *example.com*'s authoritative servers when querying for subdomains like *www.example.com*.

[10] which typically have IP addresses like `8.8.8.8` and `1.1.1.1`

[11] Not shown for simplicity are additional record types like MX (mail servers) or TXT/CNAME. In practice, multiple contiguous zones are often combined into one file. The FQDNs for the DNS servers are so-called *glue records*, less critical than for content servers — those DNS was designed to support. Since by the time you have resolved the FQDN for two.com, you generally have its DNS server's IP address already — there's no *quick* way to find the IP address of the DNS server given its FQDN — without creating another DNS layer, leading to infinite recursion. Authoritative DNS servers form a clear hierarchy with direct access to the corresponding zone files.

[12] When you visit *example.com*: First, a DNS server tells you "example.com is at 93.184.216.34". Then, the content server at that IP delivers the website. Think of DNS servers as providing directions to a building, while content servers are the building itself where the actual work happens.

[13] in practice this is done by configuring each node for every host (i.e. interface) it contains — the details of which will be discussed further in the planned follow-up volume *(Modern Networking - Software and Techniques)*

[14] APIs and formal standards serve the same fundamental purpose - defining how different components interact and ensuring compatibility. The key differences are that APIs are software-only and typically less formal. Unlike industry standards that go through lengthy approval processes and rarely change, APIs are created and modified by the software developers themselves. They can be updated more frequently, may have multiple versions running simultaneously, and don't require external certification or compliance testing. While standards like Ethernet or Wi-Fi might take years to revise through committee consensus, a company can update the API for one of its software services whenever they need to add new features or improve functionality.

[15] More accurately, the response payload corresponds to the function's primary return value, and the response header(s) are extra/meta information that complement the primary value. Together, they correspond to the fields of a *structure* or *object* the function returns.

[16] and is passed in the *Start Line(s)* in the header of an HTTP packet

[17] and together with the *path*, are passed in the *Start Line(s)* in the header of an HTTP packet

[18] *HTTP* and particularly *REST* were originally designed with the idea of being used to retrieve fixed *values* like static HTML pages or images. And URLs being a specification of how to locate and retrieve such an unchanging *resource* was a good fit at the time when most APIs were used to do this. However, modern network APIs have evolved to do a lot more than *locate and retrieve* such static resources. This is one of the reasons why REST is less "revered" than it once was, and why the definition of a URL as a *serializable representation of a network function call* (also called a *marshalled* or *remote* function/procedure call) is more accurate. A URL is like a local function call in classic programming languages. Both include a function name (e.g., the path in URLs, the function name locally) and inputs (e.g., query string in URLs; function arguments locally). The main differences come from URLs representing network requests, which must handle challenges that local calls don't face. Network calls need to also specify: (1) WHERE to find the computer and process running the function (host name and port number), and (2) HOW to communicate with it (protocol, like "HTTPS") — this sets rules (i.e. marshalling) for bundling and sending a serialized representation of the function name and inputs. Unlike local calls, where the system's built-in tools (e.g., compiler and runtime) handle this automatically, and have direct access to a function's code and inputs in memory, networks involve computers with varying setups (different operating systems, processor types, or ways of storing data), so nothing can rely on local memory or assumptions. For example, a URL like `api.example.com:443/users/123`, might be equivalent to, and actually executed on the remote machine as a local function call like `getUser(123)`. The mapping of URL *path* to local *function name* need not be 1:1 (just as one local function may ultimately call multiple other local functions), and a URL like *www.drugstore.com:443/medicines/painkillers/ibuprofen?form=liquid&size=200ml* be executed, for example, as a local call *getMedicines(type=painkiller, name=ibuprofen, form=liquid, size=200ml)*, but this does not change the fact that one can identify such a mapping nonetheless. Note that the URL need not contain *all* the information about/for a remote function, or rather the information in the URL may be supplemented e.g. by any protocol, such as HTTP, using it. HTTP adds, for example, a method name (e.g GET or POST), and possibly *POST Parameters*. HTTP packets store the inputs from the URL (path and query string) as well as the HTTP method names in the header, with additional data like POST parameters included in the payload/body

[19] URNs (Uniform Resource Names) were introduced as another attempt at the same pure-identifier concept, using a different syntax (like urn:isbn:0451450523). Despite being formally defined as a distinct type of URI in technical specifications, URNs appear to be functionally synonymous with URIs—both attempting to identify resources without location information. URNs failed to gain traction for the same reasons URIs did. Additionally, the URI syntax itself (*scheme:scheme-specific-part*) undermines the goal of separating *what* from *how*, since the scheme portion (like *http*, *urn*, *ftp*) specifies the access method or interpretation protocol — the how — not the identity of the resource. Even in its own design, URI couldn't cleanly separate identification from access method.

[20] American Standard Code for Information Interchange - the basic English letters, numbers, and punctuation that work universally across all computer systems)

[21] in addition to *Collision/Broadcast Domain* see Domain — disambiguation (caution) - which are less likely to cause confusion since, they are usually explicitly prefixed with *collision* and *broadcast* respectively

[22] It was formally called Azure Active Directory (Azure AD), is a cloud-based version of Active Directory.

[23] which also provides interoperability with Windows AD

[24] Many registrars bundle basic authoritative DNS hosting with the registration fee. Some people pay separately for DNS hosting from other providers for better performance or features. The broader DNS ecosystem — root servers and all the non-authoritative caching resolvers that speed up lookups — is also funded indirectly through various fees such as these. Also note: this is separate from hosting your actual website content, which generally requires separate payment to a hosting provider, who keeps your content servers operational. As mentioned in Figure 24, the mandatory part of an FQDN (the right-most two names) is sometimes called a "domain", and you often read about "buying a domain", but this invariably actually means leasing a subdomain.

[25] The client is by definition the party sending the initial request. The server is by definition the party patiently waiting for requests to arrive, to which it then responds.

[26] HTTP headers can only contain ASCII (American Standard Code for Information Interchange - the basic English letters, numbers, and punctuation that work universally across all computer systems) characters. This makes them easily human-readable, unlike other protocols which use binary headers (e.g., Ethernet, IP, TCP). However, for HTTP 2 and later, the client/server must first compress and encode headers into a binary format (using HPACK/QPACK) to make transmission as the payload of a layer 4 packet more efficient.

[27] A common point of confusion: query strings (the *?key=value* parts) are simply part of the URL and work with any method, not just GET. Web frameworks often hide this by automatically handling request data differently — placing it in query strings for GET requests but in the message body for POST requests — leading many developers to incorrectly assume query strings are a GET-only feature. See also POST Parameters.

[28] Otherwise they won't know how to process them and can at best ignore them

[29] This includes requests made by JavaScript code running on the page after it loads. The server signals HTTP/3 availability using the *Alt-Svc (Alternative Service)* header. Browsers that don't understand this header simply ignore it and continue using HTTP/2.

[30] In HTTP 2 and 3 the start lines are commonly called "pseudo-headers"

[31] For HTTP/1 the figure accurately depicts how HTTP packets are directly embedded in the payload of a layer 4 packet. Layer 4 (TCP) uses its own sequence numbers to reassemble all packets back into the complete HTTP message. HTTP/1 relies on this sequencing to determine which response is associated with which original request — the responses arrive in the same order as the requests were sent. For HTTP/2 and HTTP/3, the situation is more complex than depicted in the diagram — here there's an additional intermediate packet called a *Frame* (confusingly the same name used for the unrelated layer 2 "packets"). The HTTP packet is first encapsulated in one (if it fits into a single) or more (if it doesn't) of these frames. Each frame has its own header containing a *stream ID* that uniquely identifies each HTTP request-response pair. When an HTTP packet spans multiple layer 4 packets, these frame headers also contain sequencing information — somewhat redundantly, since the lower layers (TCP for HTTP/2, QUIC for HTTP/3) already handle byte-level ordering and reassembly. In either case, the HTTP header is included only in the first layer 4 packet, and the body continues in subsequent packets. This differs from lower-layer behavior: when a layer 3 packet is too large and gets split (recall Packet Fragmentation), each fragment includes a full copy of the IP header — without the IP addresses contained within it, for example, routers wouldn't know the destination IP address and couldn't deliver the fragments. HTTP headers, by contrast, are sent only once — in the first packet.

[32] In HTTP/1.1, responses arrive in the same order as requests were sent — TCP, which HTTP 1 always uses, guarantees in-order byte delivery on a single connection. In HTTP/2 and HTTP/3, each request-response pair is assigned a unique stream ID that appears in all HTTP packets of both the request and the response, allowing

multiple exchanges to happen simultaneously on one connection without confusion.

[33] The HTTP specification mandates that every HTTP request must contain a Host header (`:authority` in HTTP/2 and HTTP/3). This can contain either an FQDN (e.g., if the client looks up *example.com* in DNS getting 192.0.2.1, it includes `Host: example.com`) or an IP address (e.g., if the client uses *192.0.2.1* directly without DNS lookup, it includes `Host: 192.0.2.1`). However, using an IP address in the Host header offers no real advantages.

[34] Virtual hosting is the foundation of shared hosting plans offered by most entry-level commercial hosting providers. It also conserves IPv4 addresses by allowing multiple domains to share a single IP address—a significant benefit given IPv4 address exhaustion. With IPv6's practically unlimited address space, this conservation aspect becomes less important, though the cost benefits of shared hosting remain.

[35] The image depicts a reverse proxy forwarding based on the the HTTP Host header. Reverse proxies can also forward using other criteria (URL paths, headers, cookies) or function as load balancers distributing traffic across multiple servers. Layer 3 and 4 proxies forward based only on IP address and port number (without inspecting HTTP). More details in the planned follow-up volume *(Modern Networking - Software and Techniques)*

[36] TLS Offloading is the most commonly deployed option (and is frequently provided by cloud load balancers) because it simplifies the backends by letting them speak plain HTTP and avoids per-backend TLS certificate management. However, it also concentrates the TLS/certificate and security burden on the intermediate device (server/proxy), which must be "*up to the task*". TLS bridging maintains encryption also on the backend hop but with two separate TLS sessions. If TLS termination is not desired or possible at the intermediate device, a simpler Layer-4 proxy can use *SNI (Server Name Indication)* to perform so-called *TLS Passthrough*—the intermediate device inspects only the TLS *ClientHello*, which is sent unencrypted during the *handshake*, to read the requested hostname and then forwards all subsequent encrypted TCP/TLS packets to the selected backend. Because it does not decrypt HTTP, the backend choice is fixed for the lifetime of that TCP/TLS connection — i.e., one final destination per connection, making it less commonly used than TLS termination for HTTP-level routing and control.

[37] A "safe" operation is one that doesn't modify the system state — it only retrieves data without causing any side effects. Safe methods are read-only operations. e.g. "GET /user/123"—reading data doesn't change the system. An "idempotent" operation is one that produces the same result, no matter how many times it's performed. Making the same request once or multiple times has identical effect on the system state. e.g. "DELETE /user/123"—First call deletes user 123, subsequent calls find nothing to delete but end state is same (user 123 doesn't exist)

[38] PATCH isn't always idempotent per RFC 5789; it can be if the patch is designed that way, but the spec doesn't mandate it like it does with PUT

[39] *CRUD (Create, Read, Update, Delete*, popularized in 1983 by James Martin in his book about database management, describes the four basic operations for managing stored data in any system. REST mapped these to HTTP methods (*POST → Create, GET → Read, PUT/PATCH → Update, DELETE → Delete*), splitting *Update* into two for network efficiency, and REST's *POST* often handling operations beyond CRUD (triggering processes, complex workflows). This parallel made REST intuitive to developers familiar with data management. Unlike REST, however, which has become one option among many for APIs, CRUD remains foundational today because most applications fundamentally store and retrieve information, whether in databases or otherwise.

[40] In practice, hybrid constellations are common — e.g. when a client asks a server for resource it's not unlikely that the same server in turn (as a client) may ask another server for the resource, before returning it (as the server) to the original client. Scalability: Client-server often centralizes resources for easier management but can create bottlenecks, while P2P distributes load but may complicate coordination.

[41] For example, TCP (which HTTP/1 uses) itself follows a client-server pattern where one side initiates a connection and the other accepts it. TCP even maintains connection state that HTTP's stateless design doesn't use. Interestingly, a lower layer using a client-server model doesn't force upper layers to do the same—UDP uses peer-to-peer, yet applications built on UDP can still choose to use client-server patterns if they want. Each layer independently decides on its communication model.

[42] *HTTP* defines *methods* such as *POST* that allow a request body, but it doesn't specify the body's format—that's indicated by the *`Content-Type` header* (for example, *application/x-www-form-urlencoded* for simple key-value

pairs). The server parses the body accordingly. All HTTP methods (not just GET), including POST, can be used with a *path* and *query string* in the *packet header*. POST parameters are located in the HTTP packet body and are independent of these. This is a common point of confusion. Web frameworks often obscure this distinction by automatically handling request data differently—placing it in query strings for GET requests but as *POST parameters* in the message body for POST requests.

[43] this may involve URL rewriting, routing rules, or file system mapping

[44] This often results in the browser scrolling to the appropriate position when the response is an HTML document. This also enables page-internal navigation without server round-trips, essential for single-page applications

[45] with integrated TLS 1.3

[46] A *buffer* is a temporary holding area in memory where data waits until it can be processed —- like a shelf in the kitchen of a restaurant where ready dishes are placed until the entire table's order is complete before serving anyone

[47] separate logical channels within a single connection, each able to handle different resources (e.g. one stream for HTML, another for CSS, another for images)

[48] More accurately, the sender only retransmits if packets appear consistently missing across multiple acknowledgments (not just temporarily out of order). TCP typically retransmits after receiving the same acknowledgment value 3 times or after a timeout; QUIC uses similar logic but can detect gaps more precisely

[49] The *hyper* in hyperlink refers to the non-linear nature of these links—readers can jump directly to related content rather than reading sequentially

[50] This process happens so quickly today that it seems instantaneous, but it involves multiple round trips between client and server, *DNS - FQDNs (dotted strings) for IP addresses* lookups to find the server's address, and often requests for dozens of additional resources.

[51] Before CSS, styling was done with HTML attributes and tags like <font> and <center>, making documents difficult to maintain and inconsistent across sites. CSS lets developers write style rules once and apply them across entire websites.

[52] This is why HTTP has become the de facto protocol for most internet applications, even those that have nothing to do with traditional web pages. Mobile apps, IoT devices, and cloud services all commonly communicate via HTTP.

[53] Search engines work by following links from page to page, which is why the hyperlink structure remains fundamental to how we discover content on the Web, even though most users now start with a search rather than typing URLs or following links from bookmarked pages.

[54] These features are among those that modern web applications are increasingly incorporating that violate the principles of *REST*. Unlike HTTP where the client must initiate every exchange, WebSocket lets the server push data to the client whenever needed, enabling true real-time updates without constant polling.

[55] WebRTC still uses servers for initial connection setup and signalling, but the actual communication flows directly between browsers, reducing latency and server costs.

[56] A REST API serving JSON is somewhat web-like. A mobile app fetching data over HTTP is more web-like. A single-page application running entirely in a browser is deeply web.

[57] *FTPS (FTP Secure)* was an earlier attempt to secure FTP by adding TLS/SSL encryption. However, FTP uses separate connections for commands and data. Firewalls configured to allow FTP can recognize the command connection, but the data connection looks like unrelated traffic since the information identifying it as part of FTP is hidden inside the encrypted command channel. SFTP and SCP have become the modern standards because they run everything over a single SSH connection.

[58] While SMB is native to Windows, it has become the standard for mixed environments through native support on macOS and *Samba* on Linux. An older alternative, *NFS (Network File System)*, remains common in Unix/Linux

environments but focuses solely on file sharing; remote printing requires separate protocols like *IPP (Internet Printing Protocol)*. Windows can access NFS shares but requires additional configuration, making SMB the path of least resistance in heterogeneous networks.

[59] The *layers* we are talking about here are specifically the network layers introduced in Models – network layers. Thus, *{1–2}* is a layer set for creating layer 2 networks. Similarly, {1–2–3} for layer 3, *{1–2–3–4}* for layer 4, and *{1–2–3–4–5+}* for layer 5+ networks. For the layers as we have seen thus far, this is identical to what's more commonly called a "stack," except for the explicit grouping. When we introduce the more exotic network types below, it will become apparent that the new term is helpful.

[60] Thus, *{1–2–3–4}* is an addressing layer set, while *{1–2–3–4–5+}* is a layer set but not an addressing layer set.

[61] More specifically, Kubernetes delegates responsibility for the basic network connectivity of pods to its *Container Network Interface (CNI)*. The CNI assigns unique IP addresses to each pod. It can route messages from one pod to one another (this often involves setting up routes between different nodes). It implements network policies for pod-to-pod traffic. Doing all this is challenging as many pods may be coming and going on various nodes regularly.

[62] In general, a virtual network may be any consecutive (non-empty) subset from *{2,3,4,5+}* starting at 2 or 3So the possible layer sets that can constitute a virtual network are: *{2}*, *{2–3}*, *{2–3–4}*, *{2–3–4–5+}*, *{3}*, *{3–4}*, or {3–4–5+}

[63] The lower layer set must be an *addressing* layer set. Examples of Overlay networks are 1). VPNs with *{1-2-3}-{3-4-5+}* or *{1-2-3-4}-{3-4-5+}*, where *{1-2-3}-{3-4-5+}* means layer set *{3-4-5+}*, which is what would be sent without the VPN, is layered on top of layer set *{1–2–3–4}*. See also Figure 41. The lower layer set corresponds to the outer Russian doll set of packets, and is what provides the VPN encryption. Note that by conventionally, any uppermost 5+ (and corresponding innermost packet) is not considered part of the *overlay*. It's listed here to make it clearer where/that it is actually present, and its exclusion is merely in name, and not from the actual data sent/processed. Note that its possible in some contexts for the outer set not to need the 5+ or even 4, but it represents typical user application traffic, so we'll keep it to avoid over-complicating the discussion. 2). *VXLANs* {1–2–3–4}–{2}_, which create virtual layer 2 networks without layer 1, solving two key problems – *isolation* and *scale*. First, isolation (multi-tenancy): cloud providers need to give each customer their own private networks, guaranteed not to *see* or be able to *interfere* with each other – even malicious actors exploiting the low security at layer 2. Second, scale: because these are virtual networks without physical hardware constraints, VXLAN supports creation of up to 16 million separate VLANs (or *VXLANs*) compared to the few thousand possible with physical switches – essential for large cloud providers. The VXLAN standard allocates 24 bits for network identifiers, hence 2^24 ≈ 16 million. This was deemed sufficient for foreseeable needs. 3). Kubernetes (CNI) with *{1-2-3-4}-{2-3-4-5+}*.

[64] typically one container per pod, though a single pod can hold multiple containers that share a single network interface and IP address.

[65] This communication between the controller and devices uses a dedicated network protocol, such as *OpenFlow*, to securely push table updates and query status. OpenFlow is a layer 5+ protocol. Thus, switches, which traditionally understood only up to layer 2 (see also Layer-Specific Devices), to be SDN compatible, must operate at higher layers (up to 5+) when receiving these updates.

[66] *{2-3–4}*

[67] The virtual layer set *{2–3–4-5+}* is encapsulated inside the payload of layer 4, of the lower layer set *{1–2–3–4}*, yielding the (compound) network stack *{1–2–3–4}–{2–3-4-5+}*. You might wonder why not just *{1–2–3–4}–{3–4-5+}*, skipping the layer 2 of the outer set, since it's uncommon for Microservices to use layer 2 to communicate – after all layer 3 was designed to support flexible distributed networking. Kubernetes, however, maintains a full virtual Ethernet layer with virtual bridges and MAC addresses for compatibility – many networking tools and legacy applications expect layer 2 functionality like ARP and broadcast domains, even when running in containers.

[68] or more accurately, the CNI plugin of Kubernetes

[69] More accurately: the operating systems running on the nodes containing the interfaces, which manage the

hardware — which will be discussed further in the planned follow-up volume *(Modern Networking - Software and Techniques)*

5. Security

The aim of system security is to ensure that those, and only those, who have a legitimate right to access a system (or certain parts thereof) will actually be able to do so. In networking, this fundamental goal becomes especially critical — remote access presents opportunities for malicious actors they would not otherwise have, and the interconnected nature of modern systems means a single breach can cascade across networks.

This chapter explores how networks establish and maintain security — the mechanisms that ensure your data reaches only its intended destination, arrives unmodified, and comes from who you think it does. Security isn't implemented in a single layer, but is a set of principles and protocols woven throughout the stack you've mastered.

The journey begins with fundamental concepts: access control, identity, and credentials. You'll discover how cryptography provides the mathematical foundation for security, enabling everything from encrypted connections to digital signatures. You'll understand not just cryptographic algorithms but the crucial challenge of key distribution and trust — much like how possessing a physical key doesn't necessarily mean you have the right to use it, cryptographic keys must be not only verified as legitimate but also distributed securely. From there, we examine security in practice across each layer — seeing how switches, routers, and transport protocols each contribute to (or potentially compromise) overall security. You'll learn how identity management systems enable single sign-on across services, how tokens carry authorization between systems, and how protocols like OAuth let you grant limited access without sharing passwords.

Good security measures present minimum inconvenience to those with legitimate access rights, but maximum difficulty to those without — a balance that's particularly challenging in networks where convenience often conflicts with protection. Not all systems need the same level of security: just as a bank vault requires stronger locks than a garden shed, a banking network demands more rigorous security than a public information server. The level of security must match both the value of what's being protected and the motivation of potential attackers.

The chapter concludes with anonymous networks, showing how the same security principles can be inverted to protect privacy rather than enforce identity, creating networks within the internet that operate with very different trust models. Real-world threats like *phishing* (where attackers trick users into revealing sensitive credentials) and *ransomware* (where attackers encrypt data and demand payment to restore access) underscore why all these concepts matter. We begin with the foundational question: how do we control who can access what?

Access Control

One often speaks of **access control** when the security measures in place are not just designed to grant each person full (or no) access to the complete system, but when the possibilities are more various and fine-grained. Imagine a building that doesn't just have a single lock on the front door, but also several rooms inside, each of which may require a separate key to open them. In such cases, it can be challenging to decide what doors need locks (that require a separate key) and how secure each lock should be. More secure locks may be more expensive, and more locks may mean more inconvenience for legitimate users, who have to carry around all these keys and use them in all the appropriate locks.

A cleverly designed system may strike a balance between security and convenience in such a situation, by having certain individual keys open not just one lock, but multiple locks. And giving each person a key which opens the locks on exactly those rooms, they should be permitted access to. A guest in a hotel, for example, may have a (card) key that opens just their room. The cleaner may have a key that opens all guest rooms, and a manager may have a key that also opens the office.

> The general term *entity* is often used to refer to a person or a thing, such as a computer program (possibly acting on behalf of a person), trying to gain access to a system.

Two fundamental questions need to be answered when an entity attempts to access a security-conscious system. The first question (*authentication*) is: *whether the entity can be uniquely identified*. Identity is discussed in detail in Identity but for now, you can think of it as what clearly distinguishes the entity involved from all other entities that may legitimately attempt to gain access to the system. If the authentication succeeds, the system tries to answer a second question (*authorization*), namely: *should the (identified) entity in question be permitted to do what they are attempting to do*?

Authenticate (Identify)

Require the entity to pass valid credentials which can be used to uniquely identify them. Credentials are discussed in detail in Credentials, but for now, you can consider them to be something which vouch for the identity of the holder,[1] and possibly also what they should be allowed access to. A ticket is a form of credential which may be used at the concert, and which may have a unique ticket number printed on it to distinguish it from other tickets, and thus the holder from other ticket holders wishing to attend the concert. If the credentials are not successfully validated (*think*: the ticket is not of the specific kind used at that concert) then the entity's access request is rejected.

Authorize (Permit)

Determine whether this (authenticated) *entity has permission* to access the system in the particular way they are currently attempting to do. In the case of a concert, this may be a ticket holder trying to access the backstage VIP section. The credentials used may contain everything necessary to answer this question (*think*: a concert ticket may, in addition to the ticket number, have a label printed on it specifying whether it's a VIP ticket or a standard ticket). Or it may be necessary to look up this information separately (*think*: the staff at the concert need to look up the ticket number in a separate list, in order to determine whether this is a VIP ticket or not)

Authentication vs Authorization

If you sometimes mix up the two similar looking terms, you are probably not alone. *Think*:

- **Auth*entication*** is the *who*—confirming your name.
- **Auth*orization*** is the *what*—what is the person with that name allowed to do.

An *authentic* entity (who) may be *authorized* to do something (what).

Example: At a hotel, you show your passport to prove your name (*authentication*). The receptionist looks up your booking to see which room the person with your name paid for and whether or not breakfast is included (*authorization*).

Man-in-the-Middle

When two parties are communicating with each other, a *man-in-the-middle* is a third party through whom all their messages effectively pass. *Think*: eavesdropper. This can sometimes be legitimate, as in the case of *VPNs*, but may also be malicious, in which case one speaks of a *man-in-the-middle attack.* Here a malicious third party secretly intercepts, and possibly alters, the communication between two parties, who *fail to verify* that *who they are communicating with* is who they expect to be communicating with. *PKI* is one of the most common and effective methods of defending against such attacks.

Identity

Identity can be regarded as a *perception* of an *entity* (e.g. a person) by a particular *system*. It's not so much a characteristic of the entity itself (if the entity even exists outside the system), as the way the system perceives the entity involved. In particular, an identity clearly distinguishes a given entity from every other entity that may legitimately try to access the system.

At a concert, the staff may see your identity as the number on your ticket. As far as a banking (system) is concerned, your identity may comprise your name, date of birth, account number and other bank account details. This is all the banking system needs to know about you, when you make a cash withdrawal request. You, your family, and your friends may consider your identity to be composed of much more. You may see your upbringing, your cultural background, your taste in music etc to all be part of your identity, but the banking system may perceive you to be the collection of your bank account details. And similarly, other systems you interact with may in turn perceive you and your identity differently again.

With this in mind, we can, in the context of system security, define the (perceived) identity of an entity to be the *set of information a particular system associates with an entity that interacts with the system*. Each piece of this information can be categorized as either a *privilege* (if it pertains to permissions or roles of the assigned to the entity in the system) or an *attribute* (if it does not). Figure 34 shows typical examples of such information, but the particular set of information will vary depending on the system (and possibly the entity) in question. Compare a *simple* concert ticket where the ticket number would be an attribute, and the VIP label, a privilege.

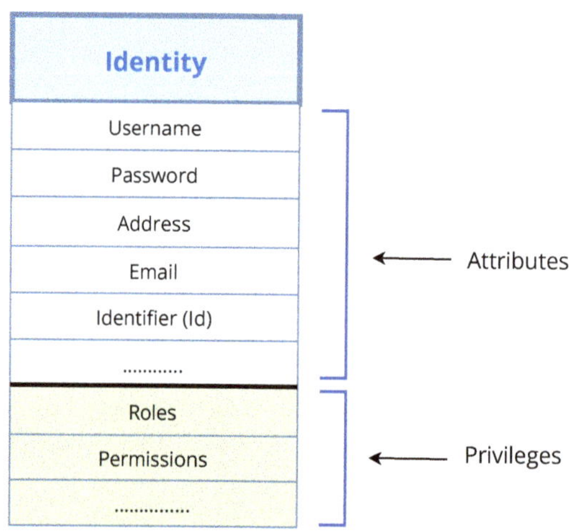

Figure 34. **Identity.** *Information a system may associate with an entity, each piece of which is either an attribute or a privilege. Identity information is stored in and managed by Identity Management systems, which can be queried for relevant data when needed.*

Digital Trust

When you hear *trust* in the context of digital security, think: *confidence*. In general, the word trust can carry connotations of wishing or hoping for a specific outcome or state, which is not the intended meaning in security-conscious computer systems. Instead, digital trust refers to a measurable confidence established through initial validation that can be relied upon for future interactions and decisions. *Cryptography* plays a central role in establishing digital trust.

Identity, Trust and Encryption

Establishing trust in communication with a trusted entity (through an identity) requires *encryption*.

Note the *threefold* trust (i.e. confidence) involved - (i) trust in the entity as a provider of valid information, (ii) trust that the identity is really that of the (trusted) entity, and (iii) trust that the information exchange through this (trusted) identity is not compromised.

Think: You are talking on the phone to your brother. (i) You trust your brother. (ii) You trust that it's your brother you identify (through the sound of his voice) on the line. (iii) You trust that only you and your brother can hear/speak on this line. Encryption is essential for establishing the third (and sometimes the second), and thus when all three are required - as is usually the case in networking.

In other sources and contexts, you may hear alternative terms for *attributes* and *privileges* as used here. There unfortunately seems to be quite a few, not all of which are particularly intuitive. But despite Humpty Dumpty having a finger in a pie here too, the concepts remain the same.

An *identifier* (which is often a part of an identity) can be used to look up (the rest of) the identity. Identifier is a simpler concept than identity, and it's not uncommon to mix the two terms up. But, thankfully, doing so is not likely to lead to serious confusion since they are generally unique and related 1:1.

It's not uncommon to find *Identity* used to mean only the attributes (and not the privileges) of an entity, which is arguably more intuitive. Unfortunately, the word is overloaded, and the most common use of the term includes both attributes and privileges, as illustrated in *Figure 34*.

Credentials

Credentials generally contain part(s) of an identity, as defined in Identity. In particular, parts which are (supposed to be kept) secret, so that being in possession of said credentials, yields *credibility* to the holder being the entity which legitimately should be in their possession. And thus credibility to the holder being the entity with which the system associates the identity in question. Just like having a key to a house yields credibility to the holder of the key being the person who legitimately should be in possession of the key (since it's presumed that the key is kept securely, and is difficult to obtain by illegitimate means or find by chance). The word credentials is derived from the Latin *credentia*, meaning *belief* or *trust*. The emphasis being that possession of the correct credentials is not an absolute proof, but still involves some measure of trust — no security measures, or combinations thereof, are absolutely secure. When used correctly, however, they can drastically reduce the chances of illegitimate access to a system.

Credentials are generally passed by the entity wishing to gain access to a *security-conscious system*[2] as part of an authentication and/or authorization process. It's not uncommon for the system to use the credentials passed to *look up* the rest of the identity. This is especially true when the credentials passed are *long-term* credentials (i.e. those whose values only rarely change). And often the system will in the process issue the entity some form of *short-term* credentials, (the contents of) which are temporarily added to their identity. Compare by analogy a possible check in process at a hotel, which may start with you needing to present your passport (a long-term credential). After validation, the receptionist may issue you with a code (or card) that opens your bedroom door (a short-term credential that you actually use to access the *system*), reminding you that check out is at noon the next day, and that thereafter the code will no longer work. Your long-term credential (passport) will still be valid thereafter, but you can't use it (directly) to get back into the room — if you want to extend your stay, you must present it at the front desk again.

Combining different forms of credentials — especially *layering* of (temporary) short-term credentials on top of long-term credentials — is a common pattern in system security. If someone finds (or steals) your passport, they still can't gain access to your room — they need the code for the door. And if they discover the code for the door, they have limited time to use it, before it becomes invalid — and they can't get a new one without your passport. (Of course, still having the code for your hotel room won't help you get through airport security the next day- but that's a different system).

Common forms of credentials are listed below. *Multi-Factor Authentication (MFA)*, as the name suggests, requires not just one, but multiple credentials. A combination of credentials of different *classes* — such as *something you know* (e.g. password), *something you have* (e.g. cryptographic key) and *something you are* (e.g. biometric scan) — is often considered more secure. Some credentials can be of multiple classes — for example, knowing an email address (so as to be able to enter it when prompted) can be of one class, whereas having access to it (so as to be able to click on a link sent to it) can be another. Such credentials are effectively multiple individual credentials (one per class).

Username, Password

Usernames are frequently used as identifiers, which means they must be unique (*think: "the chosen name already exists in this system — please choose another"*). Passwords are typically required by system administrators to change regularly and/or satisfy certain constraints (e.g. be a mix of upper and lower case, contain special characters etc), making them difficult to *guess*.[3] Occasionally, however, even well-intended security measures can have the opposite effect e.g. forcing users to change their passwords so frequently, or satisfy such difficult to remember constraints, that they may feel tempted to write passwords down they would otherwise have been able to store more securely in their heads. A password manager (such as *KeePassXC*, *Bitwarden*, and *1Password*) helps address this problem by securely storing all your passwords, so you only need to remember a single master password.

Email/SMS

Email addresses and telephone numbers are also frequently used as unique identifiers. Knowledge of them is one form of credential. Proof of access to them (typically the user is required to enter a code the system sends to the email address or telephone number in question) are regularly used as an additional credential. Unlike usernames, which the system itself must ensure are unique, external systems[4] ensure the uniqueness of (valid) email addresses and telephone numbers.

Authenticator Apps

Increasingly common are *authenticator apps* such as *Google Authenticator* and *Microsoft Authenticator*.[5] Authenticator Apps generally work using one of two methods: *Time-based One-Time Passwords (TOTPs)* and *Push Notification Approvals*. Both methods typically begin with the app scanning a QR code to receive a shared secret key from the server. With TOTP, the app combines this key with the number of intervals (typically 30 seconds long) which have elapsed since a fixed point of time in the past (typically 00:00:00 UTC on 1 January 1970) and applies a cryptographic *hash* function to produce a short, unique code. The server, using the same key and interval, performs the same calculation, and considers the credential valid if the generated codes match. With push notifications, the app simply prompts[6] the user to approve or deny on their mobile device, and considers the credential valid if the former occurs. Regardless of the method used, the initial provisioning process establishes a *shared secret*, allowing the server to verify the user's access to the authenticator as a credential.

Biometric Scan

Biometric data such as that of a fingerprint or retina may be used as a credential, but doing so requires appropriate hardware for the scan.

Cryptographic Keys

Possession of a physical key lends credibility to the holder having a legitimate right to open the door in question. *Think*: You are likely to presume someone opening a door with a key is more likely to be entering the building legitimately than someone opening the door with a crowbar. Just like with physical keys, mere possession of an appropriate digital key lends credibility to the access rights of the holder. We'll learn more about *cryptographic keys* later in the chapter.

Certificates

You can think of a certificate as a key with a label on it reading "I know the holder of the key — if you trust me, trust them", signed by someone else. They add to the credibility of possession of the key, the testament of the signer (who is often an independently trusted 3rd party). See *Figure 37* and *Digital Certificates* for more details.

Tokens

Tokens aren't so much a different kind of credential, as containers of some other kind of credential in a particular format.

Passkeys

Passkeys are gaining steadily in popularity. Like tokens, they are, however, not really a new form of credential. They are standard cryptographic key pairs — what's novel is how they're managed automatically by your browser working with a *passkey authenticator*. A passkey authenticator is software or hardware that securely stores and uses your private keys — this can be your operating system, password manager software, or an external USB/Bluetooth security device like YubiKey. When you set up a passkey with a website, your browser asks the authenticator to generate a unique *asymmetric key pair* for that specific site. The private key stays secure with the authenticator, while only the public key goes to the website, where it's stored. On future visits, your browser automatically finds the right key for that site and asks the authenticator to use it. To sign in, you unlock your authenticator locally with a different form of credential, such as a biometric scan or password. Crucially, these credentials never travel over the network (nor does the public key after the once-off setup) but are only used locally by the authenticator. Instead, the authenticator uses your private key to generate a cryptographic signature that proves your identity to the website, without revealing the key itself.[7]

Note: It's not uncommon for two parties in secure communication to each use a *different* form of credential when authenticating themselves with the other. *Think:* A police officer shows you their badge to prove they're legitimate law enforcement, while you show them your driver's licence.[8]

> Don't confuse *authenticator apps* with *passkey authenticators*. Authenticator apps generate temporary codes as a second factor alongside passwords, while passkey authenticators manage cryptographic key pairs that replace passwords entirely. Adding to the confusion, some software can serve both purposes — but these are fundamentally different forms of credentials.

Passkey Authenticators

A passkey authenticator is software or hardware that securely stores and appropriately uses your private keys. Different passkey authenticators offer different balances of convenience, security, and cross-platform compatibility:

1. **Operating System** (Platform) authenticators like *Windows Hello*, *Keychain* (macOS/iOS), or *Google Password Manager* (Android) are built directly into your device's OS.

- *Pros:* Extremely convenient with seamless OS integration, free, and leverage built-in biometrics for fast login.
- *Cons:* Tied to specific ecosystems (e.g., Apple's passkeys for Apple devices), making cross-platform migration difficult and creating vendor lock-in.

2. **Password Manager** authenticators like *1Password*, *Bitwarden*, or *KeePassXC* store passkeys alongside traditional passwords.

- *Pros:* Platform-agnostic, work across all operating systems and browsers, ideal for multi-device users, consolidate all credentials in one place.
- *Cons:* Often require subscription, entire digital security depends on one master password, reliant on third-party security practices.

3. **Hardware** authenticators like *YubiKey* are physical devices that connect via USB, NFC, or Bluetooth.

- *Pros:* Highest security level with keys on dedicated secure chip, immune to malware/phishing, highly portable across any compatible device.
- *Cons:* Must be purchased, can be lost or stolen (though PIN-protected), require physical interaction for each login.

Cryptography

Cryptography is the science of establishing digital trust. It provides the mathematical foundations that enable measurable confidence in digital interactions — allowing parties to communicate securely, verify each other's identities, and ensure that information hasn't been tampered with, even when using potentially compromised channels. Among the core components of cryptography are the *cryptographic keys* mentioned in our previous discussion of credentials, and explored in more detail below. Think of cryptography as providing digital equivalents to physical security measures we use every day. Just as we use sealed envelopes to keep letters private, locks to restrict access, and signatures to prove authenticity, cryptography gives us mathematical tools to achieve these same goals in the digital realm.

It addresses fundamental questions such as: How can two people have a private conversation over a public network? How can you prove who you are without revealing your secrets? How can you be sure a message hasn't been altered in transit? How can strangers establish trust without a prior relationship? Modern cryptography goes far beyond simply hiding information. It enables secure online banking, private messaging, software updates that can't be tampered with, digital contracts, and countless other applications that form the backbone of our digital society.

Cryptography provides effective protection against *stealth* attacks, where a malicious party tries to *steal* sensitive information from a system, or to inject malicious information into a system with the intent of affecting its behaviour (even for legitimate users) in a targeted manner. It does not protect against so-called *denial-of-service* attacks, where the malicious actor aims to overload the system with excessive input (regardless of its validity). As a result, the system is so busy rejecting it that its ability to do anything else is seriously impacted.

Applications of Cryptography

There are three main applications of cryptography: *Encryption (and Decryption)*, *Digital Signatures (and Verification)* and *Key Negotiation*.[9]

1) Encryption (and Decryption)

Encryption is concerned with keeping information confidential — ensuring only intended recipients can read (decrypt) it.

The (*forward*) process of encryption creates an encrypted output (so-called *ciphertext*), using an *encryption algorithm* (also known as a *cipher*) and a *key* (usually a secret value), from an input (so-called *plaintext*), as illustrated in *Figure 35*. Ideally, the generation should require as *little* time and computing resources as possible, but reversing the process (i.e. reconstructing the plaintext from the ciphertext), without explicit knowledge of the key (which is shared only with trusted parties) should require as *much* time and computing resources as possible[10]. Encryption plays an important role in establishing trust in communication — see *Identity, Trust and Encryption*. Decryption is the (*reverse*) process - of converting the ciphertext back into the original plaintext using a (possibly different) key and algorithm.

2) Digital Signatures (and Verification)

A handwritten signature on a physical document can be considered to be the signer vouching for the authenticity and integrity of the contents. A digital signature, as illustrated in *Figure 36*, serves the same purpose in the digital realm — proving authenticity and integrity while enabling non-repudiation. In practice, the signer calculates a *hash* of the content of the document and signs this instead of the actual document content.[11] Others can independently calculate the hash of the document and verify that the signed hash matches the value they themselves calculated. A mismatch would indicate that the contents had changed since the hash was originally calculated (and signed).

3) Key Negotiation

Key Negotiation (aka *Key Exchange*) allows two parties to use a set of keys they already securely possess to securely agree on a third key they can both use. Without anyone listening to the conversation being able to find out what the key agreed on is. It's usually used in a *TLS Handshake*.

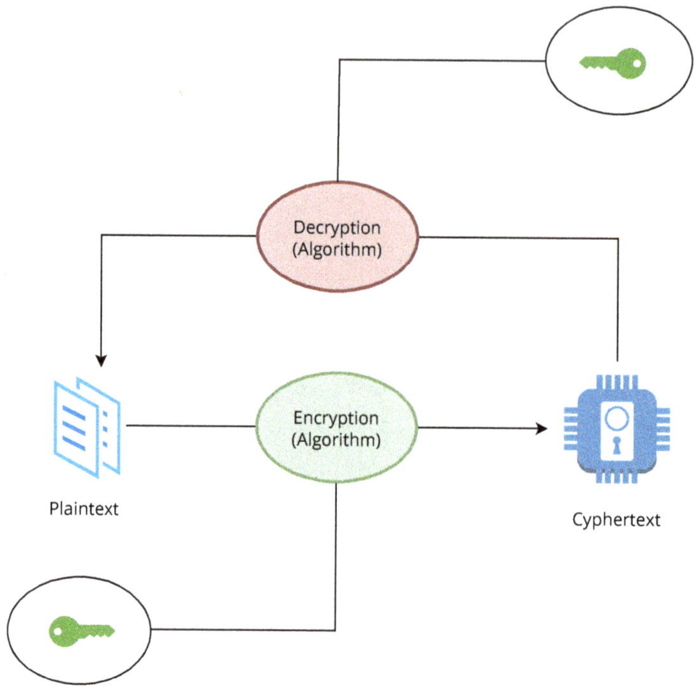

Figure 35. **Encryption** *is the (forward) process which creates an encrypted output (so-called "ciphertext"), using an encryption algorithm and a key (typically a secret value), from an input (so-called "plaintext"). Decryption is the (reverse) process of converting ciphertext back into the original plaintext using a (possibly different) key and algorithm. The algorithms are sometimes also referred to as "ciphers". If the same key is used in both processes, one speaks of "symmetric" encryption.*

The term *encryption* is used to mean both specifically the *forward* process/algorithm, *and* as an umbrella term for *both* the forward and reverse (decryption) processes.

Non-repudiation can be seen as a possible *implication* of a digital signature — in retrospect, the signer can't later claim they did not agree with the contents.

Cryptographic Keys

Cryptographic Keys Cryptographic keys are pieces of information (typically numbers or data) that are used by cryptographic algorithms. You can think of the keys as code numbers – being in their possession is a requirement for being able to lock (encrypt) and unlock (decrypt) information. And you can think of the algorithm as knowing how and where to use them. The security of encrypted data depends entirely on keeping the right keys secret from unauthorized parties – even if someone knows exactly which algorithm you used, they can't decrypt your data without the proper key. Cryptographic keys can be either *symmetric* or *non-symmetric* (of which *asymmetric* keys are the only commonly used kind today).

Beyond encryption and decryption, cryptographic keys also enable *digital signatures* (proving who created a message). Using keys effectively requires solving the challenge of getting the right keys to the appropriate people securely – a problem that becomes more complex as systems scale up. Modern solutions to this challenge include digital certificates and *Public Key Infrastructure (PKI)*, which create organized systems for distributing and verifying keys at scale.

Symmetric (Secret Key) Encryption

Symmetric encryption and decryption use the same key, but they *apply* it in different ways. Symmetric encryption can be seen as a sequence of mathematical operations (using the key). Decryption then performs the inverse of each operation, in reverse order. (Imagine an encryption algorithm with a given key involving multiplying the given (input) number by the key, and then adding the key to the result. For example, the input 3, using key 5, would be *encrypted* as 3×5 + 5 = 20. Decryption would then first subtract 5 and then divide the result by 5 – the mathematical inverse of addition is subtraction, and the inverse of multiplication is division – yielding the original number 3 again).[12] The shared key must be kept secret from all untrusted parties. Common algorithms that use symmetric keys are *AES* (most common), *Blowfish* and *Twofish* and a simple example below used only for illustrative purposes is *Caesar's Cipher*.

Symmetric (unlike asymmetric) keys are generally more resistant to quantum computing attacks. Simply doubling the key length can often be sufficient protection[13].

Example 1. Symmetric Algorithm — Caesar's Cipher using a key of 3. It is named after the Roman emperor Julius Caesar, who is said to have introduced it to protect secret messages passed in the Roman army at the time. Its simplicity makes it suitable for illustrative purposes, but unsuitable for security in modern computer systems. If you reach the end of the alphabet, you wrap around to the beginning.

```
Original Text: "HELLO"

Apply shift 3 steps (encryption with key 3):

 H becomes K (H + 3 = K)
 E becomes H (E + 3 = H)
 L becomes O (L + 3 = O)
 L becomes O (L + 3 = O)
 O becomes R (O + 3 = R)

Encrypted Text: "KHOOR"

Apply shift -3 steps (decryption with key 3):

 K becomes H (K - 3 = H)
 H becomes E (H - 3 = E)
 O becomes L (O - 3 = L)
 O becomes L (O - 3 = L)
 R becomes O (R - 3 = O)

Decrypted Text: "HELLO"
```

Asymmetric (Public/Private Key) Encryption

Asymmetric Encryption involves using a different key for the forward algorithm than for the reverse algorithm. But (unlike in the symmetric case) the forward and reverse algorithms themselves are otherwise identical. The keys used are called *public-private* and satisfy stringent mathematical conditions. The complicated mathematics involved makes it difficult to present a simple illustration like Caesar's Cipher served for symmetric encryption. Public/Private keys are the only kind of non-symmetric keys used in modern security systems. Note that the public key, falling into malicious hands, is not as dangerous as in the case of a symmetric key. All (other) holders of the public key can still be confident that anything they can successfully decrypt was encrypted by the holder of the private key. The situation is less clear for the holder of the private key, who of course can never be certain which copy of the public key might have been used to encrypt messages sent to them. As long as the private key is kept secret, however, they can always be confident that only they can decrypt messages encrypted by anyone. Common algorithms that use asymmetric keys are *RSA* and *ECDSA* (the latter is preferred for efficiency and security).[14]

Asymmetric cryptographic keys form *unique pairs* — they're mathematically linked like puzzle pieces — for each *private key*, there is a unique matching *public key*, and vice versa. You can easily check if one key was used by testing with its partner key. A private key alone can be used to (re)generate its corresponding public key (but not vice versa). This is an important reason to be careful to keep the *private* key secret while distributing the *public* key, and not vice versa.

Though the keys themselves are asymmetric, their roles in encryption are similar — each can be used to decrypt what the other has encrypted, and vice versa. But neither key can decrypt what it itself has encrypted.[15] Ciphertext created by the public key is, maybe surprisingly, as secure from hacking as that created by the private key—the computational difficulty of breaking either is equivalent when the attacker possesses neither key. What makes the private key critical is that compromising it reveals both keys, not that it produces stronger encryption.

"Layer n encryption" means *encryption of the payload of a layer n packet.*

Authenticating Cryptographic Keys

When you already have a key you trust in your possession, all is good and well, but how do you reliably *get* a key (in a trustworthy fashion) into your possession in the first place? This is also known as the *key distribution problem*. And with a public key belonging to someone else, how can you be confident who that is? i.e. who the corresponding private keyholder is? Authenticating the keys involved (and, with PKI, additionally some meta information about the owner of the private key) serves as an optional but highly valuable preamble to actually using the keys for any cryptographic purpose. Once trust is established, keys can be employed for encryption, digital signatures, or key negotiation at any network layer, including in protocols like TLS and IPSec which will be discussed later. See also Figure 34 and man-in-the-middle.

Pre-Shared Keys (PSK)

PSKs *(Pre-Shared Keys)* address the key distribution problem by distributing cryptographic material beforehand through a secure *out-of-band channel*, rather than exchanging it dynamically during communication. The material is established via a trusted mechanism, such as physical exchange, trusted couriers, manual configuration, or secure initial setup, outside the normal communication channel. While conceptually simple and avoiding real-time key exchange vulnerabilities, PSKs have significant operational limitations: they don't scale well —adding or removing parties requires (often time-consuming and/or resource-intensive) key redistribution. The keys involved can, in principle, be either symmetric keys (where all parties share the same secret) or asymmetric keys (where parties pre-exchange each other's public keys). However, pre-shared keys in group communication are usually a single symmetric key shared among all members to minimize distribution effort, as generating and securely distributing unique pairwise keys scales poorly[16]. This is common in protocols like WPA-PSK for Wi-Fi, where one PSK enables group access, though it risks broader compromise if leaked.

Trust on First Use (TOFU)

TOFU is one approach to addressing this question, and would perhaps be more aptly named *trust after first use* (and is used for example in SSH). Using TOFU is tantamount to answering the question "are you sure" the first time you use a public key, which isn't really a very thorough check. But at least it reduces the potential for problems like man-in-the-middle attacks from every use of a public key to a single use thereof. SSH, for example, asks you to verify a *fingerprint*, which is analogous to a digital signature of the public key.

Digital Certificates

A much better attempt at addressing the *key distribution problem* is the use of digital certificates. A digital certificate is essentially a (copy of a) public key, together with some extra *meta information* about the holder of the corresponding private key, all digitally signed by a third party. In effect, the signer is vouching for the public key as belonging to the entity described in the meta information, as illustrated in Figure 37. You can simply view this as a particular example of a digital signature, where the contents of the *document* being signed *happens* to be a public key of someone else and meta information about them. So if you trust the third party and already have their public key securely in your possession, you can use it to become (as) confident that the new public key is from the entity described in the metadata. But this still begs the question of how to get certificates signed by *trusted* third parties, and how to get their public keys securely into your possession (so as to be able to use them to facilitate establishing trust of keyholders they vouch for).

In effect, the question of how to get all keys you need into your possession in a trustworthy fashion, has been reduced to the question of how to get a select few (those of the signers) into your possession in a trustworthy fashion. And a standard answer to this *new* question is *Public Key Infrastructure (PKI)*, which will be discussed below.

PKI - Chain of Trust

PKI (Public Key Infrastructure) is a set of roles, policies, hardware, software, and procedures needed to create, manage, distribute, use, store, and revoke digital certificates and manage public and private keys for public-key encryption. The most important concept in PKI is its ***Chain of Trust***. One or more so-called *root authorities* trusted by everyone involved[17] verifies intermediate authorities, which in turn verify others etc. This way, when a document, such as a digital certificate, is presented as trusted (by any authority), the chain of trust can (and should) be traced back all the way to the root authority.

Imagine you are on holiday and your laptop breaks. You find a local repair shop you've never heard of. You don't trust them directly. Instead, you verify from a certificate hanging on their wall that they're licensed by a regional service center. You check online and see that regional center was certified by national headquarters, which was certified by the parent company in Taiwan—you trust them as much as you can trust anybody involved—they made your laptop. You've traced the chain backwards, link by link, until you reached someone you know. The local shop doesn't need you to trust them personally; they just need to prove an unbroken chain back to the parent company. If any link breaks—if the regional center doesn't exist or claims they never authorized the shop—you walk away.

This is exactly how your browser verifies websites: when you visit a site, it presents a certificate. Your browser traces the chain backwards (who signed this certificate? who signed theirs?) until it reaches a Root Authority already installed and trusted in your browser. If the chain is complete and valid, you see a confirmation such as in Figure 39. You're trusting strangers by verifying their connection to someone you already trust, not by knowing them directly.

When you (or your web browser) receive a certificate containing a public key and meta information about the holder of the corresponding private key, this certificate will, in general, be *signed* by a third party, as discussed in Digital Certificates. In addition, however (as prescribed by PKI), the certificate will also contain a URL where you download this third party's own certificate, containing their public key and meta information about them, all signed by a fourth party. And again, this new certificate also contains a URL pointing to the certificate of this fourth party, and so forth (in Russian doll fashion). Finally, the party (and public key) you arrive at is one of the root-authorities defined in your operating system, browser, or the network software you are using. As a convenience, all certificates necessary to follow the chain of trust may be bundled with the first. This saves you (or the network software you are using) from having to download them individually, but the concept (and security involved) remains unchanged.

Figure 36. **Signature**—*A digital signature is like a signature on paper—in applying their (digital) signature to a (digital) document, the signer attests to the validity of the document contents.*

Figure 37. **Certificate**—*A digital certificate is a (digital) signature applied to a (digital) document with a specific kind of content—one with a public key and information about the holder.*

Cryptographic (Algorithm) Schemes

Cryptographic keys are essentially just long numbers. In order to use them to do anything useful, you have to apply certain algorithms to them. These algorithms can be divided into different so-called *schemes* (*think*: families), according to the types of keys they are designed to work with (e.g. symmetric or asymmetric) and the type of application (see *Applications of Cryptography*) they are intended to be used in.

Symmetric Schemes work with *symmetric keys*. **AES** *(Advanced Encryption Standard)* is the most commonly used kind. They are much faster (and quantum resistant) than their asymmetric counterparts. They are used for the actual data transmission in a *TLS* connection. Before doing so, however, the two parties must first securely agree on a symmetric key to use. For this *key negotiation*, a separate algorithm is used—usually *ECDH* (see below).

Asymmetric Schemes work with *Asymmetric Keys*. The most commonly used kinds are:

- ***RSA*** (named after its inventors, *Ron Rivest*, *Adi Shamir*, and *Leonard Adleman*) used to be very popular, but is no longer commonly used in encrypting network traffic or signing documents. It is, however, still often used in encrypting other data, for example in *PGP* and *S/MIME*.
- ***ECDSA*** *(Elliptic Curve Digital Signature Algorithm)* is the preferred scheme for *Digital Signatures (and Verification)*. To sign a document, the forward algorithm is typically applied to a *hash* of the document. To verify the signature, the corresponding reverse algorithm is applied to a combination of both (*think*: function takes 2 parameters) the signature *and* an independently calculated *hash*, to yield a *yes/no* answer—there's no *decryption* involved—you can't recover the original hash with just the signature and the keys. A *yes* indicates the document has not changed since it was singed.[18]
- ***ECDH*** *(Elliptic-curve Diffie–Hellman)* is the preferred scheme used for *key negotiation*. A crucial property of the algorithms of this scheme is that they are commutative, which means, regardless of which order they are applied makes no difference to the outcome.[19] Its use is best illustrated with a simple example, as in *TLS Handshake* below.

Security in Practice

We saw in *Protocol Layering* how higher layers can make use of functionality (generally organized into *protocols*) in lower layers, and each layer uses data in its own *doll shell*[20]. Most of this functionality is concerned with moving packets in some way. But some is also concerned with security measures such as encrypting the packets of the layer in question. So when we speak, for example, of *layer 2 encryption* we mean encryption of the *payload* of the layer 2 packet. The layer 2 header is not encrypted in the process[21]. The same applies to encryption at other layers. And similarly for security functionality in general—when we discuss layer-specific security functionality below, we mean functionality, that, like other layer specific functionality, operates on data on its own shell, and is unaware of any higher layers, which may be using its functionality for higher level purposes.

Security protocols of layers 2, 3 and 4 are pretty much *independent*. By this, I mean that, for example, a layer 3 payload can be encrypted by layer 3 security functionality independently of whether or not the encapsulating layer 2 packet is also encrypted (independently by layer 2 functionality). *Think*: The payload of layer 2 packet may be encrypted by layer 2 security protocols. This whole packet may in turn be encrypted again as the payload for layer 3 packet, by layer 3 security protocols etc. The security protocols in the layers 2, 3, and 4 neither know nor care about that in the other layers, including whether their payloads are independently encrypted or not. In particular, *TLS* (layer 4) does not use anything from layer 3 security protocols like *IPSec* or *WireGuard*.

Some layer 5+ protocols do, however—they (re)use security functionality from lower layers, in particular from layers 3 and 4, as part of their own functionality. For example, *HTTPS* (layer 5+) uses *TLS* (layer 4) as part of its implementation, whereas *PGP* and *S/MIME* (both layer 5+) do not.

Group and individual Trust

In the context of a group[22] such as a LAN/Subnet[23], there is a difference between establishing group-wise identity and the identity of individuals in the group, as illustrated in *Figure 38*.[24] There is a similar difference between establishing trust in communication within the group as a whole and between individuals of the group—in the sense of *Identity, Trust and Encryption*.

Establishing group-wise identity can be seen as the putting of (potential) conversants into one of two categories—those trusted and those not, i.e. establishing a group-level identity for (potential) conversants. *Think*: I can pass the ball to any player on my team—they are wearing *green jerseys*. Establishing individual identity can be considered the more fine-grained ability to also distinguish (potential) conversants individually. In particular, to be able to distinguish members of a trusted group from one another. *Think*: Free kicks near the centre of the pitch are to be taken by our right midfielder—she is the player wearing a *green jersey with number 10*.

Establishing trust in communication group-wise is necessary to prevent *external sniffing*, where it's possible from outside the LAN/Subnet to eavesdrop on (or manipulate) traffic sent by members inside. Establishing trust in communication individually is necessary in order to prevent *internal sniffing*, where a member of the trusted group can eavesdrop on (or manipulate) traffic sent between other members. Every member of a trusted group having a unique (trusted) key for encryption is tantamount to establishing trust in individual communication, whereas all sharing a common (trusted) key for encryption is tantamount to establishing (only) trust in communication group-wise. The trust of any key (common or individual) can be established as described in Authenticating Cryptographic Keys.

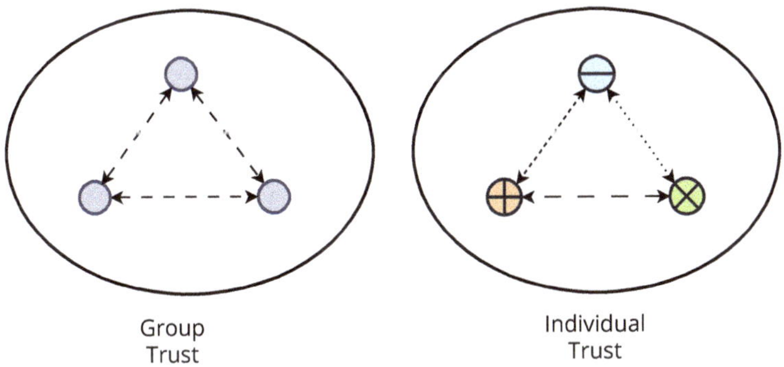

Figure 38. ***Trust*** *at the group level treats all members equally, using shared encryption (keys), allowing any member who receives a message to decrypt it. Individual level trust distinguishes each member, using unique encryption keys for each pair, preventing other group members from eavesdropping on conversations between any pair.*

Layer 2

Both Wi-Fi (using *WPA - Wi-Fi Protected Access*), and Ethernet (using *MACsec—Media Access Control Security*), can encrypt layer 2 payloads. MACsec is not enabled by default when you connect Ethernet interfaces by a cable. Doing so requires additional hardware and configuration, so encryption of Ethernet is uncommon. WPA is generally enabled by default for Wi-Fi, so encryption of Wi-Fi is standard.

Both Ethernet and Wi-Fi, in their most common versions, establish trust group-wise but not individually. These use a common PSK (pre-shared key). Due to the physical point-to-point nature of cable connections involved, Ethernet is less prone to sniffing than Wi-Fi. Both have enterprise versions, however, which do distinguish individual identities with unique keys, and also effectively prevent internal sniffing. These versions generally use PKI to do so.

Layer 3

Layer 3 security protocols encrypt the payload of layer 3 packets. It can be thought of as a *blanket encryption* of all network traffic between two interfaces. It doesn't distinguish based on port number and therefore the applications involved. This provides the advantage that no individual applications need be configured (e.g. to use specific port numbers) to actively partake in the security protocols. It, however, has the disadvantage of significantly impacting network traffic, including that of any applications which may not need the security thus provided. Layer 3 encryption is commonly used by many *VPNs*.

IPSec

IPSec (Internet Protocol Security) is the established standard for IP level encryption, standardized by the *IETF* (the same body that standardizes the rest of Layer 3 networking protocols). IPSec is highly flexible and feature-rich, supporting various encryption algorithms, authentication methods, and key exchange protocols. It can use digital certificates[25] or bare cryptographic keys for authentication. However, this flexibility comes at a cost—IPSec is notoriously complex to configure and implement correctly, similar to how XML's flexibility made it powerful but cumbersome to work with.

WireGuard

WireGuard represents a more modern approach to IP level encryption, developed as a third-party solution focused on simplicity and performance. Unlike IPSec's complexity, WireGuard follows a minimalist philosophy—*think*: JSON versus XML. It aims to do one thing well: create fast, secure encrypted connections with minimal configuration overhead. WireGuard uses only (pre-shared public/private) cryptographic keys for authentication (no certificate infrastructure required) and employs a small, carefully selected set of modern cryptographic primitives. This design philosophy makes it significantly easier to configure, audit, and deploy compared to IPSec, while maintaining strong security properties. The protocol has gained significant adoption in recent years due to its combination of simplicity, performance, and security, making it an attractive alternative to IPSec.

Layer 4

Layer 4 security protocols like *TLS* and *SSH* encrypt the payload of layer 4 packets, travelling between specific network endpoints (see *Port Numbers—interface sharing and network endpoints*). You can think of this as securing the communication pathway between two specific applications running on two different nodes. It requires the applications in question to actively partake in the encryption and decryption, for example in managing the appropriate cryptographic keys, and adhering to the layer 4 protocol in question (e.g. TLS—see below). If encryption at layer 3 can be considered *blanket encryption*, that at layer 4 can be thought of as a *Swiss Army Knife encryption*. It offers more fine-grained control, but requires more effort and skill on the part of the (developers of the) applications involved.

The Security Protocol Zoo

Why are there so many security *protocols*, and each seems to work at only one layer?

Creating a single universal security protocol that works at every layer, stays fast, remains secure, and is easy to configure, has proven intractable. So several emerged, each focusing on a specific layer.[26] Even within the same layer, protocols make different tradeoffs.[27] Each protocol answers the question: "What matters most here—flexibility, simplicity, speed, or specialized features?" differently. No single answer works for everyone.

TLS

TLS (Transport Layer Security) is the most commonly used protocol for securing (arbitrary) TCP (and UDP) based network communication. Historically, TLS evolved from *Secure Sockets Layer (SSL)*, which it has now largely replaced in modern networking. TLS is a protocol which makes use of cryptographic keys to encrypt the communication and optionally (but very commonly) digital certificates and PKI to *authenticate* and establish identity.

TLS also mandates a so-called *TLS Handshake* as part of setting up the secure connection. The main function of this handshake is for the two parties to agree on a symmetric cryptographic key, which can be used for the rest of the *conversation*. The handshake itself usually uses public/private keys,[28]. When using public/private keys as part of the handshake, TLS can optionally verify certificates through *PKI*. With PKI enabled, it requires valid certificates from a trusted certificate authority and verifies them to establish identity. More specifically, it can be configured so only one side (typically the server) presents a certificate, or both sides (client and server) present certificates—the latter being commonly (and somewhat confusingly) called *mTLS*. Without PKI verification, TLS still encrypts the connection using whatever keys are presented, but doesn't verify who owns those keys.

TLS effectively splits a single unencrypted application level *message* (such as a HTTP request or response) into one or more encrypted TLS *records*. It then passes these (encrypted) records to the underlying (insecure) layer 4 protocol as the payload. The underlying transport protocol is often TCP (as is the case for HTTPS), but it's also possible to use a different underlying protocol such as UDP, in which case one speaks of *Datagram TLS (DTLS)*

TLS also adds a checksum[29] to the encrypted payload to catch any deliberate attempts to modify the encrypted data. It acts like a digital (symmetric key) signature for each TLS record.[30]

TLS is never really used *on its own* but by many applications directly or indirectly through higher-layer protocols such as HTTPS, which use TLS to do most of the heavy lifting of encryption and identity verification.

HTTPS uses TLS to encrypt the complete *HTTP* packet. The layer 4 header is not encrypted).[31]

TLS Handshake

The *TLS Handshake* is a preamble of every TLS connection, where the parties wishing to communicate securely—first securely *agree on a symmetric key* the so-called *session key*, to use for the rest of the TLS connection.[32]

The agreement can be reached starting with either asymmetric keys (the usual case) or *Pre-Shared Keys* (the simpler case). In this simpler case with PSKs, the parties simply prove to one another that they are each in possession of the same symmetric key, and use it to derive a new symmetric key for the session. In the more common case using asymmetric keys, both parties create a new pair of (random) ephemeral asymmetric keys suitable for *key negotiation* (usually ECDH) for each new TLS connection. One or both of the parties can additionally authenticate themselves via PKI, which requires the parties to be already in possession of the associated permanent asymmetric keys suitable for signing (usually ECDSA).[33] If the parties involved are *Alice* and *Bob*, then the process involving their ephemeral asymmetric keys is roughly:

- Alice and *Bob* agree on a seed value, `g`.
- Alice computes `a(g)`, using her private key, and sends this to Bob.[34]
- Bob computes `b(a(g))`, using his private key. This is Bob's shared secret.
- Bob computes `b(g)`, using his private key, and sends this to Alice.
- Alice computes `a(b(g))` using her private key—this is the same shared secret Bob computed, due to the *commutativity* of operations involved.[35]

The common *shared secret a(b(g))* is then used to compute the symmetric key. Note that any *man-in-the-middle*, even if they observe every message sent between Alice and Bob, cannot derive from the information passed what the symmetric key they agreed upon is.[36]

The private keys a, b as well as the symmetric key they are used to create, for any TLS connection, are all *ephemeral*—and automatically deleted at the end, ensuring *perfect forward secrecy (PFS)*.[37]

Ephemeral means temporary and automatically deleted—these keys are only used once, then the system throws them away. Think of them as disposable keys, of which no record is subsequently kept.

A *seed value* is an initial value in a procedure or calculation that significantly affects the result. Imagine a board game where you have to move in a certain way —two steps up, one to the right etc. A seed value is like your choice of starting point. Even if you make all the same moves, where you end up depends clearly on where you started.

mTLS

mTLS (Mutual TLS) as a name is a bit misleading, since what it describes is more a *mutual Authentication* than a mutual TLS. In TLS both parties always participate symmetrically in the encrypted conversation (using a shared symmetric key). However, during the handshake, authentication—typically via PKI certificates—can be one-way or mutual. Standard TLS usually involves only the server authenticating itself to the client, while mTLS requires both client and server to present and verify certificates for mutual identity assurance. See also *TLS Handshake*.

Layer 5+

Some layer 5+ security protocols add higher level functionality on top of existing security protocols, and payload encyrption, that are available in lower layers. *HTTPS*, for example, defines specialized layer 5+ attributes[38] in the header of the Layer 5+ packet, enhancing security in web environments like Browsers where HTTPS is commonly used. These are in addition to the complete *encryption of HTTP packets* already provided by TLS.

Others take a roll-your-own approach, implementing full encryption and authentication independently at higher layers - duplicating what lower-layer security protocols already do (but just one layer higher - and one *doll shell* deeper).

HTTPS

HTTPS (HTTP Secure) is *HTTP* running over TLS, making it one of the most widely used applications of TLS encryption on the internet. When you see a URL beginning with *https://* instead of *http://*, the web browser and server are using TLS to encrypt all HTTP communication between them. HTTPS uses TLS with *PKI*, and the digital certificates exchanged as part of the process allow verification that the communication is with the intended server rather than an imposter. The certificate contains the server's public key and is signed by a trusted Certificate Authority (CA).

The TLS handshake in HTTPS happens transparently before any HTTP data is exchanged, establishing the encryption mechanism applied to all subsequent web traffic. This protects not just the content of web pages, but also form submissions, login credentials, and any other data exchanged between browser and server.

Web browsers are one of the most common end-user applications that use HTTPS. The Browser helps provide secure communication, handling certificate validation and GUI indicators like the *lock icon*, as illustrated in *Figure 39*. Most modern websites use HTTPS by default, and browsers increasingly warn users when visiting sites that only offer unencrypted HTTP connections, fail security checks based on HTTPS-specific Layer 5+ packet data, such as specialized headers that extend security beyond TLS authentication and encryption. Browsers manage certificate stores, which include pre-installed root certificates at the top of the chain of trust. This chain enables the browser to validate the authenticity of new certificates—verifying their signatures against already trusted certificates—before accepting and adding them at runtime, effectively extending the chain of trust. Individual browsers (operating systems, and other web applications in general) all typically maintain their own independent certificate stores.[40]

Think of these security measures used by HTTPS as complementary:

- ***PKI*** makes sure you're talking to the right person—like checking someone's ID before handing them a letter.
- ***TLS*** (*encryption*) makes sure the network is secure—like using a sealed envelope so no one can read or tamper with the letter in transit.
- ***Specialized attributes*** tell the recipient what to do once the letter arrives safely—like instructions on a bank PIN letter: "Open along dotted line", "Check seal hasn't been tampered with", "Scratch off the silver panel to reveal your PIN".

You verify who you're sending it to (PKI), the letter is sealed during delivery (TLS), and the specialized attributes add extra protection for how the content gets handled after arrival. The particular attributes are HTTPS specific, just as the instructions depend on the system the letter is using. For example, one bank may put the PIN in a scratch-off panel on the right, while another may use a tear-off section at the bottom.[41]

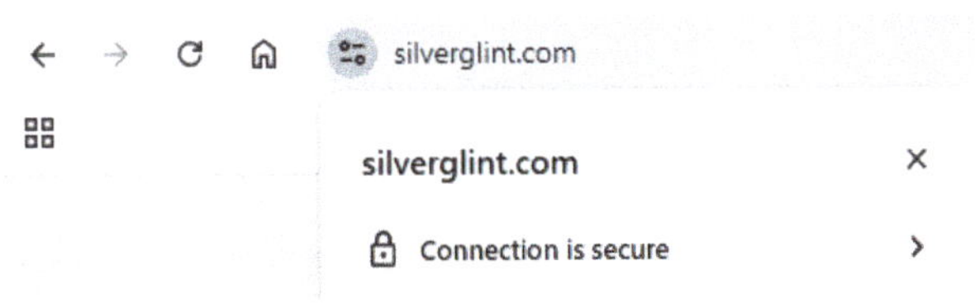

Figure 39. Web Browser confirming that the network connection to the website is using HTTPS (and thus TLS), and as a result is secure.

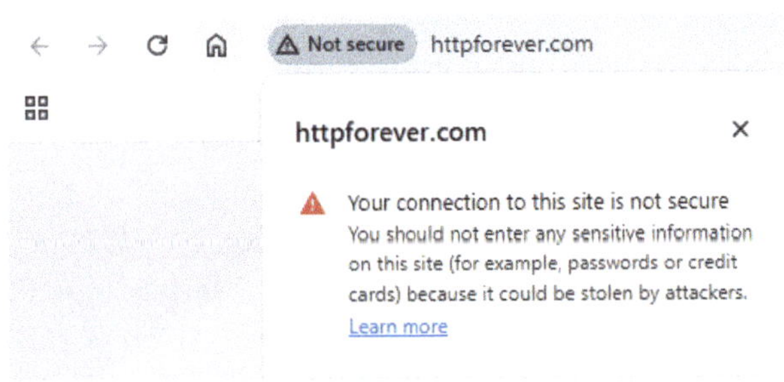

Figure 40. Web Browser warning that the network connection to the website is not using HTTPS (and thus not TLS), and as a result is insecure.

SSH

SSH (Secure SHell) can be viewed from a security perspective, as combining layer 4 encryption and authentication with specialized higher-layer functionality, such as command-line access, file transfer, and integration with applications like Git[42] and *SCP (Secure Copy Protocol)*. It is a less general purpose protocol for securing network communication than TLS. Both TLS and SSH typically use asymmetric keys for authentication,[43]—the primary difference is the trust model: SSH validates them using *TOFU* rather than the *PKI* which is standard with TLS. Like TLS, SSH typically runs on *TCP*. It excels in remote shell commands or terminal access. Once you're authenticated, the SSH server then decides what you can access (*authorization*) based on system permissions and configuration files.

Some applications like SCP, which is used for securely copying files between remote computers, use SSH behind the scenes. Some applications, like *Git*, can be configured to use either SSH or HTTPS (which in turn uses TLS). For more details and plenty of hands-on examples of using and configuring SSH, refer to the planned follow-up volume *(Modern Networking - Software and Techniques)*.

PGP

PGP (Pretty Good Privacy) is a protocol that uses public key cryptography to encrypt data. The data in question is generally local files and emails. It doesn't use PKI and its chain of trust, at the top of which sit globally trusted (root) authorities, but rather a peer-based alternative, often called a *web of trust*, containing their certificates (which contain their public keys). There are no (implicitly trusted) root authorities—everyone using PGP customizes it by explicitly adding the certificates of those they personally and directly trust to their system/software. This contrasts with PKI, where this list of explicitly trusted parties comes pre-packaged with your operating system or software. Like with PKI, however, any certificates signed by one of the trusted parties becomes implicitly trusted also as a result (expanding the web over time). Note that since you are free to add any certificates to your trusted list in PGP, you are also free to add those from the same parties as in a PKI system or software, effectively making the PGP web of trust identical to the PKI chain of trust[44].

You can use PGP (based software) to secure particular files on your computer and share these with someone else, who can read them on their computer if they add your certificate to their web of trust and vice versa. This protects the data in question from malicious third parties, even if the data is stored or transported in a manner that's in itself insecure (e.g. on a USB stick or over an insecure network). In practice, however, it's not uncommon to send such data across a secure network connection using for example TLS, in which case it's doubly encrypted. The PGP encrypted local file from your computer is encrypted by TLS in transit. Upon arrival at its destination, the network software there decrypts the TLS, leaving *just* a PGP encrypted file, which the PGP based application there in turn decrypts.

S/MIME

S/MIME (Secure/Multipurpose Internet Mail Extensions) is also a protocol for encrypting data, but unlike PGP, it's specifically designed for use with emails. More accurately, it's designed for *MIME data*, which is email's formatting standard. The disadvantage, compared to PGP, of its only working with emails, is offset by its being easier to use. This is mainly because of the native S/MIME support in operating systems and email clients, which makes certificate-based signing and encryption largely *just work* once you've installed a certificate. By contrast, PGP typically requires extra plugins or manual key management.

You can encrypt an email using an email client like Outlook, using the recipient's S/MIME certificate (from their public key). If sent over an insecure SMTP connection, the content remains secure. In practice, it's often sent via TLS,[45] so the S/MIME-encrypted email is further protected in transit. The recipient's email client, with your certificate in its trust store, decrypts the S/MIME layer after TLS is stripped away. Like TLS (and unlike PGP) S/MIME uses PKI.

Cascading Encryption Layers (Keys)

Any layer in a network stack that wants to independently use encryption to protect its payload, must first *negotiate* what cryptographic keys to use at that layer. The payload includes any higher layer packets (recursively) encapsulated, and thus these inner layer packets are automatically protected. Optionally, the keys involved may also be authenticated.[46] This is the so-called *setup phase*. The actual (encrypted) conversation happens only after the setup phase has been successfully completed, in the *conversation phase*, as illustrated in *Figure 41*.

During the conversation phase, encryption and decryption must occur in specific orders, as indicated by the direction of the arrows in *Figure 41*. Encryption proceeds from higher layers downward: the payload (inner packet data) must be encrypted first, then this encrypted blob becomes part of the lower layer's (i.e. outer packet) payload, which encrypts everything again. Conversely, decryption must proceed from lower layers upward: the outermost encrypted layer must be decrypted first before the inner encrypted content becomes accessible. The span of the arrows indicates which layers are protected by each encryption operation.

When multiple layers want to independently use encryption, security is enhanced when the higher layer performs its setup as part of the conversation phase of the lower layer(s). Critically, lower layer keys are set up first because the packets carrying the higher layer's key negotiations benefit from the outer encryption protecting them (in typical Russian doll fashion). *Overlay networks* frequently involve cascading encryption from multiple layers (where the keys originate), and these key-originating layers are typically in separate layer sets as illustrated in *Figure 41*.

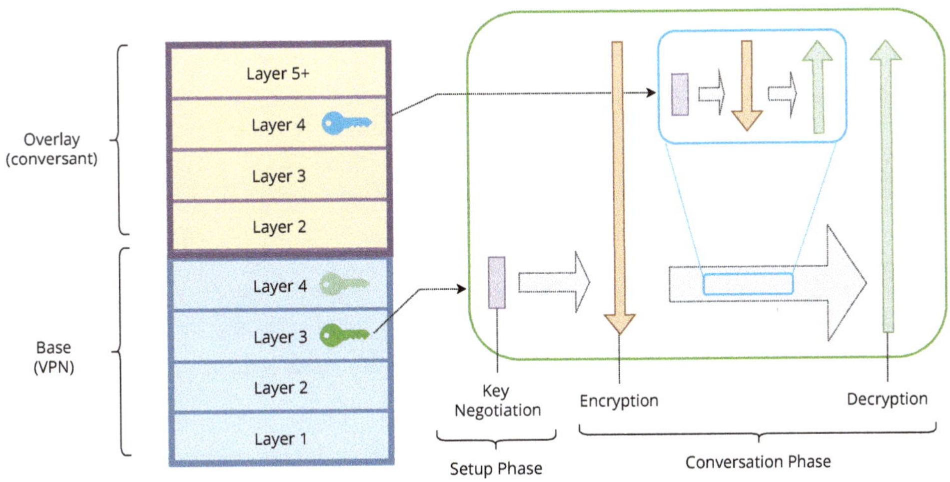

Figure 41. An overlay network stack, typically created by a VPN. The VPN encrypts all traffic inside the tenant using one set of keys, at layer 3 (or 4). Any pair of interfaces, wishing to converse, also independently negotiate different keys. The second negotiation happens through packets encrypted with the already established VPN keys. This is an example of multiple layers using (dedicated) keys, which results in independent cascading in setup (key negotiation and optional authentication), encryption and decryption phases.

VPNs

VPNs (Virtual Private Networks) are created and managed by a *VPN server* as illustrated in Figure 42. When a single VPN server (e.g., running as a cloud service with multiple independent customers) creates multiple independent virtual private networks (e.g., one for each company), each one is a so-called *tenant*. Any interface that joins such a VPN has its outgoing packets (typically layer 3 or 4) encrypted[47] and routed through VPN server, regardless of their actual ultimate intended destination. The *blanket encryption* of the VPN is performed independently of any encryption the conversants may be using (typically layer 4) themselves.

When source and destination interfaces are both inside the same tenant, traffic remains fully VPN encrypted. For destinations outside the VPN, the request gets blanket decrypted (layer 3 or 4) and forwarded by the VPN server to the external address. Any reply is again (layer 3 or 4) encrypted by the VPN server before being forwarded back to the internal interface. Each VPN tenant is an example of an overlay network.

Think of a VPN tenant as a distributed team of packaging experts together with an office in a central station (the VPN server). Each tenant gets their own office in the central station. Each user and the office itself get assigned a dedicated expert. When you want to send a letter to some other member of your tenant, you don't worry about securing it—e.g. the envelope might not have an adhesive seal or may have a translucent window showing the contents. But rather than posting it yourself, you hand it to your packaging expert, who wraps it in an additional secure outer envelope addressed to your tenant's office in the central VPN station. The letter travels through the regular postal system like any other mail. At the VPN station, another packaging expert from your team unwraps the outer envelope and checks where you actually wanted to send it. If the recipient is also in your tenant, they rewrap it (securely) and send it to that person's packaging expert. If the recipient is external, they send your inner letter out naked (only as secure as your own envelope is)—they must since this recipient does not have a packaging expert to help them remove the secure outer envelope. Throughout this process, the regular postal system (the internet) is used—the VPN is just the packaging experts and the central station.

The most important advantage of a VPN is that it handles encryption—applications and users don't need to implement their own encryption for communication within their own tenant. They can exchange data in plaintext, blissfully unaware that the VPN is securing everything at a lower layer. This offloads security concerns from users and the organization to the VPN. VPNs have the disadvantage, however, of not working transparently with PKI.[48].

Note that the interfaces (and users) in a tenant can each be located *anywhere* in the world—their encrypted packets travel through the regular internet infrastructure alongside everyone else's traffic. To join a tenant, you need to install client software for this specific VPN (think: your personal packaging expert) on your device. The VPN doesn't add any dedicated infrastructure—it's an overlay that uses existing shared internet infrastructure. Note also that an implicit assumption here is that users who share a tenant can trust each other.[49]

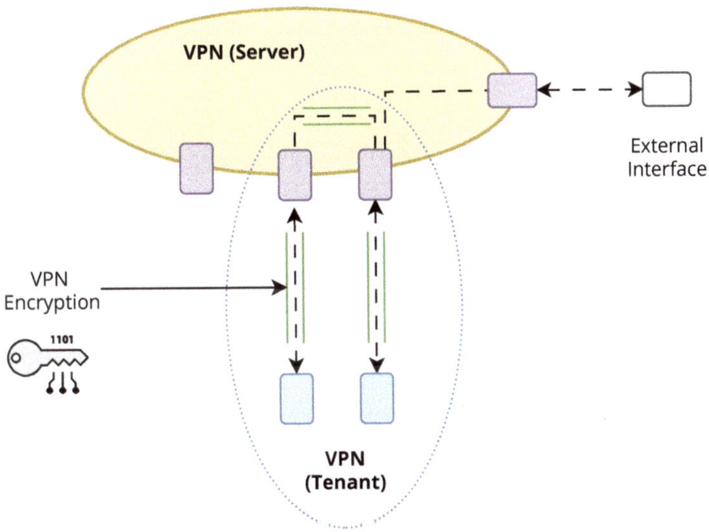

Figure 42. **VPN** *(Virtual Private Network) sits as a trusted man-in-the-middle between all interfaces in the tenant, and any external interface. It encrypts all packets (typically at layer 3 or 4) independently of any encryption the original source and final destination interfaces may be using anyway. Interfaces within the same tenant need not use encryption for internal communication. Depending on how it's configured, the server may inspect, block or alter certain packets. Communication wholly inside the tenant corresponds to the complete stack in Figure 41, whereas any communication (leg) with external interfaces corresponds only to the top half of said stack.*

Firewalls

A *firewall* is a security system that controls network traffic by enforcing a set of *rules* about what packets are allowed to pass through at a certain point and what should be blocked. Think of it as a security checkpoint that inspects packets and decides whether to let them through based on predefined criteria.

At its core, a firewall typically examines the *headers* of packets at layer 3 and above such as source and destination IP addresses, ports, and protocols — and applies rules to determine whether traffic should be permitted or denied.[50] These rules can be simple, such as *"block all traffic from IP address X"* or more complex, such as *"allow HTTPS traffic from subnet Y only to specific internal servers during business hours"*.

A firewall is like the security checkpoint at a building entrance — it checks if you're carrying prohibited items (malicious packets), if you're arriving at acceptable hours (time-based rules), or if you're trying to enter through the right door (allowed ports/protocols). Once you're past this checkpoint, *access control* takes over — like the keycard reader at each office door that verifies your identity (authentication) and only unlocks if you're authorized to enter that specific room (authorization).[51]

What kind of network component a firewall is deployed on determines its *level of operation*.[52] *Think*: security checkpoints at a country border, versus a city entrance, versus a building lobby, versus an apartment door — each controls access at a different level of granularity.

- **Subnet Gateway** firewalls are implemented in *subnet gateway routers*, which control traffic entering or leaving an entire subnet. More specifically, these gateways combine the (layer 3) function of a router with the function of a gatekeeper for all traffic (with packets typically inspected at layer 5+ and below) flowing between network segments.
- **Node** firewalls control traffic entering or leaving individual nodes (each of which may possess multiple interfaces). Every packet destined for or originating from an interface on the node passes through these rules. On Linux systems, this is commonly implemented using the *NetFilter* framework[53], while Windows systems use *Windows Firewall*.
- **Interface** firewalls apply rules to specific network interfaces. Each interface can have its own set of rules independent of others on the same node.[54] Cloud providers frequently implement interface level firewalls as so-called *security groups*.

Today's firewalls have evolved far beyond simple packet filtering. Modern deployments frequently feature *Next-Generation Firewalls (NGFWs)* — an umbrella term for firewalls that combine traditional (header-based) filtering with advanced capabilities like *Deep Packet Inspection (DPI)* that examines packet *payloads* (for instance, detecting SQL injection attempts within HTTP requests, not just allowing HTTP traffic), *Intrusion Detection and Prevention Systems (IDPS)* that identify attack patterns, and *TLS Interception* for inspecting encrypted traffic.[55]

These advanced capabilities make firewalls more powerful, but also slow down network traffic to varying degrees — simple payload inspection adds modest overhead, while decrypting and re-encrypting all encrypted traffic is far more resource-intensive than just examining headers. *Think*: upgrading from a simple ID check at the door to a system that also tracks where visitors go, what they carry, and whether they're following normal patterns for their stated purpose. Further implementation details are beyond the scope of this book,[56] but recognizing firewalls as configurable checkpoints that enforce traffic rules at different network levels provides the fundamental understanding you'll need when encountering these more sophisticated systems in other contexts.

> Firewalls control what types of traffic can flow through a network, while *access control* manages who can access specific resources via the packets that get through.

"Tunnels"

The term *tunnel* is often used in networking contexts (e.g. *VPNs*). It is, however, not a technical term but merely an analogy, presumably inspired by the superficial similarity with the connections in illustrations like *Figure 42*. Though analogies can aid in understanding, I feel *tunnel* is best avoided, as it may create impressions which are inaccurate (and unhelpful) in several ways.

Unlike an actual tunnel that provides an isolated, buried path through something like a mountain, network "tunnelling" doesn't create any alternative or invisible pathway. There's no isolated conduit, no *entering* and *exiting* a separate path, and no bypass of the public internet. Packets that enter the "tunnel" might not exit—they could get dropped inside just as easily as outside.

What actually occurs is that individual packets are encrypted and an *additional* routing point (e.g., the VPN server) is inserted in the network path. Your encrypted packets still traverse the same public internet infrastructure, routers, and ISP networks—they're simply unreadable to intermediate observers and are first routed to your VPN provider's server before reaching their originally intended final destination.

Understanding this distinction is crucial for proper security assessment, as *tunnelling* implies stronger isolation than what actually exists.

Identity Management

Identity Management (often also called *Identity and Access Management*, and abbreviated to *IAM*) describes how identities (see Figure 34) are stored and made available to those (and only those) *services* which should have access to them.footnote[Or, more precisely, made available to services being used by entities when (and only when) said entities should have access to the identities in question.]

Identities are always managed by an *Identity Provider*. A single service (*think*: small website) can act as its own identity provider—storing identities directly and verifying them itself (like a small gym issuing and checking its own membership cards). Alternatively, a dedicated identity provider can handle this for one or more services. Social Login is a typical example of a single service (*think*: website) using a separate external identity provider. When multiple related services within an organization share a dedicated identity provider—whether internal or external—this is called *Federated Identity Management,* and typically used with Single Sign-On as illustrated in Figure 43.

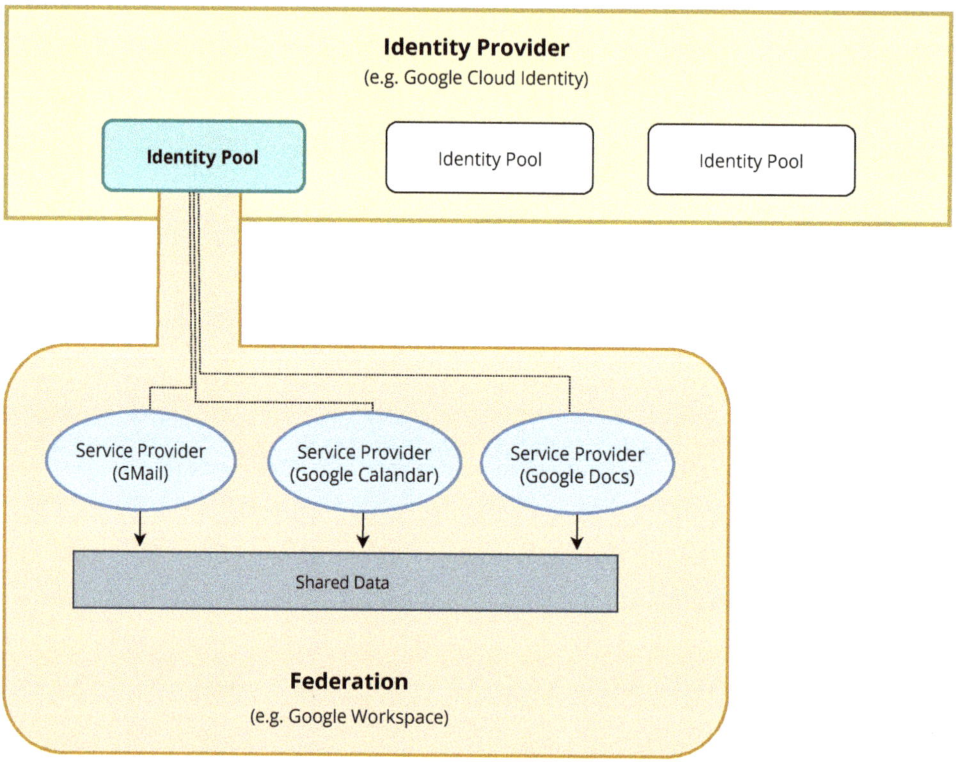

Figure 43. **Identity Management.** *An Identity Provider stores identities in independent pools. One or more service providers (typically from a single organization. e.g. Google) can form a Federation, which can share (Single Sign-On i.e. SSO) access to a single dedicated pool, and (optionally) shared data.*

Service Provider Federation and Single Sign-On (SSO)

Multiple service providers (often appearing as individual but related applications to an end user), from a single organization[57] may together form a so-called *federation*. The federated service providers can access a single dedicated pool of identities, all stored in and secured by a (separate) *identity provider*.

When an entity uses one of the services in question (*Think*: a user checks their email in Gmail using a web browser), what at a high level happens is that the service provider *asks* the identity provider for the credentials associated with the entity in question. The identity provider in turn *asks* the user for their credentials, before complying. If successful, the service provider can then access all necessary identity information about the user in question (*think*: knowing the user's email address allows the service provider to locate their emails or apply user-specific settings).

Should the user wish to access a further service provider in the federation, the identity provider recognizes that the user is already *logged on* and doesn't require them to do so again (*think*: the user doesn't get prompted for credentials when they want to access google calendar, if they have already recently used Gmail in the same web browser). Only a so-called *single sign on (SSO)* is necessary when a user uses multiple services (service provider applications). It doesn't matter which of the services they use first, once they have signed on for one, they are automatically signed on for all (for a limited period of time, after which a single sign on once again becomes necessary).

What happens at a lower level is described by the exact *flow* being used. But a typical example is that when the user tries to access a particular function in the first service (*think*: *show me my new emails*), the service automatically redirects their web browser to the identity provider, where the web browser *asks* the identity provider for a so-called *authorization code* for the entity.[58]

The identity provider prompts the user to pass their credentials (e.g. username, password and perhaps a code from an authenticator app). If the user can be successfully authenticated (i.e. the identity provider considers the credentials valid and can map them to an identity it manages for the federation in question) the identity provider saves a *(SSO) session cookie* in the browser indicating that the user has authenticated and therefore need not do so again (until the session expires). It then redirects the browser back to the service provider's callback endpoint, including a temporary *authorization code*.[59]

The service provider now needs to obtain the actual identity of the user. To do this, the service provider takes the authorization code it just received and sends it directly to the identity provider. It asks to exchange this code for identity information on the user.[60] The identity provider validates the code and replies with the requested information, packaged in a token. The service provider may use this token to retrieve further identity attributes (e.g., user ID, email, roles) and decide if this particular user should be permitted (*authorized*) to perform the particular function it is attempting to perform (*think*: *show me my new emails*).

When the user later accesses a second service in the federation, that service still redirects the browser to the identity provider just as the first service provider did,[61] but the identity provider recognizes the still-valid SSO session cookie and skips the credential prompting step, (*automatically*) redirecting the browser (with a new authorization code) back to the service provider. This time the user is not required to *"do"* anything, which is why the user experiences seamless access across all federated services without re-entering their credentials. The second service provider still uses its authorization code to query the identity provider for any other information it needs — but again this happens transparently to the user.

Protocols and Flows

How exactly which information (particularly credentials), and in what format, moves between which parties involved when using an identity management system, is governed by a protocol. Such protocols define so-called *flows* (or sometimes *authentication flow* even though it often describes the flow of information in more than just an authentication process) which can be viewed as high-level sequences or patterns outlining how the protocols are used in different scenarios. The two most widely known protocols in identity management are *SAML* and *Open ID Connect + OAuth*.

Security Assertion Markup Language (SAML)

SAML is an older XML-based protocol, that makes extensive use of certificates. It's very comprehensive but more difficult to implement, and is found most often in use inside large-scale enterprises, and legacy systems. It defines, for example, a *SAML Web Browser SSO Profile Flow*, which maps closely to the above example with Gmail/Calendar.

OpenID Connect + OAuth

This is a modern protocol, which makes extensive use of tokens (very often JWTs), is valued for its simplicity and good mobile support. It is standard in small to middle-sized organizations, and increasingly gaining traction in larger ones[62]. As the name suggests, it's (historically) a combination of two protocols, OAuth[63] and OpenID Connect, the latter adding authentication support to the authorization processes OAuth was originally designed to support. It defines an *Authorization (Code Grant) Flow* which maps closely to the above example with Gmail/Calendar. Additionally, it allows for the (optional) addition of a so-called *refresh token*, which can be used by a service provider to request the identity provider to extend the valid lifetime of the corresponding authorization token (often referred to as an *access token*).[64] This is another example of the layering of credentials of limited lifetime (the access token), which are actually used to access the system (get identity information) on top of those of longer lifetime (the refresh token) which can't be used directly to access the system.

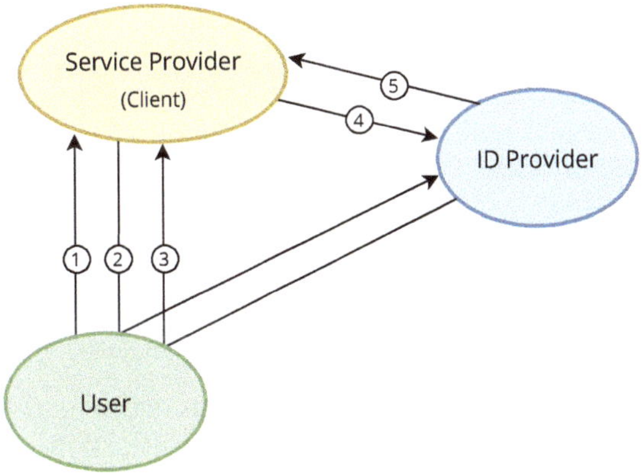

Figure 44. **Authorization (Code Grant) Flow.** *A simplified illustration of an Authorization (Code Grant) Flow. (1) The User tries to gain access to a secure Service Provider (often known as a "Client" in OAuth) (2) Provider redirects them to the Identity Provider, where they must authenticate. (3) The user returns an identifier (also called an "authorization code") to the service provider, who (4) queries the Identity Provider for any further identity information it requires about the user with said identifier. (5) The Service provider uses the identity information thus obtained, to ascertain if the user should be permitted (authorized) to perform the action they initially attempted. The service provider typically saves a (temporary) cookie in the user's browser to avoid making them reauthenticate for every subsequent request.*

Role-Based Access Control (RBAC)

When the privileges in an identity are *roles* (*think: is an administrator*) rather than fine-grained permissions (*think: _should be able to edit the values in some specific data structure*), then one speaks of *Role-Based Access Control (RBAC)*. The service provider determines from the identity what role(s) the entity using the service, has been assigned. Based on this, the service decides whether the entity should be allowed to perform the specific function they are trying to perform or not. For example, if the entity is trying to change critical values in a database that affect not only the user themselves, but also other entities that can legitimately access the service, then the service would typically only comply when the entity has been assigned a role like *administrator* (or equivalent) in their identity. Note that the definition of the roles (both names and interpretation) is completely up to the services in question. To the identity provider, there is no fundamental difference between a role and a (fine-grained) permission—they are typically just names (and possibly values) the identity provider stores and passes to the services (as part of an authentication token) when the service requests it. The service itself (or more generally, each services in a single federation) *knows* how to interpret the presence or absence of the names (and values) in question.

RBAC has gained significant popularity in recent years, because it significantly simplifies access management in large organizations by allowing administrators to manage permissions at the role level rather than individually configuring permissions for each user.

JSON Web Tokens (JWTs)

JWT is a popular *standard* defining tokens with a specific structure and content. Libraries exist in various programming languages that implement this standard which programmers can use (e.g. to create, sign, read, and validate these tokens). It's analogous to say the *zip standard* for data (often in files) compression and decompression, and the library functions available for creating and reading such compressed data, which many application developers makes use of to add zip functionality to their applications (without having to implement all the low-level details themselves).

JWT tokens are *URL-safe*, meaning that the characters used within a JWT are specifically chosen to be safely included in a URL without requiring any special encoding or escaping. This is crucial because JWTs are often transmitted in HTTP headers (like the Authorization header with the Bearer scheme) or as query parameters in the URL.

Structure of a JWT Token

Header

The header contains metadata about the token, such as the type of token and the hashing algorithm used, as JSON.

Payload

The payload contains the actual data (sometimes referred to as *claims* e.g., identity information), which the token is intended to embody, presented as JSON. JWT itself has no notion of the semantics of the token content (payload) - that's left to the application/framework using the token (~ zip archives).

Signature

A signature (optional according to the standard, but highly recommended in practice) ensures that the token hasn't been altered after it was signed. It's created using the header, payload, and a secret key or a public/private key pair. OAuth, for example, is a framework that (can) uses JWT for its tokens. It defines specific semantics for the content of the JWT payload.

Social Login

Websites that offer users an option, like *Sign on with GitHub* or *Sign on with Google*, have become increasingly popular in recent years. The websites in question wish to be able to uniquely distinguish their users, with something like an identifier from an associated identity, however. Doing so (securely) requires significant effort—*think*: securely storing and managing user credentials (in compliance with international data regulations), implementing two-factor authentication, etc. And as always in security, the consequences of doing so incorrectly creates a window of opportunity for malicious actors, which may result in not only theft/corruption of the user's data but also a loss of reputation of the company behind the website, should any such successful attack become public knowledge.

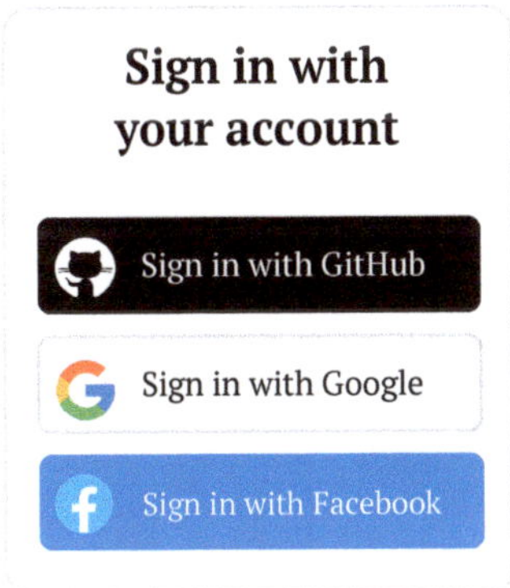

Figure 45. A typical **Social Login** *dialog, often shown in a web browser, offering visitors of a website the opportunity to authenticate using a 3rd party website xx.*

Some enterprises who already have a well established and tested identity management platform, and a large body of existing users (like GitHub and google) offer an authentication service to 3rd party service providers, on behalf of the (already registered) users at the large enterprise. Effectively when a user wants to *log on* to a 3rd party website, the website in question redirects them to the identity provider, and after successful authentication, the identify provider sends them back to the website with an authentication token, just like it does with the services in the federation. However, unlike the federation services, the 3rd party website cannot use this token to get any further identity information related to the user (which the federated services can do as part of an authorization process, for example).

Effectively, the 3rd party website (securely) gets enough information (typically a unique ID) about the user in question to recognize them (e.g. if/when they have logged on before) and to distinguish them from any other user of the system. They do not know *who* the user is, in the sense that any other identity information in the enterprise system is off limits to the 3rd party website (at least without the explicit consent of the user), but this is often more than enough.

The user benefits from not having to safely maintain a further set of credentials. The 3rd party website benefits from being able to concentrate on the business logic that is its domain of expertise. The enterprise with the identity provider benefits from a further source of revenue (and advertising).[65]

Delegated Authorization

A website like *github.com* can be perceived as a service which interacts with an identity provider of the (confusingly) same name. After a user logs into their account at GitHub, they can interact with the service—e.g. view and edit their repositories and other settings. In order to enable users to also use more specialized git clients, services like GitHub enable *delegated authorization* of such 3rd party applications. The user no longer uses the service (e.g. GitHub website) directly, but through a 3rd party application. The two most common ways of (securely) doing so are:

SSH Based

The user (securely) uploads a public ssh key to the service (e.g. GitHub website, where it is stored as part of their profile). The user additionally makes the private key (locally and securely) available to the trusted 3rd party application, which uses it to *authenticate* itself on behalf of the user with the remote service, when the user wants to use the application to perform a function (e.g. push a git commit) which requires corresponding permission.

Ssh keys when used in this way typically grant an *all or nothing* access to the remote services. The application effectively *becomes* the user from the perspective of the remote service. Everything the user is allowed to do when interacting with the service directly, the application is generally allowed to do on the user's behalf. This approach violates the *principle of least privilege*, whereby such an application should be given only the permissions it needs to do its job, and no more. For this reason, despite ssh keys being the more convenient option for delegated access, they are generally considered less preferable than the following option.

OAuth Authorization Grant Flow (TLS Based)

The service provider issues the 3rd party application with an authentication token, which it must present to the service when it's attempting to perform (secure) service functions on behalf of the user. The token can (and should) contain specific privileges that allow the application to perform those, and only those, secure functions it should be performing on behalf of the user, as doing so reduces the possibility of unintended actions (both malicious and erroneous). It's also possible to issue tokens with a limited valid lifetime, which increases security in the use of applications for which granting permanent access is not necessary (nor desirable).

An example of a 3rd party application, which can be configured to use either option, is illustrated in Figure 47. If you chose the *OAuth Authorization Grant Flow* you can verify at the *github.com* website which privileges exactly have been granted.[66]

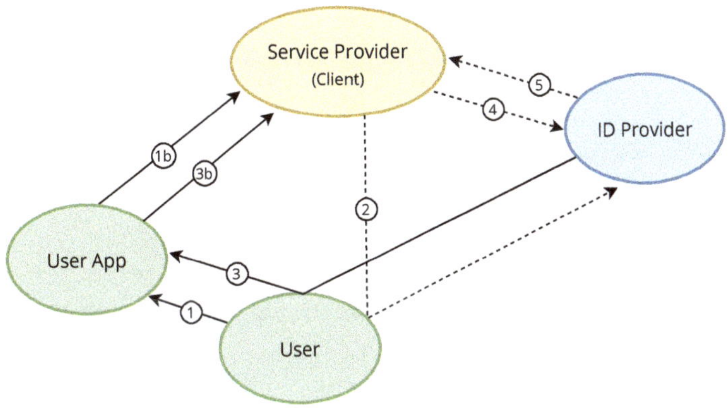

Figure 46. **Delegated Authorization Flow.** *A simplified illustration of a Delegated Authorization Flow. Steps (2), (4) and (5) are depicted with dotted lines—and are essentially the same as for the (usual) authorization flow depicted in Figure 44. (1) The user triggers their app to try to (2) perform an operation which requires access to a secured service on the provider. After authenticating and receiving an identifier from the ID provider (as usual) the user (browser) passes the identifier on to the App, which in (3b) presents it to the service provider. The Service provider (as usual) uses the identity information thus obtained, to ascertain if the user app should be permitted (authorized) to perform the action they initially attempted. The service provider typically saves a (temporary) cookie in the user's browser as usual, and additionally the app securely stores (temporary) tokens from the service provider (e.g., access and refresh tokens), to avoid making them reauthenticate for every subsequent request.*

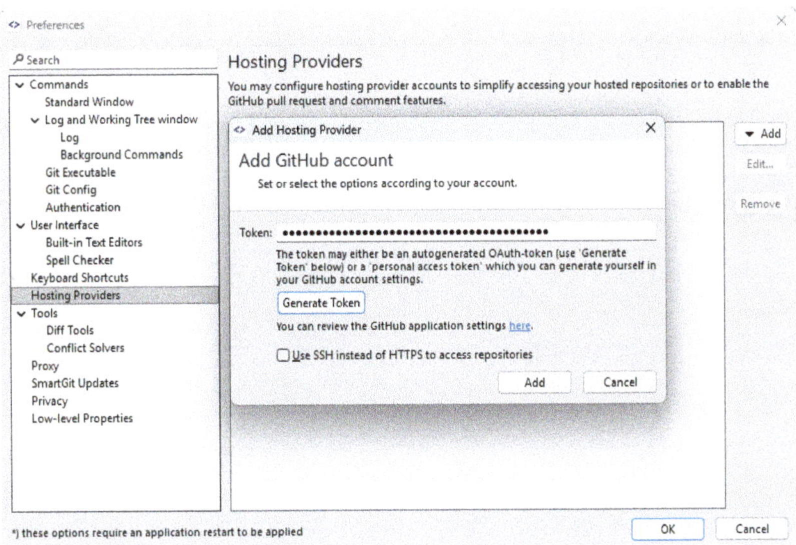

Figure 47. **Configuring delegated authorization for a secure service.** *The 3rd party application SmartGit[39] can be granted delegated authorization to a remote service (e.g. github.com) by using either ssh keys or a (OAuth) token, which it passes as needed to the service in question via HTTPS. You can enter the token from the GitHub website manually, or have SmartGit do so automatically.*

Web Browsers

When thinking about network security, a classic image one often has in mind is of a user interacting with a remote system using local (client) software (such a web browser). During which, the remote system (and the data it maintains) needs to be secured against possibly malicious (or erroneous) users. Many access control mechanisms (such as authentication and authorization) are designed with this scenario in mind.

But the converse is equally true—the client software is also a system, connected to a network which needs securing—from possibly malicious (or erroneous) servers. And in the case where the client software is a web browser, the possibly many websites a single browser (simultaneously) interacts with need protection from one another.

Browser security protects the client's environment, some of which is locally stored data (such as tokens) from different websites. Browsers are more susceptible to security issues than regular applications, because:

- It's a single application, effectively running multiple *virtual applications* (one per website). Furthermore, these virtual applications are loaded dynamically from independent sources.
- Browser extensions from 3rd parties offer a further potential security vulnerability.
- Regular applications are at least to some extent isolated by the operating system (e.g. can store data in separate isolated application-specific directories, protected by operating system permissions). It's up to the browser itself, however, to keep its virtual applications as isolated as necessary to maintain security without causing excessive *overhead*.[67]

Modern web browsers are a remarkable feat of engineering, often taken for granted.

Anonymous Networks — Dark Web

Anonymous networks are networks which are designed to keep the identity of both initial sender and final destination *secret*, [68] of which the *Tor network* is by far the biggest. This anonymity can be useful to journalists, activists, privacy-conscious individuals, and yes, sometimes criminals — just like any communication technology. Using them usually requires special software.

You can consider the dark web to be the web content hosted within anonymous networks. The term *dark web* is misleading, since there's nothing inherently dark (nor illegal) about anonymous communication, and much of what happens on anonymous networks isn't *web* at all — networks like Tor can anonymize any TCP traffic, not just HTTP.

These anonymous networks are not really separate from the rest of the internet. The nodes and interfaces involved use PKI and IP addresses, just like in *regular* networks. They just additionally build more layers of abstraction on top of these to maintain the desired anonymity of interfaces involved.

Understanding how anonymous networks work is an excellent exercise in applied cryptography, network protocols, and security design. It demonstrates how clever combinations of well-established techniques (public key cryptography, symmetric encryption, and proxy chains) can solve complex privacy problems.

The term *dark web* refers specifically to the *web* content accessible through anonymous networks — essentially, the *web part* of all anonymous networks on the internet. This includes websites with *.onion* addresses on Tor.

You've probably heard explanations like *your data bounces through so many random servers that it's impossible to trace back to you* or *your data is encrypted in so many (onion) layers that it's infeasible to decrypt*. This sounds plausible, but is fundamentally wrong. Computers can easily track arbitrarily long paths, and given knowledge of the keys involved, they can also easily decrypt effectively arbitrary many layers of encryption. The real anonymity mechanism is much more sophisticated and relies on cryptographic separation of knowledge, rather than using too many hops to follow. In fact, there are typically just three main hops between source and final destination interfaces.

The anonymity of dark web networks is created by careful cryptographic separation of knowledge among a few (typically 3) so-called *relay nodes* (illustrated in *Figure 48*) not by involving *"distractingly many"* hops as some explanations misleadingly suggest.

Tor

Tor is the most widely used anonymous network and using it requires the *Tor Browser*.[69]. When someone wants to communicate with a remote interface through the Tor network, the Tor browser first downloads a list of available Tor *relays* and their public keys. It selects 3 of these relays and an overlay network is created containing the interfaces on these 3 relays together with the source and destination. A setup phase is performed during which a cascade of key negotiations takes place. This means that the packets leaving the source is encrypted 4-fold. The first relay strips away one layer of encryption, send out a packet 3-fold encrypted, and so on until the final node receives packets with just one layer of encryption. These multiple layers of encryption, and the way they are successively *peeled away* one at a time at the nodes on the path, are reminiscent of layers of an onion, which is what gives Tor its nickname of the *onion network*.

These multiple layers of encryption, make the network very secure, but what guarantees the anonymity is the fact that each successive node in the chain receives and passes on IP addresses solely on a *need-to-know* basis, as illustrated in Figure 48. The overlapping ellipses in the figure represent each node's sphere of knowledge—notice how no single ellipse encompasses both source and destination, ensuring anonymity through separation.

Apart from the IP addresses of their own interfaces, each relay node only knows the IP address of

- Node 1 (*Entry Guard*): the source IP address, and that of facing interface on Node 2.
- Node 2 (*Middle Relay*): the facing interfaces on Node 1 and Node 3.
- Node 3 (*Exit Relay*): the facing interfaces on Node 2 and that of final intended destination.

No single relay ever sees both the source IP address and that of the (final intended) destination[70]. The initial source knows the address of its own interface, that of the facing interface on the first relay, and also always knows the IP address of the final destination[71]. The final destination is typically unaware of the IP address of the source interface, unless the source voluntarily and explicitly reveals it as part of the encrypted payload. And no node except the final intended destination can decrypt the innermost payload.

Tor also uses PKI to verify the identity of the nodes involved, but with its own *chain of trust* and *root authorities* separate from the ones used by regular websites. This protects against potential government coercion of traditional certificate authorities.

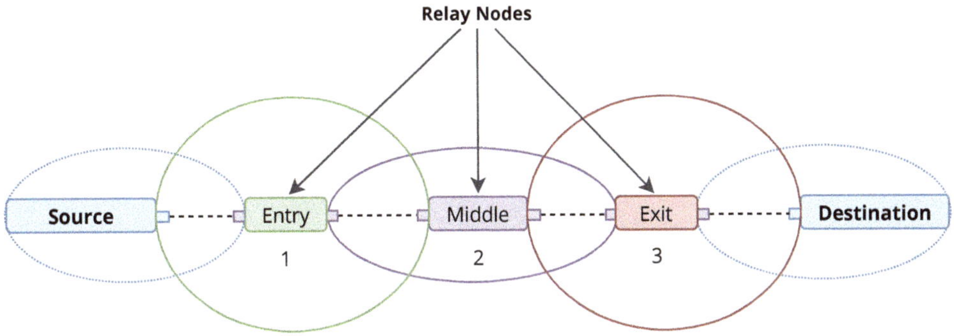

Figure 48. **Tor Architecture**. *Each node knows (only) the addresses of its own interfaces, as well as those on the previous and next and hops, respectively. The source is an exception—it also knows the IP address of the final destination interface. The 3 nodes in the middle are called "relay nodes" — they are service nodes of the Tor network.*

Summary

- The main aim of system security is to ensure that those, and only those, who have a *legitimate right* to access a system (or certain parts thereof), will actually able to do so.
- *Networked* computer systems can be accessed remotely, which makes securing them both more difficult and important.
- An *entity* is a person or thing (e.g. computer program) that may attempt to gain access to a system.
- *Identity* is the set of information a particular system maintains about such an entity, for the purposes of (future) access control.
- The information in an identity can be conceptually divided into 2 categories: *privileges* and *attributes*.
- When using *Role-Based Access Control (RBAC)*, the privileges are a few broad *roles* rather than numerous specific permissions.
- *Credentials* come in various forms (e.g. username, password, tokens) and generally (effectively) contain part(s) of an identity. In particular, parts which are (supposed to be kept) secret, so that being in possession of said credentials, yields credibility to the holder being the entity which legitimately should be in their possession. And thus, credibility to the holder being the entity with which the system associates the identity in question.
- Access control for computer system is often separated into two stages: authentication and authorization.
- *Authentication* is the establishment of the identity of the entity attempting to gain access to the system. This involves determining which (previously stored) identity is that of the entity in question. The entity typically has to provide the system with credentials in the process.
- *Authorization* is the use of the privileges in the already established identity, to determine if that particular entity should be allowed to access the system in the particular manner they are attempting.
- *Cryptography* is the science of establishing digital trust, using advanced mathematical techniques.
- Encryption and digital signatures are two of the main applications of cryptography.
- Encryption uses a key to transform (i.e. *encrypt*) data into a form that is unrecognizable without a corresponding key to transform (i.e. *decrypt*) the data back.
- Encryption of network traffic, and related security functionality, can be implemented (independently) in different layers—i.e. payloads of packets of a particular layer (and thus in the corresponding Russian doll shell) can be independently encrypted.
- A *digital signature* allows an entity to attest to the validity of (the contents of) a digital document.
- When the digitally signed document contains a public key and meta information about (who)

the holder (is), it's called a *digital certificate*. Usually, the signer is a (trusted) 3rd party. PKI is a collection of best practices and technologies for creating and using them. Using digital certificates according to PKI represents the most secure method of generally distributing (public) cryptographic keys in a trustworthy fashion.

- *Symmetric* keys are created independently of any other key, and can be shared by multiple entities.
- Asymmetric keys come in so-called *public-private pairs*. The pairs are unique in that for each private key, there is a unique matching public key and vice versa. It's only safe to distribute the *public* key, since the private key can be used to generate the public key (but not vice versa).
- Various competing *schemes* govern cryptographic keys and their use. In particular, how exactly to generate the keys and what algorithm should be applied when using them to in a particular application (use-case). *AES* is most popular for symmetric scheme, while *RSA*, *ECDSA* and *ECDH* are the asymmetric scheme. RSA used to be predominant but is not used as much in networking any more.
- *TLS* is the most widely used (TCP or UDP based) protocol for encrypting network communication using cryptographic keys. Using TLS with keys and certificates according to PKI, helps ensure that the communication is encrypted using keys from known, trustworthy sources — and thus protected against attacks such as *man in the middle*. TLS is used by many applications and higher-level protocols such as HTTPS, directly or indirectly.
- *SSH*, like HTTPS, is a layer 5+ protocol that is used for secure network applications. Unlike HTTPS, however, it doesn't use TLS to do the low level cryptographic lifting, but implements it itself. Unlike (the implementation used by) TLS, it cannot be layered on top of UDP, but only TCP. It's not generally used with PKI or certificates — the question of how to distribute trusted keys securely is not one SSH tries very hard to address. It, however, excels at communication that involves executing remote (shell) commands or terminal interaction, which is why many applications choose to use it (behind the scenes).
- *Identity Management* describes how identity information is stored and made available to services that have a legitimate right to access it securely on behalf of specific entities. Related services can form (*single sign-on*) federations to make access control more convenient for the entities in question. *Delegated Authorization* happens when such services allow (with the consent of the entity in question) 3rd party applications to access some or all of the identity information (of the entity) the services themselves are privy to.
- An *Identity Provider* is what actually stores and protects the identities in an identity management system. It may provide *authentication as a service* also known as *social sign-on* to an arbitrary application — i.e. not one of the services which has a dedicated pool of identities secured by the identity provider, with the entities consent.
- Protocols such as *OpenID Connect* + *OAuth* and *SAML* describe the detailed manner in which specific information should be passed between the parties involved in identity management systems. They often use named *flows* (each of which represents a typical access control scenario) to do so.

- *JSON Web Tokens (JWTs)* is a popular standard defining tokens with a specific structure and content
- *Anonymous networks*, such as the *Tor network*, are networks which are designed to keep the identity of both initial sender and final destination *secret*.

Conclusion

In this chapter, you've successfully navigated the complex landscape of network security — from fundamental concepts of identity and access control through the cryptographic foundations that make secure communication possible. You now understand how authentication proves who you are, how authorization determines what you can do, and how cryptography ensures your data remains confidential and unmodified in transit.

You've seen how security is woven throughout the network stack, with protocols like TLS and SSH creating secure channels, PKI providing the infrastructure for digital trust, and identity management systems enabling seamless yet secure access across multiple services. Technologies like OAuth, OpenID Connect, SAML, and JWTs aren't just acronyms anymore — you understand how they work together to enable delegated authorization and single sign-on, balancing the competing demands of security and convenience.

Most importantly, you've learned that security isn't absolute but contextual — different systems require different levels of protection based on their value and threat landscape. You've seen how the same cryptographic principles that protect banking transactions can be inverted to enable anonymous communication, demonstrating that security is ultimately about controlling information flow according to specific trust models.

With this foundation, you're equipped to understand not just how security-conscious systems work, but why they're designed the way they are — the trade-offs they make, the threats they counter, and the trust relationships they establish. As networks continue to evolve and new threats emerge, these fundamental principles will remain your guide to designing, implementing, and maintaining systems that protect what matters while enabling the connectivity modern life demands.

[1] The entity involved need not always be a single person. Credentials can, in principle, be shared among a group or team (though this is generally discouraged since it makes it impossible to trace actions back to specific individuals). The system then uniquely identifies that group as a single entity.

[2] sometimes also known as a *hardened system*. While the term *secure system* is also not uncommon, it can be misleading as it implies absolute security, which no system can guarantee — all systems have potential vulnerabilities and attack vectors.

[3] Performing repeated guessing in an attempt to gain illegitimate access to a system is known as a *dictionary attack*

[4] *IANA (Internet Assigned Numbers Authority)* assigns top-level domains (e.g. *.com*) and *registrars* (like *Hostinger*, *GoDaddy*) allocate subdomains e.g. *mydomain.com*, and the owner of mydomain.com can allocate addresses like me@mydomain.com. *International Telecommunication Union (ITU)* assigns country level telephone codes, and national bodies such as *Federal Communications Commission (FCC)* in the United States, or *Bundesnetzagentur (BNetzA)* in Germany, allocate telephone numbers within their respective countries

[5] While mobile apps dominate this space, desktop alternatives exist including Authy Desktop, WinAuth (Windows), and password managers with built-in *TOTP (Time-based One-Time Password)* support like *1Password*, *Bitwarden*, and *KeePassXC*.

[6] which, in contrast to TOTP, requires an active internet connection between app and server

[7] Passkeys follow the FIDO2/WebAuthn standards, which define how clients (web browsers and native apps via OS APIs) communicate with authenticators. Each passkey is bound to a specific website domain (e.g., example.com), and the client (browser for web, OS APIs for apps) automatically enforces this binding, making phishing much harder because it won't use a passkey for the wrong site. Most (web) services let you add multiple passkeys per account, name them (e.g., 'phone', 'laptop'), and rotate/revoke individual ones without affecting the others. Many sites also maintain traditional password login as a fallback, allowing you to recreate passkeys if lost — though some security-focused sites may disable password access once passkeys are configured. *Note*: You could manually achieve the same security with traditional key files: generate a key pair, send the public key to the website, then for each login, use your private key to sign a challenge from the server and send back the signature. But you'd have to manually store keys securely, remember which key goes with which site, run the signing commands yourself, and send the results back to the website. Passkeys automate all of this, and additionally add the automatic site-binding phishing protection. Where private keys are stored depends on the authenticator: OS-based authenticators store them in the device's secure enclave or TPM chip and may sync them (encrypted) via cloud services; password managers store them in encrypted databases; hardware keys like YubiKey store them non-exportably on their secure chip.

[8] for example, in *HTTPS* the server often uses a certificate, whereas the client often a token.

[9] *Key Negotiation* is an *egg waiting for chicken* — see The Chicken and the Egg — patience please :-)

[10] typically, however, increasing the latter requires a similar increase in the former

[11] for performance reasons, since signing the actual contents would be unfeasible for large documents. Additionally, signing hashes prevents certain attacks where raw RSA signatures can be exploited due to their multiplicative property—if a target message m can be factored into $m_1 \times m_2$, an attacker can get legitimate signatures for these seemingly harmless factors, then multiply those signatures to forge a valid signature for m without the private key. This vulnerability is one reason ECDSA is increasingly preferred for digital signatures.

[12] this simple example is just for illustrating what is meant here by *inverse operation* and *reverse order* and is not a safe form of encryption, which would typically involve a much longer sequence of more complicated mathematical operations

[13] if a symmetric key of a certain length provides a measure of protection against an attack from a classical computer, then doubling the length of the key will provide the same measure of protection from such an attack from a quantum computer—all other things being equal

[14] ECDSA achieves stronger security with smaller keys than RSA. For example, a 256-bit ECDSA key offers similar

protection to a 3072-bit RSA key, making operations faster and requiring less storage. Alternatively, for the same key size, ECDSA provides stronger security than RSA.

[15] *Indirectly a private key can*, in the sense that it can be used to generate the public key, which can then be used to decrypt.

[16] requiring $O(n^2)$ keys for n members

[17] each browser, each operating system, and much software designed with network access in mind, including packet managers like python's *pip*, maintains its own list of trusted Root Certificate Authorities (CAs)

[18] Unlike with RSA where there is "decryption involved"—the reverse algorithm does yield the original hash. This is then compared to the independently calculated value and checked for a match. Note also that *EdDSA (Edwards-curve Digital Signature Algorithm)* is a newer alternative gaining adoption in SSH keys and some modern protocols, but ECDSA remains dominant in TLS and most established systems.

[19] RSA and ECDSA are not commutative—a property which is essential for their use-cases. In particular, the maintenance of the integrity of a chain-of-trust. Being able to reverse who signed in which order would defeat the purpose—*think*: me verifying a statement the government makes vs the government verifying a statement I make

[20] a layer may sometimes also use data from lower layers i.e. outer doll shells

[21] but the headers of higher layers are, since the layer 2 payload contains all of the higher layer packets (including their headers) in inner doll shells

[22] *Group* here just means multiple individuals - no special technical or mathematical meaning.

[23] consisting of more than two members

[24] the difference becomes immaterial when there are only 2 conversants in the group

[25] typically X.509 certificates, often from internal Certificate Authorities

[26] Layer 3 protocols must encrypt all traffic automatically without applications knowing—perfect for connecting entire office networks. Layer 4 protocols need applications to actively manage their connections—perfect when your web browser needs different security than your email client. It's possible to combine multiple security protocols as discussed in *Cascading Encryption Layers (Keys)*.

[27] **IPSec** offers many configuration options and authentication methods, but setup complexity increases with that flexibility. **WireGuard** uses only one modern approach with minimal configuration, but you can't adapt it to unusual requirements. **TLS** works for any application but needs certificate infrastructure to verify identities. **SSH** is streamlined for remote terminal access with simpler key exchange

[28] using a symmetric key, agreed upon during a handshake that itself uses asymmetric keys (in particular those in which trust has been established by certificates/PKI) is no less secure than using asymmetric keys for the complete communication. It provides the benefit of improved performance, however, as encrypting/decrypting with symmetric keys is faster and easier. For added security, the two parties often agree on not just one, but multiple symmetric keys—e.g. separate keys for encrypting messages in each direction (client-to-server and server-to-client)

[29] a so-called *Message Authentication Code (MAC), not to be confused with _Media Access Control (MAC)* address - see *MAC Address*, with which it is unrelated

[30] Note that the underlying transport protocol may also use such checksums for catching unintentional data corruption or loss in transit, as TCP for example does. The TCP checksum, however, resides in the (unencrypted) header, and is thus itself unprotected from deliberate modification—an attacker could modify the TCP checksum to balance any modification they make to the (encrypted) payload

[31] Technically, it inserts new *TLS packets* (which are usually called *records*, but like all other packets we have discussed, each consists of a header and a payload) as the layer 4 payload. The HTTP packets becomes the payload of these TLS packets, which are encrypted in their entirety, but the TLS packet headers are not.

[32] during which the actual data is exchanged. They want to use a symmetric scheme for as much due to their superior performance over asymmetric counterparts

[33] In standard TLS, the server must authenticate themselves, and the client may. To do so, each pass the other party a certificate with their permanent public key and other identity information about the holder. The other party can verify that the permanent key they use in the keys negotiation matches this certificate. When both parties authenticate themselves, one speaks of *mTLS*. Note that neither is the handshake generally encrypted using the permanent keys, nor are they used to generate the ephemeral ones. The permanent keys are only used for authentication.

[34] More accurately, g is a well-known fixed *generator point* on the elliptic curve—chosen to make things very secure. The value chosen does not have to be kept secret for the rest of the handshake to be secure. For *"a(g)" read*: "Alice applies her (ECDH) algorithm to the value, g, using her ephemeral private key". *a(g)* is, in fact, Alice's *public key*. For *"b(g)" read:* "Bob applies his (ECDH) algorithm to the value, g, using his ephemeral private key". *b(g)* is, in fact, Bob's *public key*. For *"b(a(g))" read*: "Bob applies his (ECDH) algorithm to the value a(g), using his ephemeral private key".

[35] this is only holds for (EC)DH algorithms. Other cryptographic algorithms are, in general, not commutative

[36] unless they also have the permanent private key of one of the conversants, AND are actively eavesdropping during the key negotiation. Past recorded sessions cannot be decrypted even with the permanent private key, since the ephemeral keys are never stored. Usually, *multiple keys* are derived from the shared secret: e.g. separate keys for encrypting messages in each direction (client-to-server and server-to-client).

[37] whereby if the permanent (asymmetric) keys of one of the original conversants are compromised at some later stage, their past conversations remain secret. This is because the ephemeral private keys a and b are randomly (re)generated for each new TLS connection, independently of the permanent keys, which are at most used for initial authentication

[38] e.g., *Content-Security-Policy* for blocking *XSS*, *X-Frame-Options* for preventing *clickjacking*, and *Secure/HttpOnly* cookies for mitigating session hijacking

[39] available from *syntevo.com*, with which I have no affiliation, but can heartily recommend

[40] This can make integration of VPNs that re-sign certificates (so-called *inspecting VPNs*) challenging, as each store must be updated independently to recognize the new custom root certificates (of the VPN).

[41] This particular combination of PKI, TLS, and specialized attributes is specific to HTTPS. Other systems combine these security measures differently. For example, IPSec or WireGuard might be used for encryption instead of (or in addition to) TLS, and different layer 5+ protocols define their own specialized features suited to their needs.

[42] Git is a tool that tracks changes to files over time, letting multiple people work on the same project without overwriting each other's work. It's become the standard way software developers collaborate—most code projects use it.

[43] though both can be configured to use (symmetric) *Pre-Shared Keys* instead. SSH can even be configured to use password authentication, but this is now deprecated

[44] PGP certificates, which PGP calls *key blocks*, have a different format to that (X.509) used by PKI

[45] e.g., SMTP STARTTLS

[46] Each layer in question can independently decide, for example, what keys to use for the encryption, but it automatically protects not only the payload of packets of its own layer, but also automatically, the complete packets of all higher layers, since they are encapsulated (Russian doll style) in the encrypted payload of this layer's packets. In the case of protocols like TLS and IPSec, that use public/private key pairs to negotiate a symmetric key, there are actually two key *negotiations* – agreeing what public/private keys to use and then using these to agree on a symmetric key, which is then used for the actual conversation. In the case of PSK, the *negotiation* is trivial – the keys have been *installed* and are available, or they are not. In open systems like the internet, this typically involves PKI-based authentication. In closed systems like *Kubernetes* clusters, where pre-shared keys (PSK) are common, the authentication is correspondingly simpler. The parties involved effectively confirm that the other also has the same correct key, by ensuring that they decrypt what they have encrypted and vice versa.

[47] Layer 3 encryption, particularly using IPSec used to be standard in VPNs, but layer 4, particularly using TLS, have gained significant popularity for remote access due to easier deployment, better firewall traversal, and no need for dedicated clients. VPN (blanket) encryption means that all packets — including any layer 4 packets already encrypted by applications e.g. browsers using HTTPS, are encrypted (again) by the VPN

[48] in order to sit as a trusted man-in-the-middle between you and any site you want to communicate with using (PKI) certificates, they need to re-sign the certificates using their own keys. More accurately, they need to if they wish to inspect the payload of the messages (which enterprise/corporate VPNs like *Zscaler* usually do), since it has to be able to encrypt and decrypt messages going in both directions. This often works less transparently than one would wish — partly because operating systems and various networking applications running on them often have independent *certificate stores*, and configuring them all to trust the keys of the VPN server can be a challenge. Additionally, all VPNs, like transparent proxies, need to rewrite source IP addresses (e.g. via NAT) when accessing 3rd party websites. This address rewriting is often marketed as a feature in consumer VPNs, allowing users to hide or spoof their geographic location by appearing to browse from the VPN server's location instead of their own. However, this location masking can be defeated through other means such as browser fingerprinting, DNS leaks, or websites simply blocking known VPN server addresses. More in the planned follow-up volume *(Modern Networking - Software and Techniques)*

[49] unlike company VPNs where employees typically share a tenant with other employees, users of consumer/personal VPNs like NordVPN typically get allocated their own separate tenant.

[50] While it's technically possible to filter at layer 2 (e.g., by MAC address), this is rarely done by what we call firewalls — such filtering is usually handled by switches, and is applied only at layer 2

[51] Your firewall might allow HTTPS traffic to reach your web server (the traffic type is acceptable), but it's your authentication system that verifies username/password and your authorization system that determines whether that specific user can view confidential documents or just public pages. Firewalls protect the perimeter and regulate traffic flow; access control protects individual resources by verifying identity and permissions. Note that *Next-Generation Firewalls (NGFWs)* blur these lines by incorporating some access control features — for example, applying rules based on user identity through integration with Active Directory or LDAP. However, the fundamental distinction remains: firewalls primarily govern traffic flow, while dedicated access control systems manage resource permissions.

[52] Other characteristics of firewalls include their *mode of operation* — whether they are *stateless* (evaluating each packet independently) or *stateful* (tracking connections and automatically allowing related return traffic). Most modern firewalls operate in stateful mode, which simplifies configuration since you only need rules for initiating connections, not for every packet in both directions. Additional characteristics such as *rule types*, as well as implementation details — from configuring *NetFilter* with *nftables* commands to writing *eBPF* programs for advanced packet processing — are covered more extensively in the planned follow-up volume *(Modern Networking - Software and Techniques)*.

[53] NetFilter is a framework built into the Linux kernel that provides hooks at various points in the packet processing path. Applications like *iptables* (the traditional tool) and *nftables* (its modern replacement) use these hooks to inspect and filter packets.

[54] *Workload/Process level* firewalls provide the finest granularity, controlling which specific applications or processes can communicate over the network. This approach, sometimes called *micro-segmentation*, allows rules like "*only the nginx process can connect to the database server.*" These are often implemented using which is a technology that allows small programs to run safely in the Linux kernel without modifying kernel source code. For firewalls, this means you can write custom packet filtering logic that executes at kernel speed, with fine-grained control over which processes can send or receive specific types of traffic. Micro-segmentation can also be implemented using specialized security agents.

[55] TLS interception works by having the firewall act as a *man-in-the-middle* — it presents its own certificate to internal clients (who trust it because IT administrators have configured their systems to do so), decrypts the traffic for inspection, then re-encrypts it using the real server's certificate. This requires explicit configuration and raises both security and privacy considerations. It can be considered a special case of TLS Bridging, because, like TLS

bridging in general, it terminates the client-side TLS session and establishes a separate TLS session to the server; the "special" aspect is that this is done specifically to enable content inspection and policy enforcement on the decrypted traffic.

[56] more in the planned follow-up volume *(Modern Networking - Software and Techniques)*

[57] identified by a domain such as my_organization.com

[58] more specifically, it sends the web browser to a dedicated identity provider endpoint specifically for such queries, passing any necessary parameters, such as the federation ID, which can be used to uniquely identify the federation, and a *callback* endpoint in the service provider. Note that *standard flow* being described here is commonly known as the *Authorization (Code Grant) Flow*, and is typical in the case of an end user using a web browser to log into a website with a security conscious backend. Other flows like the *Client Credentials* and *Authorization Code + PKCE* are typical in other situations. For more information see the planned follow-up volume *(Modern Networking - Software and Techniques)* and the companion website for the book modern-networking.com (and in particular, its companion repository where some example flows are implemented)

[59] The cookie is used by the id provider to *short circuit* the need to ask the user for credentials should they come back before the session cookie expires. The use of a cookie here creates a potential opening for *Cross Site Request Forgery (CSRF)*—not in that a 3rd party site can hijack the session of one of SPs—it can't access their identity token, but it could in principle, use the cookie to *obtain a token of its own*. More in the planned follow-up volume *(Modern Networking - Software and Techniques)*. The authorization code is typically included as a query parameter in the URL, or as part of the response body. Crucially, this is *not* the token itself; it is a temporary ticket that the browser merely passes to the server to be exchanged for the actual token.

[60] which parts of the identity it's requesting is specified as a set of so-called *scopes*

[61] and just like the first service provider it sends along the same federation ID, from which the identity provider can determine that both service providers are in the same federation

[62] somewhat reminiscent of the popularity of the more heavyweight XML ceding to newer more lightweight data interchange formats like JSON and YAML

[63] which you will often see explicitly referred to as OAuth2 to emphasise the significant differences introduced since the original OAuth version, which was not designed to work with an authentication protocol like OpenID Connect

[64] OAuth prefers the term *Client* over the (arguably more intuitive) *Service Provider* favoured in SAML documentation. And strictly speaking, the identity provider returns a completely new access token rather than extending the lifetime of an existing one.

[65] even Humpty Dumpty is happy, because the *social* in the *social sign on* is inapt enough to engender at least the occasional confusion

[66] currently this is shown at the *github.com* website under *Settings-Integrations-Applications-Authorized OAuth Apps*

[67] Techniques involved include *sandboxing*, and *same-origin policy*

[68] more accurately, secret from all except the initial sender and final destination interfaces themselves. Intermediate nodes may know one of these, but no intermediate node knows both

[69] unlike regular web browsers, the Tor browser can communicate not only using HTTP but many TCP-based protocols

[70] in fact, 2 relay nodes would be sufficient to create this separation of knowledge. But the addition of a further relay makes it harder to *guess* which nodes are involved by traffic analysis — by monitoring traffic in and out of one of the relay nodes, even if the nodes themselves are not compromised

[71] it must, since they must *decide* what destination IP address to connect to

Afterword

Congratulations! You've reached the end of this journey through the fundamental concepts of modern networking. Take a moment to appreciate what you've accomplished – you've navigated through layers of abstraction, untangled complex protocols, and connected the dots between physical signals and the applications we use every day.

Previous feelings of mystery that once surrounded networking have largely lifted, and disconnected pieces of knowledge – packets, protocols, port numbers, and addresses – should now form a clear, logical mosaic. You understand not just what happens when you browse a website or send a message, but why and how it happens at each layer. The *chicken-and-egg* problems we encountered throughout this book should now resolve themselves naturally. You can see how DNS depends on IP networking, which depends on routing, which depends on addressing, which depends on physical connectivity – and how each piece supports and enables the others. This interconnected understanding is your foundation for everything that comes next. The *Humpty Dumpty* confusion of terms – where the same word meant different things in different contexts – should be largely resolved. You're now aware of these linguistic traps and potential pitfalls, and better equipped to navigate them when encountering new sources or documentation.

With these fundamentals firmly in place, you're no longer forced to blindly follow recipes or copy-paste commands without understanding their purpose. You know what happens when you configure network settings, why port numbers matter, how packets find their way across the internet, and what role each layer plays in the grand scheme. This understanding transforms you from a passive user to an active participant – someone for whom networking is no longer a black box. When you encounter new technologies or troubleshoot problems, you'll approach them with confidence, knowing you have the conceptual framework to make sense of what's happening.

In a world where technologies have notoriously short shelf lives, networking remains a core technology with remarkable staying power. The fundamental concepts you've learned haven't changed significantly in decades, even as the applications built on top of them have evolved dramatically. Many rising technologies – cloud computing, IoT, edge computing, distributed systems, AI model training across GPU clusters, distributed inference (running large AI models across multiple machines) – all have networking at their core. Your solid understanding of these fundamentals positions you to leverage not just today's technologies but tomorrow's as well. The effort you've invested in learning networking will pay dividends as you encounter new systems and platforms, all of which ultimately depend on the same foundational principles you now understand.

The planned follow-up volume *(Modern Networking - Software and Techniques)*, picks up exactly where this book leaves off. While this volume focused on the why, the next focuses on the how — the practical, hands-on techniques that professionals use daily. You'll dive into software networking with *Docker* and *Kubernetes*, seeing how containerization leverages the networking concepts you now understand. You'll configure firewalls using *nftables* and *eBPF*, knowing exactly which layers you're protecting and why. *SSH* configuration will make perfect sense because you understand port numbers, encryption, and authentication. The command-line tools — *ping, traceroute, netcat, tcpdump, nmap* — will become extensions of your understanding rather than mysterious incantations. You'll work with *sockets*, seeing through *Python* code examples how the operating system provides you with access to the networking stack it guards and manages. You'll debug browser traffic and explore how modern protocols like *QUIC* and *HTTP/3* achieve smooth streaming by building on the foundation you've learned here. This separation between concepts and techniques was deliberate. By mastering the fundamentals first, you'll find the practical applications not just easier to learn, but genuinely intuitive. The next volume will expect you to know these fundamentals already, briefly summarizing at most and referring back to this book for the detailed explanations. If you would like to be kept up to date on the progress or review early drafts, please let me know at modern-networking.com.

The networking landscape continues to evolve, but the fundamental concepts you've learned here remain constant. Whether you're building cloud infrastructure, securing enterprise networks, or simply understanding the technology that powers our connected world, you have the knowledge base to adapt and grow. The journey continues, and with your newfound understanding, you're well-equipped for whatever networking challenges lie ahead. Bon Voyage!

Index

@

3G, 4G/LTE, 5G, 39

A

A records, 100
AAAA records, 100
access control, 138
Address Discovery, 40
address realms, 92
addressing, 25
Administrative Domain, 107
advanced routing, 112
Advanced Routing Techniques, 112
AES, 149
Aetheria, 8
anonymity, 179
Anonymous networks, 179
Anycast, 78
API, 103
API endpoint, 86
APIs, 103
Applications of Cryptography, 147
ARIN, 76
ARP, 66
Asymmetric (Public/Private Key) Encryption, 151
asymmetric key pair, 151
asymmetric keys, 151
authenticate, 152
Authenticating Cryptographic Keys, 152
Authentication, 139
authenticator apps, 144
Authorization, 139
Authorization (Code Grant) Flow, 173
Autonomous System (AS), 76

B

backhaul, 46
Best Path Problem, 42
BGP, 79
binary, 59
Biometric Scan, 143
bits, 26
Bits and Bitstreams, 26
Blowfish, 149
border routers, 77
broadcast, 37
Broadcast and Collision Domains, 16
Broadcast Domain, 16

C

cache, 68
cached, 68
caching, 68
Caesar's Cipher, 150
CAM Tables, 35
cascade of key negotiations, 165
Cascading Encryption Layers (Keys), 165
cascading layer of encryption, 165
Cat6, 40
Cat7, 40
CDNs (Content Delivery Networks), 93
Cellular, 39
Cellular, 37
Certificate Authorities (CAs), 153
Certificates, 144
Chain of Trust, 153
checksum, 29
CIDR, 62
circuit-switched, 38
client, 117
client-server, 117

Cloudflare, 93
CNAME records, 100
Collision Domain, 16
Containers, 123
Content servers, 101
Content-Security-Policy, 187
conversation phase, 165
copper cables, 40
Cost, 72
Credentials, 142
cryptographic algorithms, 149
Cryptographic Keys, 143, 149
cryptographic keys, 149
cryptographic purpose, 147
Cryptography, 146

D

dark web, 179
Datagram TLS (DTLS), 159
Decimal, Binary, and Hexadecimal, 59
default gateway, 69
delegated authorization, 176
Delegated Authorization Flow, 177
DELETE, 115
Destination Address Types, 37
Digital Certificates, 152
digital signature, 147
Digital Signatures (and Verification), 147
digital trust, 141
DNAT, 92
DNS, 95
DNS - FQDNs (dotted strings) for IP addresses, 95
DNS Domain, 107
DNS name tree, 98
DNS Records, 100
DNS Resolver, 99
DNS servers, 101
Docker, 123
Docker or Kubernetes, 123
DOCSIS (Data Over Cable Service Interface Specification), 38
domain name registration, 107
domain registrar, 107
Domains, 107
Domain – disambiguation (caution), 16
DSL (Digital Subscriber Line), 38
Dynamic Host Configuration Protocol (DHCP), 102

E

eBGP (external Border Gateway Protocol), 79
eBPF (extended Berkeley Packet Filter), 188
edge routers, 77
electromagnetic wave, 27
Electromagnetic Waves and the Role of Media, 27
Encapsulation, 84
encrypt, 147
encryption, 147
encryption of HTTP packets, 160
Endpoint, 86
ephemeral, 161
Ethernet, 19
Ethernet cables, 40
example DNS resolution, 99
external Border Gateway Protocol (eBGP), 77

F

FCS, 31
Federated Identity Management, 170
Fibre Optics, 37
Firewalls, 167
flexibility, 97
flows, 172
FQDN, 95
Fragmentation Needed, 82
Fragmentation Needed, 82
Frames, 29
Fundamental Theorem of Software Engineering, 54

G

gateway, 69
gateways, 69
GET, 115

GraphQL, 93
Group and individual Trust, 156
group communication, 156

H

Handshake, 160
hash, 29
hexadecimal, 59
home router, 72
hop, 68
Host, 79
host, 105
Host Configuration, 102
Host Header and Advanced Routing, 112
Hosts—layer 3 interfaces, 79
HTTP, 108
HTTP/3, 119
HTTP/3 and QUIC, 119
HTTPS, 161

I

iBGP (internal BGP), 79
ICMP, 81
Identifier, 141
Identity, 140
Identity Management, 170
Identity Provider, 170
Identity, Trust and Encryption, 141
IETF, 158
IGPs (Interior Gateway Protocols), 79
IMAP, 122
infrastructure, 13
interface, 29
Interfaces, 29
Internet Protocol (IP), 58
Intrusion Detection and Prevention Systems (IDPS), 168
IP, 58
IP Address Ranges, 61
IP Addresses, 60
IPSec, 158
IPSec (Internet Protocol Security), 158
iptables, 188
IPv4, 58
IPv5, 61
IPv6, 58
IS-IS, 93

J

JSON Web Tokens (JWTs), 174
JWT, 174

K

key negotiation, 147
Kubernetes, 123
Kubernetes CNI, 123

L

LANs, 35
Layer 2, 28
Layer 2 Limitations, 40
Layer 3, 52
Layer 4, 83
layer set, 123
Layer-Specific Devices, 18
Layers of Abstraction, 17
Link, 28
Link-Local Addresses, 92
Logical Addressing, 52
Lower Layer Landscape, 37

M

MAC, 31
MAC Address, 31
MAC spoofing, 41
MACsec—Media Access Control Security, 157
man-in-the-middle, 139
Media, 25
methods, 115
Metropolea, 50
Microservices, 117
model, 18
Models — network layers, 18
mTLS, 161
multicast, 37
multilayer switches, 65

MX records, 100

N

NAT (Network Address Translation), 78
negotiate, 147
neighbour discovery, 66
NetFilter, 168
network endpoint, 86
Network Topology, 34
  Mesh, 34
  Ring, 34
  Star, 34
Next-Generation Firewalls (NGFWs), 188
next-hop, 67
nftables, 188
NIC, 15
nodes, 11
Nodes and Ports, 11
NS records, 100
Number Systems, 59

O

OAuth, 172
Official Standards, 19
OpenID Connect, 172
OSPF, 93
overlay network, 124
Overlay networks, 123
overlays, 123

P

Packet Encapsulation, 55, 84
packet forwarding, 72
Packet Fragmentation, 80
packet interception, 41
Packet Too Big, 82
packet-switched, 38
passkey authenticator, 145
Passkeys, 144
PATCH, 115
path, 105
PDU—Protocol Data Unit, 45
Peer-to-Peer, 117
PGP, 164
physical networks, 25
PKI, 153
Podman, 123
pods, 125
point-to-point, 36
Points of Presence (PoPs), 93
POP3, 122
port, 11
port number, 83
Port Numbers—interface sharing and network endpoints, 83
ports, 12
POST, 115
POST Parameters, 117
private IP addresses, 78
Private Subnet, 92
Protocol Layering, 57
protocols, 55
Protocols and Flows, 172
PSKs *(Pre-Shared Keys)*, 152
Public/Private Keys, 151
PUT, 115

Q

query string, 105
QUIC, 119

R

Regional Internet Registries (RIRs), 76
Request-Response pairs, 110
REST, 115
REST Principles (Theory vs. Practice), 116
REST semantics for HTTP methods, 115
Reverse Proxies, 112
RIPE, 76
Role-Based Access Control (RBAC), 173
Root Certificate Authorities, 153
router, 67
Router Modes, 72
Router Repackaging, 71
Routers, 67
Routing Domain, 107

routing domain, 78
Routing Domains, 78
routing modes, 72
routing policy, 78
Routing Protocols, 79
routing protocols, 79
Routing Table example, 70
routing tables, 69
RPC (Remote Procedure Call), 122

S

S/MIME, 164
Samba, 134
SAML, 172
SCP (Secure Copy Protocol), 122
SDNs, 126
Secure/HttpOnly, 187
Security, 130
seed value, 161
Segment, 28
server, 117
setup phase, 165
SFTP (SSH File Transfer Protocol), 122
shortcut connections, 76
Sign on with GitHub, 175
Sign on with Google, 175
signature, 147
Single Sign-On, 171
single tree model, 76
SmartGit, 177
SMB (Server Message Block), 122
SMTP (Simple Mail Transfer Protocol), 122
SNAT, 92
SNI (Server Name Indication), 133
Social Login, 175
socket, 93
software networks, 124
Software-Defined Networks, 126
software-defined networks, 123
Specialized attributes, 162
SSH, 163
SSO, 171
standard, 19
stateful mode, 188
Stateless Address Autoconfiguration (SLAAC), 102
stream of bits, 26
subdomain, 96
subnet, 61
subnet gateway routers, 69
subnet mask, 91
Subnet – reserved addresses, 75
Subnets, 61
switch, 32
Switches, 32
symmetric keys, 149

T

table update, 72
TCP, 85
The Chicken and the Egg, 3
The Internet (Realistic), 76
The Internet (Simplified), 73
TLS, 159
- *Bridging*, 114
- ClientHello, 114
- Handshake, 160
- *Interception*, 168
- mTLS, 161
- *Offloading*, 114
- *Passthrough*, 114
- *Termination*, 114

TOFU, 152
token, 144
Tor network, 179
trust, 141
trust after first use, 152
tunnel, 169
Twofish, 149
TXT records, 100
type of action, 115

U

UDP, 85
unicast, 37
URIs (Uniform Resource Identifiers), 106

URL, 104
URLs, 104
Username, Password, 143

V

Virtual Devices and Interfaces, 123
Virtual Hosting, 112
virtual networks, 123
virtual networks and software-defined systems, 123
Virtual Private Networks, 166
VLAN, 39
VLANs, 39
VoIP (Voice over IP), 38
VPN, 166
VPNs, 166
VXLAN, 124

W

Web, 120
web, 120
web browsers, 178
WebRTC, 122
WebSockets, 122
WebTransport, 122
Wi-Fi, 19
Windows Firewall, 168
WireGuard, 158
World Wide Web, 120
WPA (Wi-Fi Protected Access), 157
WPA-PSK, 152
WPA2/WPA3, 46
WPA3, 47
WPA3-Enhanced Open, 47
WPA3-Enterprise, 47

X

X-Frame-Options, 187
X.509 certificates, 186
XSS, 187

Z

Zone files, 100

www.ingramcontent.com/pod-product-compliance
Lightning Source LLC
LaVergne TN
LVHW071335210926
848486LV00003B/148

9783000849763